Modelling for Added Value

Springer
London
Berlin
Heidelberg
New York
Barcelona
Budapest
Hong Kong
Milan
Paris
Santa Clara
Singapore
Tokyo

Macredie, Paul, Anketell, Lehaney and
Warwick (Eds)

Modelling for
Added Value

With 39 Figures

Springer

Robert Macredie, BSc(Hons), PhD
Ray Paul, BSc, MSc, PhD

Department of Information Systems and Computing, Brunel University,
Uxbridge UB8 3PH, UK

Dervarajan Anketell, DipTech, MSc

Anketell Management Services Ltd., 608 Kingston Road, Raynes Park,
London SW20 8DN, UK

Brian Lehaney, BA, MSc
Shamim Warwick, BSc, MSc

Department of Computing, University of Luton, Luton, UK

ISBN 3-540-76108-X Springer-Verlag Berlin Heidelberg New York

British Library Cataloguing in Publication Data
Modelling for added value
    1. Information storage and retrieval systems   2. Database management
    3. Databases
        I. Macredie, Robert
    005.7'4
ISBN 354076108X

Library of Congress Cataloging-in-Publication Data
Modelling for added value / Macredie ... [et al.], eds.
        p.   cm.
    Includes bibliographical references and index.
    ISBN 3-540-76108-X (paperback: alk. paper)
1. Management information systems.   2. Decision support systems.
I. Macredie, Robert, 1968- .
T58.6.M6123 1998   98-3911
658.4'0352--dc21   CIP

Typesetting: Gray Publishing, Tunbridge Wells, Kent
Printed and bound at the Athenæum Press Ltd., Gateshead, Tyne and Wear
34/3830-543210 Printed on acid-free paper

Contents

Theme II: Modelling for Information Systems

Theme III: Modelling for Decision Support

List of Contributors

D. (Rajan) Anketell
Anketell Management Services Limited, 608 Kingston Road, Raynes Park, London SW20 8DN, UK
Tel: +44 181 543 4729; Fax: +44 181 543 1801;
e-mail: rajan.anketell@mcmail.com

J.S. Busby
Cranfield University, Cranfield, Bedfordshire MK43 0AL, UK

Chuing-Yao Chen
Power Development Department, Taiwan Power Company, Taipei, Taiwan

Steve Clarke
Department of Business Systems, University of Luton, Park Square, Luton, Bedfordshire LU1 3JU, UK
Tel: +44 1582 734111; Fax: +44 1582 743143;
e-mail: Steve.Clarke@Luton.ac.uk

Elayne W. Coakes
Westminster Business School, University of Westminster, Well Street, London W1P 3FG, UK

Hilary Duckett
Oxford Brookes University, School of Business, Wheatley Campus, Wheatley, Oxfordshire OX33 1HX
Tel: +44 1865 485874; e-mail hrduckett@brookes.ac.uk

Jasna Kuljis
Department of Mathematical and Computing Sciences, Goldsmiths College, University of London, New Cross, London SE14 6NW, UK
Tel: +44 171 919 7868; Fax: +44 171 919 7853; e-mail: j.kuljis@gold.ac.uk

Brian Lehaney
Department of Business Systems, University of Luton, Park Square,
Luton, Bedfordshire LU1 3JU, UK
Tel: +44 1582 734111; Fax: +44 1582 743143;
e-mail: Brian.Lehaney@Luton.ac.uk.

Anne Leeming
Department of Management Systems and Information, City University
Business School, Barbican Centre, London EC2Y 8HB,UK
e-mail: A.Leeming@city.ac.uk

Anthony Lucas-Smith
Design and Innovation Discipline, The Open University, Walton Hall,
Milton Keynes MK7 6AA, UK
Tel: +44 1908 655022; Fax: +44 1908 654052;
e-mail: a.j.h.lucas-smith@open.ac.uk

Robert D. Macredie
Department of Information Systems and Computing, Brunel University,
Uxbridge, Middlesex UB8 3PH, UK
Tel: +44 1895 203374; Fax: +44 1895 203391;
e-mail: Robert.Macredie@brunel.ac.uk

Kim Merchant
University of Luton, Park Square, Luton, Bedfordshire LU1 3JU, UK

Brian J. O'Connor
B J. O'Connor International Ltd, 10 Aldenholme, Ellesmere Road,
Weybridge, Surrey KT13 0JF, UK
Tel: +44 1932 851334; Fax: +44 1932 854298

Anthony R. Ovenden
22 Tower Road, Tadworth, Surrey KT20 5QY, UK

Ray J. Paul
Department of Information Systems and Computing, Brunel University,
Uxbridge, Middlesex UB8 3PH, UK
Tel: +44 1895 203374; Fax: +44 1895 203391;
e-mail: Ray.Paul@brunel.ac.uk

Nandish V. Patel
Department of Information Systems and Computing, Brunel University,
Uxbridge, Middlesex UB8 3H, UK

Stephen K. Probert
School of Computing and Information Systems Management, Cranfield
University, RMCS Shrivenham, Swindon, Wiltshire SN6 8LA, UK
Tel: +44 1793 785738; Fax: +44 1793 782753;
e-mail: s.k.probert@rmcs.cranfield.ac.uk

Carl Sandom
Department of Information Systems and Computing, Brunel University,
Uxbridge, Middlesex, UB8 3PH, UK
Tel: +44 1895 203374; Fax: +44 1895 203391

David Shaw
Department of Management Systems and Information, City University
Business School, Barbican Centre, London EC2Y 8HB, UK
e-mail: d_shaw@compuserve.com

Alfred D. Vella
University of Luton, Park Square, Luton, Bedfordshire LU1 3JU, UK
e-mail: alfred.vella@luton.ac.uk

Jon Warwick
School of Computing, Information Systems and Mathematics, South
Bank University, 103 Borough Road, London SE1 0AA, UK

Shamim Warwick
University of Luton, Park Square, Luton, Bedfordshire LU1 3JU, UK

G.M. Williams
Cranfield University, Cranfield, Bedfordshire MK43 0AL, UK

Andrew Williamson
Cranfield University, Cranfield, Bedfordshire MK43 0AL, UK
e-mail: A.S.Williamson@Cranfield.ac.uk

Theme I

Modelling for Evaluation and Change

1 Modelling for Change: An Information Systems Perspective on Change Management Models

Robert D. Macredie, Carl Sandom and Ray J. Paul

Abstract

This paper will focus on the topic of organisational change and its management from an information systems perspective. The paper will examine the issues raised during a review of the change management literature – looking at the major approaches to change management, namely, the planned, emergent and contingency approaches – as background to the issues raised in other papers in this theme of the book. As in the Management In The 90s (MIT90s) study, a very broad definition of the term IT is used to include: computers of all types, hardware, software, communications networks, and the integration of computing and communications technologies. The paper will then examine change management within the context of information systems (IS) theory and practice. This will lead to a discussion of an emerging model by Orlikowski and Hofman which will be briefly reviewed to provide insight into the types of models which are likely to provide a focus for research in the area in the near future. The model also provides a strong and interesting framework against which to view some of the papers that follow in this theme of the book.

1.1   Introduction

As we approach the twenty-first century there can be little doubt that successful organisations of the future must be prepared to embrace the concept of change management. Change management has been an integral part of organisational theory and practice for a long time, however, many theorists and practitioners now believe that the rate of change that organisations are subjected to is set to increase significantly in the future. Indeed, some even go so far as to suggest that the future survival of all organisations will depend on their ability to successfully manage change (Burnes 1996; Peters 1989; Toffler 1983).

It could be argued that the study of organisational change management should be the preserve of the social scientist or the business manager. After all, much of the theory has evolved from social and business studies and not from the field of computer science. However, information systems do not exist in a vacuum and it is widely accepted that technology, particularly information technology (IT), is one of the major enablers of organisational change (Markus and Benjamin 1997; Scott-Morton 1991). The successful development of any information system must address sociological issues including the effects of the system itself on the organisation into which it is introduced. Paul (1994) maintains that information systems must be developed specifically for change as they must constantly undergo change to meet changing requirements. Clearly, organisational change is an important issue.

This chapter will focus on the topic of organisational change management from an information systems perspective. The chapter will examine the issues raised during a review of the change management literature as background to the issues raised in other chapters in this theme of the book. As in the Management In The 90s (MIT90s) study (Scott-Morton 1991), a very broad definition of the term IT is used to include: computers of all types, hardware, software, communications networks and the integration of computing and communications technologies.

1.2   Overview of the Field

Many of the theories and models relating to the management of organisational change have evolved from the social sciences (Bate 1994; Burnes 1996; Dawson 1994). Information systems (IS) research is, of course, a much newer discipline. However, the socio-technical nature of information systems is now recognised and many of the IS theories and models have been adopted and adapted from the social sciences (Benjamin and Levinson 1993; Yetton *et al.* 1994).

This chapter presents a discussion on the change management literature drawn from a social science perspective which is then related to an IS perspective of IT-enabled change. We will begin by giving a broad overview of change management and examining the nature of change and its applicability to the IS field. We will then briefly examine the foundations of change management theory. Specifically, the three main theories that underpin the different approaches to change management are examined which concentrate on individual, group and organisation-wide change, respectively.

This chapter will then examine the major approaches to change management, namely the planned, emergent and contingency approaches. The planned approach to change, based on the work of Lewin (1958), has dominated change management theory and practice since the early 1950s. The planned approach views the change process as moving from one fixed state to another. In contrast, the emergent approach, which appeared in the 1980s (Burnes 1996), views change as a process of continually adapting an organisation to align with its environment. The contingency approach is a hybrid approach which advocates that there is not 'one best way' to manage change.

Change management within the context of information systems (IS) theory and practice will then be examined. In particular, this chapter will investigate the fundamental characteristics of IT-enabled change and will discuss how this is different to the management of change in pure social systems.

Finally, the Improvisational Change Model proposed by Orlikowski and Hofman (1997) will be examined in detail. This model is based on the same principles as the emergent approach to change management and, similarly, Orlikowski and Hofman (1997) maintain that their model is more suitable than the traditional Lewinian models for modern, networked organisations using adaptive technologies.

1.3   Change Management

Although it has become a cliché, it is nevertheless true to say that the volatile environment in which modern organisations find themselves today mean that the ability to manage change successfully has become a competitive necessity (Burnes 1996; Kanter 1989; Peters and Waterman 1982). The aim of this section is to provide a broad overview of the substance of change and of change management.

Organisational change is usually required when changes occur to the environment in which an organisation operates. There is no accepted definition of what constitutes this environment, however, a popular and practical working definition is that the environmental variables which influence organisations are political, economical, sociological and technological (Jury 1997).

Change has been classified in many different ways. Most theorists classify change according to the type or the rate of change required, and this is often referred to as the substance of change (Dawson 1994). Bate (1994) proposes a broad definition for the amount of change which he argues may be either *incremental* or *transformational*. Bate maintains that incremental change occurs when an organisation makes a relatively minor change to its technology, processes or structure, whereas transformational change occurs when radical changes programmes are implemented. Bate also argues that modern organisations are subject to continual environmental change and consequently they must constantly change to realign themselves.

Although there is a general recognition for the need to successfully manage change in modern organisations, questions regarding the substance of change and how the process can be managed in today's context remain largely unanswered. There are numerous academic frameworks available in the management literature that seek to explain the issues related to organisational change and many of these frameworks remain firmly rooted in the work of Lewin (1958). Dawson (1994) points out that, almost without exception, contemporary management texts uncritically adopt Lewin's Three-stage Model of planned change, and that this approach is now taught on most modern management courses. This planned (Lewinian) approach to organisational change is examined in detail later in this chapter.

Information systems are inherently socio-technical systems and, therefore, many of the theories and frameworks espoused by the social sciences for the management of change have been adopted by the IS community. Consequently, even the most modern models for managing IT-enabled change are also based on the Lewinian model (Benjamin and Levinson 1993). Figure 1.1 depicts the most popular and prominent models for understanding organisational change which are examined in detail in later sections of this paper. These models will be subsequently be compared with the main change management models adopted by the IS community.

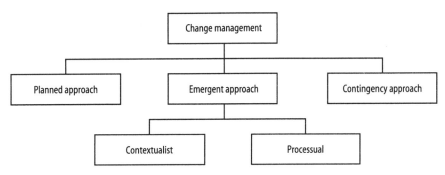

Figure 1.1. Principal change management models.

1.4   Theoretical Foundations

Change management theories and practice originate from different, diverse, social science disciplines and traditions. Consequently, change management does not have clear and distinct boundaries, and the task of tracing its origins and concepts is extremely difficult. This section will briefly examine the foundations of change management theory as these foundations underpin later discussions concerning the most prominent models for understanding organisational change.

Whatever form change takes and whatever the required outcomes of any change initiative, managers responsible for implementing change must address the management issues at either an individual, group or organisational level. It may also be argued that a successful change programme must address the management issues at all levels. Three of the main theories upon which change management theory stands are the individual, group dynamics and the open systems perspectives which are summarised in the remainder of this section.

1.4.1   The Individual Perspective

The individual perspective school is divided into two factions know as the Behaviourists and the Gestalt-field psychologists. Behaviourists believe that behaviour is caused by an individual's interaction with the environment. The basic principle of this approach, which originates from Pavlov's (1927) work, is that human actions are conditioned by their expected consequences. Put simply, this means that rewarded behaviour is repeated while ignored behaviour tends not to be repeated. Gestalt-field protagonists, however, believe that behaviour is not just caused by external stimuli, but that it arises from how an individual uses reason to interpret these stimuli. Behaviourists attempt to effect organisational change by modifying the external stimuli acting upon the individual, whereas Gestalt-field theorists seek to change individual self-awareness to promote behavioural and thus organisational change.

1.4.2   The Group Dynamics Perspective

Group dynamics theorists believe that the focus of change should be at the group or team level, and that it is ineffectual to concentrate on individuals to bring about change as they will be pressured by the group to conform. The group dynamics school has been influential in developing the theory and practice of change management and of all the schools they have the longest history (Schein 1969). Lewin (1958) maintains that the emphasis on effecting organisational change should be through targeting group behaviour rather than individual behaviour as people in organisations work in groups and, therefore, individual behaviour must be seen, modified or changed to align with the prevailing values, attitudes and norms (culture) of the group. The group dynamics perspective manifests itself as the modern management trend for organisations to view themselves as teams rather than merely as a collection of individuals.

1.4.3   The Open Systems Perspective

Proponents of the open systems perspective believe that the focus of change should be neither on the individual nor on the group but that it should be on the entire organisation (Burnes 1996). Organisations are viewed as a collection of intercon-nected sub-systems and the open systems approach is based on analysing these sub-systems to determine how to improve the overall functioning of the organisation. The sub-systems are regarded as *open* because they interact not only internally with each other but also with the external environment. Therefore, internal changes to one sub-system affect other sub-systems which in turn impact on the external environment (Buckley 1968). The open systems perspective focuses on achieving overall synergy rather than on optimising any one individual sub-system (Mullins 1989).

Burke (1987) maintains that this holistic approach to understanding organisations is reflected in an different approach to change management which is driven by three major factors: interdependent sub-systems; training; and management style. An organisation's sub-systems are regarded as interdependent and Burke argues that change cannot occur in one sub-system in isolation without considering the impli-cations for the other sub-systems. He also argues that training cannot achieve organisational change alone as it concentrates on the individual and not on the organisational level. Burke also maintains that modern organisations must adopt a consultative management approach rather than the more prevalent controlling style epitomised by Taylor's (1911) famous work.

1.5   The Planned Approach

Much of the literature relating to the planned approach to organisational change is drawn from Organisational Development (OD) practice and numerous OD protag-onists have developed models and techniques as an aid to understanding the process of change (Dawson 1994). The origins of most of the developments in this field can be traced to the work of Lewin (1958) who developed the highly influential Action Research and Three-phase models of planned change which are summarised in the remainder of this section.

1.5.1   The Action Research Model

Lewin (1958) first developed the Action Research (AR) Model as a planned and col-lective approach to solving social and organisational problems. The theoretical foun-dations of AR lie in Gestalt-field and Group Dynamics theory. Burnes (1996) maintains that this model was based on the basic premise that an effective approach to solving organisational problems must involve a rational, systematic analysis of the issues in question.

AR overcomes "paralysis through analysis" (Peters and Waterman 1982, p. 221) as it emphasises that successful action is based on identifying alternative solutions, evaluating the alternatives, choosing the optimum solution, and, finally, that change is achieved by taking collective action and implementing the solution. The AR approach advocates the use of a change agent and focuses on the organisation, often represented by senior management. The AR approach also focuses on the individ-uals affected by the proposed change. Data related to the proposed change are col-lected by all the groups involved and are iteratively analysed to solve any problems. Although the AR approach emphasises group collaboration, Burnes (1996) argues that cooperation alone is not always enough and that there must also be a 'felt-need' by all the participants.

1.5.2   The Three-phase Model

Lewin's ubiquitous Three-phase Model (1958) is a highly influential model that underpins many of the change management models and techniques today (Burnes 1996; Dawson 1994). The main thrust of this model is that an understanding of the critical steps in the change process will increase the probability of successfully managing change. Lewin (1958) also argues that any improvement in group or individual performance could be prone to regression unless active measures are take to institutionalise the improved performance level. Any subsequent behavioural or performance change must involve the three phases of unfreezing the present level, moving to a new level and refreezing at the new level. Lewin (1958) argues that there are two opposing sets of forces within any social system; these are the driving forces that promote change and the resisting forces that maintain the status quo. Therefore, to unfreeze the system the strength of these forces must be adjusted accordingly. In practice, the emphasis of OD practitioners has been to provide data to unfreeze the system by reducing the resisting forces (Dawson 1994). Once these negative forces are reduced the organisation is moved towards the desired state through the implementation of the new system. Finally, refreezing occurs through a programme of positive reinforcement to internalise new attitudes and behaviour. Burnes (1996) argues that this model merely represents a logical extension to the AR Model as unfreezing and moving, respectively, equate to the research and action phases of the AR Model.

Lewin's Three-phase Model of planned change has since been extended by numerous theorists to enhance its practical application, including Lippitt *et al.*'s (1958) seven-phase model and the Cummings and Huse (1989) eight-phase model. All these models are based on the planned approach to change management and, according to Cummings and Huse (1989), they all share one fundamental concept: "the concept of planned change implies that an organisation exists in different states at different times and that planned movement can occur from one state to another".

The implications of this concept are that an understanding of planned organisational change cannot be gained by simply understanding the *processes* which bring about change, it is also necessary to understand the *states* that an organisation passes through before attaining the desired future state (Burnes 1996).

1.6   The Emergent Approach

Within the social sciences, an approach described by Burnes (1996) as the emergent approach is a popular contemporary alternative to the planned approach to the management of change. The emergent approach was popularised in the 1980s and includes what other theorists have described as processual or contextualist perspectives (Dawson 1994). However, these perspectives share the common rationale that change cannot and should not be 'frozen' nor should it be viewed as a linear sequence of events within a given period as it is with a planned approach. In contrast, with an emergent approach, change is viewed as a continuous process.

The modern business environment is widely acknowledged to be dynamic and uncertain, and, consequently, theorists such as Wilson (1992) and Dawson (1994) have challenged the appropriateness of a planned approach to change management. They advocate that the unpredictable nature of change is best viewed as a process which is affected by the interaction of certain variables (depending on the particular theorist's perspective) and the organisation.

Dawson (1994) proposed an emergent approach based on a processual perspective which he argues is not prescriptive but is analytical and is thus better able to achieve a broad understanding of change management within a complex environment. Put simply, advocates of the processual perspective maintain that there cannot be a prescription for managing change due to the unique temporal and contextual factors affecting individual organisations. Dawson succinctly summarises this perspective, saying that "change needs to be managed as an ongoing and dynamic process and not a single reaction to adverse contingent circumstance" (Dawson 1994, p. 182).

For advocates of the emergent approach it is the uncertainty of the external environment which makes the planned approach inappropriate. They argue that rapid and constant changes in the external environment require appropriate responses from organisations which, in turn, force them to develop an understanding of their strategy, structure, systems, people, style and culture, and how these can affect the change process (Dawson 1994; Pettigrew and Whipp 1993; Wilson 1992). This has, in turn, led to a requirement for a 'bottom-up' approach to planning and implementing change within an organisation. The rapid rate and amount of environmental change has prevented senior managers from effectively monitoring the business environment to decide upon appropriate organisational responses. Pettigrew and Whipp (1993) maintain that emergent change involves linking action by people at all levels of a business. Therefore, with an emergent approach to change, the responsibility for organisational change is devolved and managers must take a more enabling, rather than controlling, approach to managing.

Although the proponents of emergent change may have different perspectives there are, nevertheless, some common themes that relate them all. Change is a continuous process aimed at aligning an organisation with its environment and it is best achieved through many small-scale incremental changes which, over time, can amount to a major organisational transformation. Furthermore, this approach requires the consent of those affected by change – it is only through their behaviour that organisational structures, technologies and processes move from abstract concepts to concrete realities (Burnes 1996).

1.7   The Contingency Approach

Burns and Stalker (1961) established a contingent relationship between an organisation and its environment and the need to adapt to that environment. Perhaps more importantly, they also showed that there was more than 'one best way' to do this. In contrast to both the planned and the emergent approaches to change management, the basic tenet of the contingency approach to change management is that there is no 'one best way' to change.

Although British theorists acknowledge that contingency theory has contributed significantly to organisational design theory, they do not acknowledge that it has had the same impact on change management theory (Bate 1994; Burnes 1996). However, within North America and Australia a rational model of change based on a contingency perspective has prevailed, therefore this section will briefly discuss this approach (Dawson 1994).

A contingency approach has been taken by Dunphy and Stace (1993) who proposed a model of organisational change strategies and developed methods to place an organisation within that model. Dunphy and Stace (1993) maintain that their model reconciles the opposing views of the planned and emergent theoretical protagonists.

Environment

Approaches to change

Figure 1.2. The change management continuum (from Burnes 1996, p. 197).

It can be argued that the planned and emergent approaches to change management are equally valid but that they apply to different organisational circumstances.
For example, an organisation facing constant and significant environmental
changes may find an emergent approach to change management more appropriate
than a planned approach. In short, a model of change could embrace a number of
approaches with the most suitable approach being determined by the organisation's
individual environment. The resultant continuum can be seen in Figure 1.2.

Contingency theory is a rejection of the 'one best way' approach taken by the
majority of change management protagonists. This approach adopts the perspective
that an organisation is 'contingent' on the situational variables it faces and, therefore,
organisations must adopt the most appropriate change management approach.

1.8   IT-Enabled Organisational Change

Previous sections of this chapter have dealt with the different approaches to managing organisational change taken from a social science perspective. Regardless of
which model is adopted, the requirement for an organisation to change is generally caused by changes in its environmental variables which many academics and practitioners agree are political, economic, sociological and technological (Jury 1997;
Scott-Morton 1991). This section will focus on one of these environmental variables,
namely technology, in the specific form of information technology (IT), and will
examine the major issues that are particular to IT-enabled change.

Woodward's (1965) study demonstrated the need to take into account technological variables when designing organisations and this gave credibility to the argument for technological determinism which implies that organisational structure is
'determined' by the form of the technology. However, despite the general acceptance
that the application of change management techniques can considerably increase
the probability of a project's success, many IT-enabled change projects have failed
for non-technical reasons. Some projects, such as the London Ambulance Service
Computer Aided Dispatch System, have failed with fatal consequences (Benyon-
Davies 1995). Markus and Benjamin (1997) attribute this to what they describe as
the magic bullet theory of IT, whereby IT specialists erroneously believe in the magic
power of IT to create organisational transformation. Some academics argue that
although IT is an *enabling* technology it cannot by itself *create* organisational change
(Markus and Benjamin 1997; McKersie and Walton 1991).

McKersie and Walton (1991) maintain that to create IT-enabled organisational
change it is necessary to actively manage the changes. They also argue that the
effective implementation of IT is, at its core, a task of managing change. The

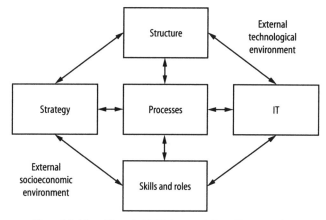

Figure 1.3. Adapted from the MIT90s framework (Scott-Morton 1991).

Management In The 1990s (MIT90s) programme (Scott-Morton 1991) proposed a framework for understanding the interactions between the forces involved in IT-enabled organisational change. A simplified adaptation of this framework is shown in Figure 1.3.

Proponents of the MIT90s model maintain that to successfully manage IT-enabled change it is necessary to ensure that the organisational choices, the technology and the strategic choices depicted in Figure 1.3 are properly aligned (Scott-Morton 1991). In contrast, Yetton (1994) challenges the view that the critical issue in managing IT successfully is alignment. They argue that IT can be used deliberately to modify an organisation's strategy and also that the MIT90s framework is a static model that does not address the dynamic nature of change. Nonetheless, despite this criticism, the MIT90s study has been highly influential to IS academics and practitioners (Benjamin and Levinson 1993; Yetton 1994). The MIT90s study concluded that the benefits of IT are not generally being realised by organisations because investment is biased towards technology and not towards managing changes in organisational processes, structure and culture.

Benjamin and Levinson (1993) maintain that IT-enabled change is different from change which is driven by other environmental concerns. They argue that skills, jobs and organisational control processes change radically. Zuboff (1988) also described the revolutionary changes in jobs and control processes within organisations that take full advantage of IT as workers become 'informated' and thus empowered. Ives and Jarvenpaa (1994) provide a vision of the effect of IT-enabled changes on basic work methods as organisations become global networked organisations to take advantage of collaborative work methods. IT-enabled changes also span across functions and organisations as technology enables increased inter- and intra-organisational coordination with decreased transaction costs (Kalakota and Whinston 1996).

Many academics and practitioners would agree that IT-enabled change is different from more general change processes and that change must be managed to be successful (Benjamin and Levinson 1993; Yetton 1994). Clearly, the change process must be understood to be managed and a number of models have been proposed for this. One such model is Benjamin and Levinson's (1993) which draws on the general change management literature to develop a framework for managing IT-enabled change. This framework is typical of many IS change models (Orlikowski and Hofman 1997) which have been adopted and adapted from the social sciences, and are based on the Lewinian unfreeze, change and refreeze approach to change management discussed previously. However, in a situation reminiscent of the developments within the social sciences, a number of new IT-enabled change management models are now emerging which are based on the emergent or contingent approaches to change management.

1.9 Orlikowski and Hofman's Improvisational Change Model

A key example of this type of model is presented by Orlikowski and Hofman (1997). We will review this model here to provide insight into the types of models which are likely to provide a focus for research in the area in the near future. The model also provides a strong and interesting framework against which to view some of the papers that follow in this theme of the book. Theirs is an improvisational model for managing technological change which is an alternative to the predominant Lewinian models. They maintain that IT-enabled change managers should take as a model the Trukese navigator who begins with an objective rather than a plan and responds to conditions as they arise in an ad hoc fashion. They also argue that traditional Lewinian change models are based on the fallacious assumption that change occurs only during a specified period, whereas they maintain that change is now a constant. This is similar to the arguments of the proponents of the emergent change management approach which were examined earlier in this chapter.

The origins of Orlikowski and Hofman's (1997) Improvisational Change Model can be found in a study by Orlikowski (1996) which examined the use of new IT within one organisation over a 2-year period. The study concluded by demonstrating the critical role of situated change enacted by organisational members using groupware technology over time. Mintzberg (1987) first made the distinction between deliberate and emergent strategies, and Orlikowski (1996) argues that the perspectives which have influenced studies of IT-enabled organisational change have similarly neglected *emergent* change. Orlikowski challenges the arguments that organisational change must be planned, that technology is the primary cause of technology-based organisational transformation and that radical changes always occur rapidly and discontinuously. In contrast, she maintains that organisational transformation is an ongoing improvisation enacted by organisational actors trying to make sense of, and act coherently in, the world.

1.9.1 Model Assumptions and Types of Change

Orlikowski and Hofman's (1997) Improvisational Change Model is based on two major assumptions. First, that changes associated with technology implementations constitute an ongoing process rather than an event with an end point after which an organisation can return to a state of equilibrium. Second, that every technological and organisational change associated with the ongoing process cannot be anticipated in advance. Based on these assumptions, Orlikowski and Hofman (1997) have identified three different types of change.

- *Anticipated change*: anticipated changes are planned ahead of time and occur as intended. For example, the implementation of e-mail that accomplishes its intended aim of facilitating improved communications.

- *Opportunity-based change*: opportunity-based changes are not originally anticipated but are intentionally introduced during the ongoing change process in
response to an unexpected opportunity. For example, as companies gain experience with the World Wide Web they may deliberately respond to unexpected
opportunities to leverage its capabilities.
- *Emergent change*: emergent changes arise spontaneously from local innovation
and that are not originally anticipated or intended. For example, the use of
e-mail as an informal grapevine for disseminating rumours throughout an
organisation.

Orlikowski and Hofman (1997) maintain that both anticipated and opportunity-
based changes involve deliberate action in contrast to emergent changes which arise
spontaneously and usually tacitly from organisational members' actions over time.
Furthermore, they contend that the three types of change usually build iteratively
on each other in an undefined order over time. They also argue that practical change
management using the Improvisational Change Model requires a set of processes
and mechanisms to recognise the different types of change as they occur and to
respond effectively to them.

1.9.2 Critical Enabling Conditions

Orlikowski and Hofman (1997) suggest that there are certain enabling conditions
which must be fulfilled to allow their Improvisational Change Model to be successfully adopted for implementing technology within an organisation. The first of these
enabling conditions is that dedicated resources must be allocated to provide ongoing support for the change process which Orlikowski and Hofman (1997) maintain
is inherently continuous. They also suggest that another enabling condition is the
interdependent relationship between the organisation, the technology and the
change model as depicted in Figure 1.4.

Orlikowski and Hofman's (1997) research suggested that the interaction between
these key change dimensions must ideally be aligned or, at least, not in opposition.
Their research also suggested that an Improvisation Change Model may only be
appropriate for introducing open-ended technology into organisations with adaptive cultures. Open-ended technology is defined by them as technology which is
locally adaptable by end users with customisable features and the ability to create
new applications. They maintain that open-ended technology is typically used in different ways across an organisation. Orlikowski and Hofman appear to share similar views to the contingency theorists discussed earlier as they do not subscribe to
the view that there is 'one best way' for managing IT-enabled change.

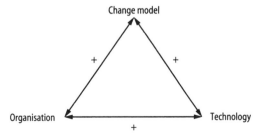

Figure 1.4. Aligning the key change dimensions (from Orlikowski and Hofman 1997, p. 18).

Orlikowski's (1996) research, upon which Orlikowski and Hofman's (1997) Improvisational Change Model is based, concluded that further empirical research was needed to determine the extent to which an improvisational perspective of organisational change is useful in other contexts and how different organisational and technological conditions influence the improvisations attempted and implemented. Orlikowski and Hofman's (1997) Improvisational Change Model is a first attempt at moving this research theme forward and it is an area which is likely to grow in importance over the next few years.

1.10 Summary

The dominant theories and models relating to the management of change have evolved from the social sciences. IS research is relatively much newer and the socio-technical nature of information systems has caused most IS theories and models to be adapted from the social sciences. The main theories that provide the foundation for general change management approaches are the individual, group dynamics and the open systems perspectives. The planned approach to change management tends to concentrate on changing the behaviour of individuals and groups through participation. In contrast, the newer emergent approach to change management focuses on the organisation as an open system with its objective being to continually realign the organisation with its changing external environment.

Lewin's (1958) model is a highly influential planned approach model that underpins many of the change management models and techniques today, and most contemporary management texts adopt this three-phase unfreeze, change and refreeze model. The rationale of the newer emergent approach is that change should not be 'frozen' or viewed as a linear sequence of events but that it should be viewed as an ongoing process. Contingency theory is a rejection of the 'one best way' approach taken by planned and emergent protagonists. The contingency approach adopts the perspective that an organisation is 'contingent' on the situational variables it faces and, therefore, it must adopt the most appropriate change management approach.

Many IT-enabled change projects fail despite the general acceptance that change management can considerably increase the probability of a project's success. This is often attributable to the misconception that IT is not only an *enabling* technology but that it can also *create* organisational change. The highly influential MIT90s framework is useful for understanding the interactions between the forces involved in IT-enabled organisational change which must be aligned to create successful organisations.

IT-enabled change is different from changes driven by other environmental concerns and the process must be understood to be managed. Consequently, many IS change models have adopted and adapted the Lewinian unfreeze, change and refreeze approach to change management. However, in a situation reminiscent of the developments within the social sciences, a number of new IT-enabled change management models are now emerging which are based on the emergent or contingent approaches to change management.

Orlikowski and Hofman (1997) have proposed an improvisational model for managing technological change as one alternative to the predominant Lewinian models. This improvisational model is based on the assumptions that technological changes constitute an ongoing process and that every change associated with the ongoing process cannot be anticipated beforehand. Based on these assumptions Orlikowski and Hofman (1997) have identified three different types of change, namely, anticipated, opportunity-based and emergent. Both anticipated and opportunity-based changes involve deliberate action in contrast to emergent changes which arise spontaneously and usually tacitly from organisational actors' actions over time. These three types of change build iteratively on each other in an undefined order over time. Orlikowski and Hofman (1997) suggest that the critical enabling conditions which must be fulfilled to allow their Improvisational Change Model to be successfully adopted for implementing technology are aligning the key dimensions of change and allocating dedicated resources to provide ongoing support for the change process.

The review of models of change presented in this chapter provides background for the following papers in this theme, and provides a developing research perspective against which to view the issues discussed by the other authors.

References

Bate, P (1994) *Strategies for Cultural Change*. Oxford:Butterworth-Heinemann.

Benjamin, RI and Levinson, E (1993) A framework for managing IT-enabled change. *Sloan Management Review*, Summer: 23–33.

Benyon-Davies, P (1995) Information systems failure: The case of the London Ambulance Service's Computer Aided Dispatch Project. *European Journal of Information Systems*, 4: 171–184.

Buckley, W (1968) *Modern Systems and Research for the Behavioural Scientist*. Chicago, IL: Aldine Publishing.

Burke, WW (1987) *Organization Development: A Normative View*. Wokingham: Addison-Wesley.

Burnes, B (1996) *Managing Change: A Strategic Approach to Organisational Dynamics*. London: Pitman.

Burns, T and Stalker, GM (1961) *The Management of Innovation*. London: Tavistock.

Cummings, TG and Huse, EF (1989) *Organisational Development and Change*. St Paul, CN: Southwestern.

Dawson, P (1994) *Organisational Change: A Processual Approach*. London: Paul Chapman Publishing.

Dunphy, D and Stace, D (1993) The strategic management of corporate change. *Human Relations*, 46(8): 905–920.

Ives, B and Jarvenpaa, SL (1994) The global network organisation of the future: information management opportunities and challenges. *Journal of Management Information Systems*, 10(4): 25–57.

Jury, GM (1997) Managing technology: the environment in which technology is managed. *IEE Engineering Management Journal*, 7(1): 27–32.

Kalakota, R and Whinston, AB (1996) *Frontiers of Electronic Commerce*. Reading, MA: Addison-Wesley.

Kanter, RM (1989) *When Giants Learn to Dance: Mastering the Challenges of Strategy Management and Careers in the 1990s*. London: Unwin.

Lewin, K (1958) Group decisions and social change. In *Readings in Social Psychology*. Swanson, GE, Newcomb, TM and Hartley, EL (Eds). New York: Holt, Rhinehart and Winston.

Lippitt, R, Watson, J and Westley, B (1958) *The Dynamics of Planned Change*. New York: Harcourt Brace and World.

Markus, ML and Benjamin, RI (1997) The magic bullet theory in IT-enabled transformation. *Sloan Management Review*, Winter: 55–68.

McKersie, RB and Walton, RE (1991) Organisational change. In *The Corporation of the 1990s: Information Technology and Organisational Transformation*. Scott-Morton, MS (Ed.). London: Oxford University Press.

Mintzberg, H (1987) Crafting strategy. *Harvard Business Review*, July–August: 66–75.

Mullins L (1989) *Management and Organisational Behaviour*. London: Pitman.

Orlikowski, WJ (1996) Improvising organisational transformation over time: a situated change perspective. *Information Systems Research*, 7(1): 63–92.

Orlikowski, WJ and Hofman JD (1997) An improvisational model for change management: the case of groupware technologies. *Sloan Management Review*, Winter: 11–21.

Paul, RJ (1994) Why users cannot 'get what they want'. *International Journal of Manufacturing Systems Design*, 1(4): 389–394.

Pavlov, IP (1927) *Conditioned Reflexes* (translation). London: Oxford University Press.

Peters, TJ (1989) *Thriving on Chaos*. London: Pan.

Peters, TJ and Waterman, RH (1982) *In Search of Excellence: Lessons from America's Best Run Companies*. London: Harper and Row.

Pettigrew, A and Whipp, R (1993) Understanding the environment. In *Managing Change*. Mabey, C and Mayon-White, B (Eds). London: Open University/Paul Chapman Publishing.

Schein, EH (1969) *Process Consultation.* Reading, MA: Addison-Wesley.

Scott-Morton, MS (Ed.) (1991) *The Corporation of the 1990s: Information Technology and Organisational Transformation.* London: Oxford University Press.

Taylor, F (1911) *The Principles of Scientific Management.* New York: Harper.

Toffler, A (1983) *Future Shock.* London: Bodley Head.

Wilson, DC (1992) *A Strategy of Change.* London: Routledge.

Woodward, J (1965) *Industrial Organisation: Theory and Practice.* London: Oxford University Press.

Yetton, PW (1994) Computer-aided architects: a case study of IT and strategic change. *Sloan Management Review,* Summer: 57–67.

Zuboff, S (1988) *In the Age of the Smart Machine: The Future of Work and Power.* Oxford: Heinemann Professional.

2 Information Systems as Powerful Forces of Change

D. (Rajan) Anketell

Abstract

This paper makes a brief journey through time in order to describe some of the landmarks in the evolution and development of information systems. These observations indicate that information systems have from the very earliest times in the history of our planet exerted a very great influence. At first, and for a very long period, information systems based on natural biological systems were predominant. These appeared to act in a harmonious and self-regulatory manner which resulted in stable ecosystems. More recently the mantle of change has been passed to information systems based on technological advances made by mankind. While many of these advances have provided great benefits, the manner in which some of these are being used is causing some concern and giving rise to the question of whether our knowledge is outstripping our wisdom.

2.1   Introduction

Throughout the history of this planet information systems (IS) have made a significant contribution to the rise and fall of whole species, civilisations, religions, governments and commercial organisations. Other factors such as climatic changes have also played their part and there have been periods of stability followed by times of great upheaval. Our own era appears to be one of almost unprecedented change. The explosive advances in our knowledge and technology are forcing many local and global changes in the way that individuals, commercial organisations and governments conduct their affairs. The first part of this chapter contains a short historical account of information systems in nature and in developing civilisations. The second part examines some of the more recent advances and questions whether adequate provisions are being made to realise the tremendous potential gains while avoiding the dangers. Has our knowledge outstripped our wisdom?

2.2   Natural History

Natural history enthusiasts and television viewers who have followed Sir David Attenborough's *Life on Earth*, and other related series, will be aware that information systems are an essential inherent feature of the life forms which first appeared on this earth millions of years ago. In order to survive, grow and regenerate even the simplest life forms needed to process information relating to both their external and internal environments. The reliance on information systems increased when individual cells combined to form larger and more complex tightly knit interdependent units. These mergers could not succeed unless the actions of individuals within the whole were coordinated and this created the need for specialisation, a system of internal communication and memory. These early systems were very crude. However, new life forms and their information systems were developed and refined by the evolutionary forces of natural selection over millions of years. Many species with inferior information systems were displaced by superior progeny and over this very long period a harmonious balance was remarkably maintained. As a result there is today a varied and wonderful selection of interdependent life forms. Superior information systems support those at the higher levels of the food chain, with man elevated to the apex with the aid of a complex nervous system controlled by a large powerful brain. Indeed, life itself could be considered to be a complex information system because DNA and genes, the very essence of life, appear to be nothing more than packets of information containing the very complex set of coded instructions required to create and sustain the rich diversity of life.

Later on in the history of our planet, some of the more advanced insects and animals found that further advantages were to be gained by forming into groups for protection, procreation and the acquisition of food. In order for these independent individuals to act in concert in the determination and achievement of common goals, it was necessary for them to develop information systems containing elements of recognition, communication and decision making. How life began remains a mystery, but there can be no doubt as to the prominent position occupied by information systems.

2.3 Early Glimmers of Technological Leverage

All life is a struggle for survival against the vagaries of nature and, until relatively recently, all species had to depend on their inherent mental and physical powers. This began to change with the evolution of those species that resulted in our own *Homo sapiens*. Individuals in these species discovered how to enhance their physical powers through the use of tools. They also began to enhance their inherent information systems by developing more elaborate methods of visual and vocal communication. Vocal communication reached a high degree of sophistication in man and was a major factor in the fight for survival over other life forms. It reinforced the drive towards group activity and helped knowledge to be passed on by word of mouth from a few gifted individuals to others and from generation to generation. This led to the development of a wide range of tools and implements, and helped the move towards increasing specialisation supported by families, religious sects, secret societies, professional and trade groups, etc. A few thousand years ago man's inherent information systems were further leveraged by external data storage through the use of various symbols on stone and clay tablets. Although difficult to reproduce, a few copies could be made and transported to other locations. These early attempts at external data storage and communication over distance enabled knowledge to be more easily distributed and helped man to distance himself even further from other species. It also played a part in differentiation within our own species. The use of paper made from papyrus reeds reinforced the development of writing, but it was the invention of the printing press which provided a very much cheaper method of disseminating and storing information. It transformed the nature of society by making information more accessible to a much wider audience. This helped to strengthen the move towards greater democracy and also weaken the influence of the Church in Europe. Those organisations which developed and exploited superior information systems (whether civil, military or commercial) tended to be more successful. Each new major advance brought great changes to the structure of societies and to the relationships within them as the size of groupings increased from families, clans, cities, city states, kingdoms to the nations of the present day and to the first tentative steps of the infant virtual society in the global village.

2.4 Developments in Technology

The pace of change has continued to increase sharply over the last 50 years with advances in branches of mathematics, science, bio-technology and engineering. These have contributed to the invention of the transistor, the integrated circuit, satellites and networks which form the basis of the continuing development in computing, information and communication technology. These developments, which are summarised below, have already been instrumental in many significant changes to our industries, commercial organisations, education systems and society with the promise of even more radical changes.

2.4.1 Mainframes

The first commercial electronic computers that were developed in the 1960s were very large and expensive, and were only affordable by the military organisations of the major powers and a few of the larger academic and commercial organisations. These machines, which subsequently became known as mainframes and heralded the dawn of the age of computing, were difficult to use and program. Most of the early applications were relatively simple and the computers were used mainly as transaction-processing machines. They helped to remove much of the drudgery of many low-level repetitive operations. They were also able to perform many numerical iterative computations that were not previously possible by other methods, and this proved to be of great help in some branches of mathematics, science and engineering.

2.4.2 The Mini

As hardware technology developed thermal vacuum tube valves were replaced by the transistor, the integrated circuit and by other products of increasing miniaturisation. This resulted in the development in the late 1960s and early 1970s of powerful smaller 'mini' computers. Programming languages also progressed from the difficult machine languages and assemblers to higher-level languages such as COBOL, FORTRAN and RPG. The new minis were much easier to use and were also much cheaper. This fuelled a mini explosion and the numbers of computers in use multiplied rapidly. The governments of smaller countries and smaller organisations were able to install them and begin to reap some of the benefits of automation. Industry was able to profit from automation in some process-control systems in many areas of engineering production. Commercial organisations also obtained further benefits in the white-collar area. With these developments came the first signs of potential social problems in relation to redundancies in unskilled sectors.

2.4.3 The Information Technology (IT) Revolution Begins

Further important developments in technology resulted in the production of even smaller desk-top computers in the late 1970s. These microcomputers were almost as powerful as the early mainframes. Mass production greatly reduced the prices of the hardware and operating systems. Off-the-shelf software for applications such as accounting and word processing became available. The combination of cheap hardware and software put computing power within the reach of the very small organisation and even the individual. This gave rise to the generic name of the 'personal computer' (PC). Small, powerful processors also helped further improvements to be made in process control and manufacturing methods. More manual operations were de-skilled. Some companies linked to older technologies were unable to adapt and passed into oblivion. Fortunately, new IT-related industries were born and some new jobs created. The industrial nature of many countries was dramatically changed. Whole industries moved across frontiers and economic power began to shift from the Atlantic basin to the Far East and the Pacific basin.

2.4.4 Memory Chips and Central Processors

Developments in engineering technology have enabled an increasing number of transistors and other components to be manufactured in integrated circuits on a single microchip. In 1964 Gordon Moore, a co-founder of Intel, noticed that their number on a single chip doubled every year. His prediction that this would continue has proved to be roughly correct over almost 30 years. If, as is likely, this progression continues PCs will soon have gigabyte memory chips enabling their users to have many gigabytes of memory at their disposal. Microprocessors have also been increasing in power. Intel's target (in 1994) for the year 2000 was 2000 million instructions per second (mips) and some other manufacturers are hoping for 10 000 mips at a cost of about 10 cents per mip. This means that the fast processors (250 mips) in some of today's mainframes costing many millions of dollars will probably be considered for use only in appliances such as television, washing-machines, etc., and the intelligent house and office will move from the realm of fantasy to reality.

2.4.5 Off-line Storage

There is no reason to doubt that similar improvements will be made to the capacities of off-line storage media such as magnetic diskettes, cartridges, tapes, discs and optional storage systems. This would allow for the widespread use of document image processing systems, and automate departmental and company-wide workflow.

2.4.6 Communications

The speeds at which data are transmitted over the public services networks have also been increasing but at a slower pace. This means that it has not been possible to transmit effectively and cheaply large packets of data such as those associated with multimedia applications. However, the great demand for these services is likely to result in an early breakthrough.

Local area networks have enabled individual PCs to be linked together and share common components such as printers and data storage. The hardware developments are being complemented in the software arena with applications for cooperative working, workflow and electronic conferencing.

Personal mobile communications have been in use for some years. At present they are expensive and are restricted to a limited geographical area. As with all other new products, there will be improvements in cost and service. This will bring their use within the reach of most individuals and thus help increase their level of personal security, a feature that will be of particular benefit to the more vulnerable members of society such as children, women and senior citizens.

At the other extreme, advances in communication systems have led to a shrinking of global distances. The widespread dissemination of information has helped to bring about a greater understanding between peoples of different nations and made it difficult for governments to act in total isolation. It has also altered trading patterns and helped in the creation of the great multinational commercial organisations.

2.4.7   Open Systems

There is an increasing demand for standardisation and for so-called 'open systems'. To some this means the use of UNIX and to others the use Microsoft Windows as the standard. To many others it means that every hardware and software component should be interchangeable, i.e. be the same, and proprietary systems abolished. At first glance these may appear to be reasonable views because the benefits seems to be great. However, history has demonstrated that those with the superior information systems have the edge. Therefore, competition from all quarters (especially the users of information systems) will ensure that such openness (equality) will never be achieved. A more realistic objective is inter-connectivity between different proprietary systems in a manner that is transparent to the user. This is why the systems pioneered on the Internet are now replacing client server systems as Intranets (internal systems) and Extranets (special inter-company secure systems). This 'openness' is more likely to succeed and is a major step towards the achievement of very powerful information systems.

2.4.8   IS as an Aid to Decision Making

The early software systems used the processing power of the computer for low-level data processing. The information produced was subsequently manipulated manually in order to provide management with a higher level of information as an aid to decision making. More sophisticated software was developed in an attempt to remove completely the element of manual processing. However, these systems were only as good as their designers and had many limitations. This prompted Professor Russell Ackoff to express the view that the problem was not the lack of information but too much misinformation. Subsequently other variations of the software were developed under labels such as decision systems, economic models, strategic information systems, executive information systems, etc.

Many of these systems were based on sets of initial assumptions and rules (models) which had little flexibility. Their introduction was much heralded but they proved to have limited value especially in complex situations. On the other hand, biological systems possess great flexibility with the ability to learn. The need to incorporate these desirable features initiated research into the development of 'intelligent systems'.

2.4.9   Artificial Intelligence, Expert and Knowledge-based Systems

The development of artificial intelligence is a daunting task and it is unreasonable to expect man to achieve in a short time a state which has taken Nature millions of years. An attempt at simplification was made with the definition and development of some of the component elements of 'intelligence'. One of the early class of systems enabled the encapsulation of the experience (knowledge) of experts, and new languages such as Lisp were devised for this purpose. The aim of these systems was to help less-skilled personnel make informed decisions. Subsequent simple sets of rules were included in order to automate some of the decision-making processes. Expert systems have moved from the laboratory into some areas of industry and commerce. They have been used by Barclaycard to help uncover cases of fraud by detecting variations in normal patterns of credit card use. They have also been used in insurance and manufacturing systems. At present there is a high cost in developing, amending and testing these systems. This makes them unsuitable for use in situations that are subject to frequent change. Their limitations are providing the impetus for research into neural networks and systems that are flexible and can learn. However, there is much to be done. The Daleks of Dr Who are fortunately a long way off.

Audio and visual pattern recognition is another area of artificial intelligence under investigation. Recent developments have enabled great improvements in photography and in the manipulation of visual images and audio signals.

Most man-made transmission systems are based on digital techniques where very small errors could result in very large errors in data. For example, an error of one bit could make the difference between a very large or small number, or between yes or no (fight or flight). Although some error-detection and correction mechanisms have been devised, they are far from perfect. Biological transmission systems, on the other hand, use impulse frequency as a measure of magnitude. This means that a small error in the transmission is unlikely to have a significant impact on the meaning of the message. Current developments in technology may enable this form of transmission to be used, particularly in safety-critical systems.

2.4.10   Mice, Windows, Touch Screens, Voice and Multimedia

The use of graphical user interfaces, mice and touchscreens have made computer systems much easier to use both at home and at work. Touchscreens, for example, are used in a number of sales outlets. Developments in vocal systems have been slower but are gathering pace. Their use will further simplify the man–machine interface. The ability to manipulate audio and visual images have been combined in some applications. A few years ago the hardware and software costs of multimedia systems were in the region of £250 000. Now it is possible to obtain simple systems for under £5000. As a result these systems are beginning to find uses in education, electronic conferencing, marketing and sales.

2.4.11   Simulation and Virtual Reality

One of the main planks of the 'scientific method' is the development and testing of alternative theories by observations and experimentation. Unfortunately, it is not always possible to study the effects of alternatives in a real-life situation. This is because the studies would be very expensive, complex, take too long to complete or result in the destruction of the system. Under these circumstances recourse has to be made to the use of models which can be used to simulate those aspects of the system under investigation. Clearly, the more closely the model represents reality, the better the results. Advances in mathematics and computer technology have helped simulation make a great contribution to many branches of engineering, general management and training. For example, design engineers have been able to study the behaviour of bridges even to the point of destruction under a variety of conditions of traffic and weather; and flight simulators have been used to reduce risk and cost in training.

Commercial organisations have also begun to make use of simulation to help them improve their service to customers at reduced cost.

2.5 Some IS-induced Changes and Implications

Some of the major developments in the individual hardware and software components of IS have been discussed above. Most have resulted in massive increases in power and reductions in cost. Taken together, they have been instrumental in some of the great changes that have already taken place and further upheavals can be expected. Below are a few examples that have been selected from diverse areas such as banking, insurance, departmental and organisation structure, home working, and education.

2.5.1 Banking

Developments in information systems continue to have a profound effect in all areas of banking. Until recently, personal banking facilities were almost the sole province of all the major banks with many high street branches operating at high cost. In the early 1990s First Direct (owned by the Midland Bank) was formed to provide banking by telephone. It had no high street branches but by September 1992 had collected about 300 000 customers. In 1995 this was increasing at the rate of 10 000 per month. In 1995 the National Westminster Bank had about 700 000 customers using Action Line, its home electronic banking system. Home banking is cheaper for the customers, as well as for the banks. Therefore, this trend will accelerate and many other financial services are likely to be offered. Operating costs will be dramatically reduced by maintaining only a very small core of branches (like the building societies). This will increase unemployment and add to the number of vacant office premises.

Another major change brought about by a complementary use of their information systems is the entry into personal banking by some large retailing organisations such as supermarkets. This competition is forcing the more conservative conventional banks to re-examine their practices in order to survive.

2.5.2 Insurance

The initial benefits of computer quotation systems and electronic data interchange (EDI) have helped the insurer, the intermediary and the public. There are, however, some disturbing trends for a number of the participants. The first to be adversely affected is the high street intermediary. Banks have moved into this area and some insurers are bypassing the intermediary. Other big organisations such as department stores and building societies are beginning to make use of the new information technologies and offer insurance services directly to the public. There are only a few quotation systems available and some of the big insurers have either completely taken over suppliers of these systems or have taken large stakes in them. This means that, in future, smaller insurance companies may well be discriminated against and, without protective legislation, may well disappear. As personal computers increase in power and become more widespread, customers will be able to deal directly with their insurers. This may result in the demise of many insurance intermediaries leading to further redundancies.

2.5.3   Retail Applications

Multimedia systems are beginning to make an impact on the way some retail business is conducted, with some Scandinavian countries leading the way. They have been used by estate agents to reduce the average number of visits prior to purchase from six to two. Motor car sales have also been improved by their use. In another example, from the United States, the sales of shoes have been boosted by the use of multimedia kiosks with PCs replacing sales staff. Many organisations in a number of countries appear to be conducting pilot studies. Further changes to purchasing patterns would be made by linking these systems to PCs in the home.

Data Warehousing and Data Mining are two other innovative uses of information systems which are helping to transform the retail industry. The ability to store detailed information on customers and their purchasing habits enables retailers to target individuals with specific sales and marketing information. It has also helped some large organisations to enter the financial services market.

Some retailers are now doing business solely on the Internet. An example is the Internet Book Company in the United States which quickly gained a significant share of the market.

2.5.4   Virtual Organisations

In the past, companies would use mergers and takeovers in vertical integration of supplier, manufacturer and retailer as a method of improving control and, hence, profitability. They were not always successful for a number of reasons. These included problems with investment, a disproportionate initial expenditure in time and money, and subsequent organisational problems. Many of the benefits of physical mergers with none of the disadvantages have been achieved by the vertical integration of the information systems of independent organisations. Levi Strauss in the United States and its trading partners have been able to achieve this by linking their IS. This enables all parties to know almost immediately what is being bought by the customer and enables the correct inventory levels to be maintained all along the whole supply chain from the retailer to the raw-material supplier.

Another example of a virtual organisation is that of the supplier who takes orders for customised PCs over the Internet. Payment is made via the Internet to a bank and the order is completed by a number of different organisations in different locations (which could be in different countries), who supply the components and assemblies, and the final product is shipped to the customer within a short period. This method helps to keep the overall cost of production and supply to a minimum while providing a high level of customer service.

2.6   The Intranet and Major Internal Organisational Changes

Information systems provided by the use of Intranets have already brought about many changes in the work patterns within organisations. A few examples are provided to give an indication of the tremendous potential of the technology.

2.6.1   Electronic Mail, Workflow and Document Image Processing

All these features can and have been integrated in order to improve efficiency within the workplace. They avoid the usual problems of manual systems such as bottlenecks and missing files. Incoming mail can be scanned and the images stored, indexed and routed from operator to operator. The actions of each operator can be automatically checked prior to release to the text. Two or more operators can even work on the same document at the same time. Further advantages are to be gained by linking these systems with the existing traditional data-processing systems

2.6.2   Concurrent Engineering

Concurrent engineering (CE) is a method used to improve efficiency and complement other developments in industry such as 'total quality' and 'just-in-time manufacturing'. Many different departments are involved in the introduction of a new product. These include design, marketing, purchasing, manufacturing, quality management and senior executives. In the past there was little integration among these various functions. CE enables them to act in concert through the use of a highly automated flow of computerised product information. CE systems and the use of multidisciplined teams with the inclusion of an IS representative are being used by a number of organisations to improve efficiency and competitive edge. One of them, Martin Marrietta Areo & Naval Systems Division in Baltimore, USA, was able to bid 20–30% lower on some jobs because less time and material was wasted in manufacturing.

In a further development of this principle, global organisations can follow the sun and work 24 hours around the clock using fresh teams by passing partially completed work from office to office. This enables them to gain a competitive edge through a reduction in the lead time of some large projects.

2.6.3   Electronic Publishing

There is increasing use of the Internet by organisations publishing their catalogues and service manuals. Other service organisations such as United Parcels are providing up to date information on progress through access to their databases via the Internet. In both cases not only have costs been dramatically reduced but the level of customer service has also been significantly increased.

2.6.4   Home Computing and Teleworking

As the cost of computer systems and their power increases, more households will be able to obtain the benefits of their use. Most of the benefits relate to the ability to make purchase decisions and even purchases without the need to leave home. The increase in teleworking will also reduce the need to travel. Academic education could also be undertaken from home. The implications of these changes will include a big reduction in white-collar workers; many retail, office and even educational premises falling vacant; and a reduction in the use of transport systems.

2.6.5   Genetic Testing and Bio-engineering

The final example is one in which mankind is attempting to improve on Nature by altering the genetic codes of the fundamental building blocks of life. These experiments are causing considerable controversy because they have the potential not only for great benefits but also great harm.

2.7   Conclusions

Information systems have been seen to be essential. They have also been seen as powerful forces of change. Many of the changes have brought great benefits. However, there are signs of potential problems of great magnitude. Nature had developed the information systems and the intrinsic power of species in a manner that maintained a balance. The ability of man to develop and use technologies of great power appears to have upset this balance.

Much money, effort and ingenuity has been expended in the development of information and other technologies. Much less time has been devoted to the study of environmental and social problems caused by these development; and there is now a danger not only of self-destruction but of destruction of the whole ecosystem. Attention has been focused on short-term gain at the expense of long-term security and survival, and it is vital that this situation is reversed quickly.

There is no simple answer to this problem. However, it has to be faced by everyone, the public, commercial organisations and governments. One way to proceed may be to use a proportion of the profits from new technologies to fund research into possible consequences of their use. Information can be a source of wealth and power. We have the power. Let us use it wisely.

3 How the Open University Uses Information Technology to Provide Distance Learning in a Competitive Market

Anthony Lucas-Smith

Abstract

The education field has become very competitive. This chapter describes some of the ways in which the Open University (OU) is using information technology (IT) to make radical changes in its operation, in order to provide high value distance education and maintain its competitiveness. It is finding new ways to improve the learning experience, to develop new material and to assess students' performance. IT has been progressively used to make the OU a realistic alternative to traditional universities. The 1980s saw a huge growth in the use of personal computers (PCs) by students, particularly for simulation exercises in many subjects. In the late 1990s CD-ROM technology is enabling the bulk transmission of text, sound, interactive software, still and moving images. Even training in the use of the petrological microscope can be CD-ROM assisted. Communication networks are being used to re-orientate the role of lecturers and tutors, and enable students to form tutorial groups and carry out collaborative activities. Ultimately electronic communications will be used for the distribution of most course material. Finally, this chapter considers business process re-engineering (BPR) in the context of distance learning, aimed at achieving a more effective response to students' needs and faster updating of learning material.

3.1 Introduction

3.1.1 What is the OU and What Does it Do?

Many people are aware of the OU but have a hazy idea of where it exists beyond the educational programmes of early morning television. It was founded 28 years ago and survived in the face of much opposition to become known world-wide for its distance education methods. The late Harold Wilson and Jennie Lee were the champions whose persistence and vision sustained its early growth. Since then many successors have kept the wheel turning up to and beyond its 25th anniversary in 1994. The OU has a large campus in Milton Keynes, UK, with academics, researchers and administrative staff, but no undergraduates on-site. OU students are spread around Europe and elsewhere, on land and in ships, supported by a network of regional offices, mainly in the UK. All undergraduates are distance learners, many in full-time employment, having to juggle the demands of day-to-day living, family and study in pursuit of a degree.

The OU is 'open' in several senses, with the explicit mission of being:

- *open as to people*, with an increasingly large and diverse student population;
- *open as to places*, throughout Europe and more widely in the world;
- *open as to methods*, distance teaching and new learning technologies;
- *open as to ideas*, dedicated to the expansion, refinement and sharing of knowledge.

To give some idea of the scale and nature of operations and recent statistics, taken from OU (1996, 1997):

- over 2.5 million people have studied with the OU;
- more than 200 000 people study with the OU each year, equivalent to 14 Oxford universities;
- around 25 000 people are taking OU courses outside the UK, many from Russia and the East European republics;
- over 70% of students are in full-time employment, 50% are women, 2–3% are severely disabled;
- OU students represent around 37% of all part-time UK higher education;
- the OU employs around 3700 full-time staff and 7600 part-time tutors;
- distribution via the post is over 1000 tons per annum and includes 120 000 video cassettes and 37 000 home experimental kits;
- around 25 000 students are interconnected via the Internet.

3.1.2   How Does it Operate in Comparison With Other Universities?

In the early days the Open University had to overcome a credibility problem. Distance learning was often considered a poor compromise for those unable to attend a traditional university. Teaching texts, radio and TV programmes, audio material (long-play records originally), home experimental kits (HEKs) and occasional tutorials were seen as an inferior package to the traditional 3 years of lectures, tutorials and laboratory experimentation. Gradually the perception shifted. High-quality teaching material on paper and video cassette, experimental work on HEKs with PC assistance, supported by regular tutorials were seen to provide an advantage over much traditional (and often hastily prepared) teaching. The OU degree steadily became accepted in its own right and attracted imitators.

The current operation uses any available and appropriate communication media, including computer networking and CD-ROM. Assessment of students is partly by traditional written examinations, but also has a strong element, typically 50%, of continuous assessment through tutor- and computer-marked exercises. Tutorials are optional; self-help groupings of students abound and many courses include a residential summer school.

3.2   Current Trends in University Education

3.2.1   Economic Pressures

Considerable pressure is being applied nationally to expand higher education across a wider section of the populace, in terms of social class, sex and age range. The

Association of University Teachers AUT (1995) recommended an increase of 4% per year in full-time undergraduate places, aiming for 200 000 places by 2010. This is probably a conservative figure, and likely to be far exceeded by the number of part-time students studying for a range of purposes and qualifications.

The cost per student has to decrease while standards are to be maintained or improved. The Dearing Report (Dearing 1997) was uncompromising in its message that the massive expansion underway in higher education will not be funded to any great extent by public revenue. Funding constraints, league tables, research and teaching assessments all encourage universities to examine market conditions and develop strategies for survival by expansion. One of the results is that the OU model for distance learning is being widely imitated and adapted.

A familiar controversy amongst academics is the polarised perception of higher education: at one extreme a business to be maximised, at the other a high-quality service to be provided with little regard to profitability. The reality is that good education requires dedication and enthusiasm in its development but must operate in an increasingly competitive market. The same forces that are compelling many organisations to re-engineer their business processes apply equally to universities.

3.2.2   The Convergence of Distance and Traditional Learning Institutions

The OU's 25th anniversary in 1994 was an opportunity to celebrate the achievements of a unique institution. It also served to highlight the urgent need for major strategic changes. One perception of the OU was that it was more like a publisher than a university, producing and distributing large quantities of information in text and video form, with its publications often seen as becoming too static. Teaching material in rapidly changing subjects has to be updated regularly section by section, rather than reissued a year or more after the event, like new editions of a book. IT was urgently needed to enhance and replace many existing operational systems which had given good service but were batch-oriented and no longer able to respond fast enough. IT, in the form of electronic mail and more sophisticated forms of computer conferencing, could also improve communications amongst the OU community.

Meanwhile, traditional universities, under pressure to educate increasing numbers of students, were adopting distance-learning techniques to reduce the need for traditional lectures and tutorials. The OU had a reputation for pioneering effective distance education and perhaps even considered that it had cornered the market. Gradually it became clear that its activities were converging with many other initiatives and the OU would soon face stiff competition in its own traditional market sector.

3.2.3   Collaborative Working

In most industrial and public organisations fragmentation is taking place. Slow moving, centralised, hierarchical control is being replaced by a more flexible arrangement in which smaller autonomous groups associate and collaborate on multi-disciplinary tasks. Sometimes the collaboration is for short-term projects in which the different parties provide specialist skills for a particular phase and then disassociate; sometimes it is a more enduring relationship which brings economic benefit to all by symbiosis rather than by rivalry. These changes require people who not only have technical skills but are used to working in teams and have some understanding of related disciplines. The narrow specialist, although still required, is being steadily replaced by more widely skilled workers with the ability to collaborate within a team.

This change must be reflected in:

- the range and depth of skills universities attempt to teach, including communication skills;
- the tasks set for students to carry out (more collaborative, less individual);
- the support networks provided for tutorial and self-help;
- the manner in which academics develop courses.

3.3   Organisational Needs and Examples of IT at the OU

The rapid growth of distance learning at the OU has been highly dependent on IT. Broadly, IT usage can be categorised as follows:

- administrative support (application handling, computer-marked assessments);
- learning material within courses (simulations, computer-based instruction);
- Student communication and tutoring (computer-mediated conferencing);
- Dissemination of course material (CD-ROM and the Internet);
- Course development (conferencing, collaborative design and production).

A few examples will illustrate the wide range of IT applications that are in use and considered to be invaluable in supporting the programmes of study.

3.3.1   Computer-marked Assignments (CMAs)

For years CMAs have been the stock in trade of many OU courses. They enable assessment in a range of subjects based on multiple-choice questions, answered by marking boxes on computer-readable forms. They are a cheap and simple means of assessing the understanding of concepts by large numbers of students and their ability to apply techniques. Lecturers must use considerable skill in designing CMAs but are then relieved of the tedium of marking large numbers, often thousands, of answers.

3.3.2   Assessment Administration

Another significant use of IT is the support system for assessment of students' achievements in following a course. To assign a pass grade, or fail, to a student, lecturers must for most courses consider scores for both examinations and continuous assessment. Boundaries need to be set, to distinguish between grades by reference to a number of considerations, such as the difficulty of the assessment questions compared with previous years. The two sets of scores result in boundaries which are two dimensional, so that examination boards need to view the complex situation in a two-dimensional form. The support system, amongst its many features, provides scatter diagrams to represent the combined scores of all students (ranging from hundreds to thousands) completing a course. This support system, long established, is essential IT to enable the assessment of large numbers of distance-learning students.

3.3.3 Computer Conferencing

Another example arising from the need to reduce the isolation of students spread across rural areas, such as in Scotland, is the use of computer conferencing. Students and lecturers who rarely meet each other need more substantial and cheaper communication than the telephone can provide. The solution has been evolutionary, starting from little more than communal electronic mail. The next stage has been the steady increase in the use of organised computer conferencing using FirstClass (registered trademark of SoftArc software), within which groups and subgroups of course participants freely exchange information quickly and at low cost. Real-time conferencing has occasionally taken place enabling widely separated participants to hold tutorial discussions. This may be seen as an inferior substitute for 'real' meetings but it is very welcome to students who cannot travel, because of distance or disability, and who can feel very isolated.

3.3.4 Virtual Summer School

An interesting example of real-time computer conferencing was the first 'virtual summer school', held in 1994. It was an attempt to replicate many of the interactive experiences of summer school for a small group of students who had difficulty in attending a residential centre. Based on the subject of cognitive psychology, 12 students attended 'electronically' from their own homes using a computer, telephone and modem. They held group discussions, ran experiments, participated in experiments as subjects, received one-to-one tuition, listened to lectures, asked questions, conducted literature searches, browsed journal publications, worked in project teams, undertook statistical analyses, prepared individual and joint reports, took part in plenary sessions with simultaneous UK and US participation, and even socialised, all without leaving their homes. The organisers even claim the event finished with a virtual disco.

The experiment called for a range of software facilities and considerable overheads for setting-up and familiarisation by students. To assist the establishing of the summer school metaphor, a virtual campus map appeared on students' desktops and navigation relied on room icons to describe meeting places and bulletin boards. The technology comprised three main categories:

- *communication and groupwork tools* (e-mail, Internet conferencing, remote presentation software, interactive whiteboard);
- *support and infrastructure software and hardware* (Macintosh or Windows PC, mobile telephone support and voice conferencing, remote diagnostic support, software-guided tours, World Wide Web with Mosaic, FirstClass conferencing server);
- *academic project software* (AI packages, academic papers, interactive programs).

Evaluation after the event revealed the expensive nature of the project because it used a wide range of software resources and substantial human effort. However, the concept is clearly viable and shows much promise, supporting other related initiatives: Berge and Collins (1995) and Hutchison (1995) for example.

3.3.5 Compact Discs (CD-ROMs) and Electronic Distribution

Another compelling example has been the growing use of multimedia in which text, sound, computer programs, moving and still images can be inextricably mixed. The geographic separation of academic staff from distance-learning students has always been a stimulus to strive for communication which is clear and revealing. As multimedia features become available and affordable they often stimulate the imagination of an academic to teach a technique or explain a concept more effectively. The use of CD-ROM allows the assembly of multimedia-learning material in a form that is easy to distribute. Manufacturing and sending a single disc in a padded envelope is much simpler than providing a package of assorted printed matter, videotapes and floppy discs. CD-ROMs might, however, be considered as an interim technology, to be at least partially replaced by electronic distribution using the Internet. The growth of fibre optic cable, ISDN and faster communications processing and transmission will make it even easier to distribute multimedia material. At last, students will be able to download only the material they need, and only when they need it.

3.3.6   Virtual Microscope

With good reason the OU does not attempt to teach chemical and civil engineering. The requirements for practical experimentation would be daunting. On a smaller scale, the teaching of petrographic microscope techniques presents a problem of cost and availability that can be overcome by IT and is a good example of how CD-ROM can be particularly useful. There is no substitution for examining real rock sections with a real petrological microscope (as carried out at summer school). However, the difficult and time-consuming process of learning the techniques can be assisted using the OU's *virtual microscope* on a CD-ROM. It was originally developed to help disabled students with a visual or dexterity handicap, but was soon adopted as an ideal way to introduce all students to microscope work. The CD-ROM images are derived from real rock sections viewed under a number of optical conditions.

Features of the virtual microscope include:

- low magnification of rocks, or 'hand lens view';
- high magnification of a range of igneous and metamorphic rocks in thin section (basalt, peridotite, gabro, pumice, granite, gneiss, schist, slate, etc.);
- plane-polarised and crossed-polarised light modes, viewable simultaneously (a real bonus as this is not otherwise achievable);
- adjustment of magnification and light level;
- images of similar quality to a typical college introductory microscope, sufficient to demonstrate zoning, twinning, cleavage, pleochroism and birefringence.

The technique is still being developed but has shown itself useful in speeding up the learning process for a large number of students. If further embedded within a multimedia package it could be even more suited to self-instruction. There is scope here for revitalising student interest and expertise in petrographic techniques.

3.3.7   Virtual Reality

Virtual reality of the type used in industrial design, and requiring very large computer power, is clearly unavailable to most OU students. However, forms of 'experiential' graphics are being made cheaply available using CD-ROM. One example comprises a collection of photographic images of the Sir John Soane Museum in London, a building of considerable architectural interest. Students can explore the building visually, by 'clicking' their way from room to room, looking in different directions, at distance and close up. A similar example, but of smaller scale, is the examination of a crystal's symmetry by allowing it to be viewed at any desired angle. The technique can be adapted to the many subjects in which flexible visual exploration is required.

3.3.8 Virtual Design Studio

A third-level course, called "Mechatronics: Designing Intelligent Machines", uses PC simulations, and a home experimental kit (HEK). The HEK is a mobile 'buggy' assembled by students, operating under artificial intelligence control and utilising a simple scanner to recognise plane shapes such as alphanumerics, and linked to the PC by infra-red communications. The cost and international requirements for electromagnetic conformance currently prohibit producing it in large numbers and distributing the course internationally.

One solution under development is to set up a number of these HEKs in a laboratory and have them accessed remotely via the Internet. They will be available at any time of day and as demand increases more can be added. Furthermore, they offer the opportunity for remotely investigating the interaction between HEKs. The concept is feasible, as has been demonstrated by the University of Western Australia's "Telerobot on the Web" which allows access to its laboratory robot in something approaching real time. One can dial up and control it via the Internet from anywhere in the world. It is, of course, no trivial task to ensure that such experimentation is workable and that students can experience the practicalities via the medium of a PC screen.

This technique could be extended to enable the *virtual design studio*, allowing remote handling of prototype artefacts by a number of designers. Industrial design teams have, in the past, collected all the necessary expertise in one location at the same time, or suffered the inefficiencies of constant travelling and communication delays. Improved computing and electronic communication now make this new concept workable. Designers remotely located are having to cooperate in cyberspace, developing new working protocols to ensure timely, effective and coherent development. The OU must practise what it preaches, carrying out its own design through virtual teams and enabling students to experience the processes they will increasingly meet in their work.

3.3.9 New Course: "Communicating Technology"

Many of the themes described above have their expression in this new second-level course. As implied by the double meaning of its title, students learn about the technologies of communication *and* practise the skills required to communicate on technological subjects. Rather than experiencing these as two separate subjects, students soon find that the subjects are inextricably mixed. A collaborative exercise, in which a group of remotely located students combine their efforts in producing a substantial technological report, encourages students to develop a range of skills. The exercise entails software set-up and manipulation; learning about communications technology; writing clear, correct English; preparing Hypertext documents and communicating effectively with fellow students using conferencing software.

3.4 The OU and Business Process Re-engineering (BPR)

BPR requires *restructuring the activities* of an organisation such that business processes are better aligned to the requirements of the 'customer' or 'client', namely students in the case of the OU. Coulson-Thomas(1994) questions the concepts of BPR: whether change is to be revolutionary (step changing) or evolutionary (increment changing), whether IT drives BPR or is its facilitator. CCTA (1994) amongst many commentaries proposes a methodology for achieving BPR. One big question is whether BPR is applicable in a university context. A recent survey by a research group based at Strathclyde University found that, of 70 UK universities responding, 23 reported activity using BPR tools and techniques. Clearly there is more than passing interest in the use of IT to achieve radical change. In the OU context BPR would result in changes where:

- the responsibility for business processes would reside with someone who has control over all activities which handle customer inputs and outputs;
- internal specialist functions would be avoided so that autonomy would no longer be in the hands of skill or occupational groups;
- parallel or simultaneous engineering would be introduced to make the design and production functions no longer sequential but run as much as possible in parallel, and help the distribution function to disappear by making all information accessible electronically.

Taking perhaps the most obvious example: students receive a variety of teaching materials associated with a course; (in OU parlance a course relates to subjects such as "Artificial Intelligence for Technology" or "State, Economy and Nation in Nineteenth Century Europe", not a whole B.A. or B.Sc. degree). Traditionally it has taken 2 years or more for a course team of lecturers to devise the course and write the study material. Many acclaimed courses have been designed in this manner. After a short period the course settles down and it then runs, largely unchanged, for around 7 years, after which it may be revised to take new developments into account. Production is mostly sequential, in that it is first devised and written by a team of academics, then designed and illustrated by specialists such as editors, artists and video makers; production is then scheduled; course material is bulk produced on paper, video, audio cassette, floppy disc, CD-ROM, and finally distributed via the postal system. The result is that course production takes a long time, lacks flexibility and relies on coordination amongst several departments (see Figure 3.1(i)).

This is analogous to traditional manufacturing in which a model, such as a car, takes a long time to develop and put into production and is then sold, with few changes, for a number of years. In education, as in manufacturing, this approach is no longer an option. Technologies and customer requirements change rapidly and if an organisation cannot keep up with them it loses its competitive edge.

In the fully 'BPRd' Open University (see Figure 3.1(ii)), a course will be designed and issued by a team under a leader with responsibility for all aspects of serving the students' needs related to the course. The team might be a virtual team, with members spread over a number of locations but bringing their specific expertise to the course (as well as to developments run by other virtual teams). Most course material will be available via the Internet, including text, sound, computer simulations, and still and moving images. As the course progresses teaching material can be regularly updated so the course evolves to keep it up-to-date. Aspects of this transition have already taken place and IT developments are keenly awaited to speed up the process.

3.5   Conclusions

An important conclusion is that the teaching and learning business is stimulated by the continual convergence of telecommunications and the ability of computers to

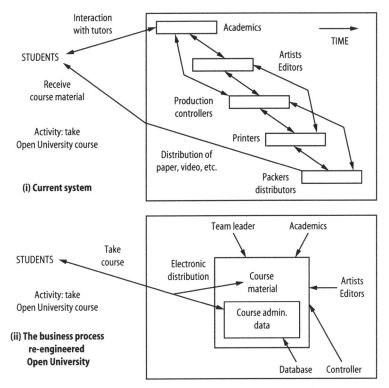

Figure 3.1. The transition to business process re-engineering (BPR).

illustrate and simulate. However, universities engaged in distance learning must not get carried away by the latest technology. Academics must always explore their own subject areas and ask how the functionality of IT can best be used to *enhance* learning experiences, as well as checking if the solution is cost-effective? In addition, they must strike a balance between exploitation of the latest, most expensive technology and the ability of students to afford it.

Dazzling technology does not on its own automatically produce good distance-learning material. IT provides the learning infrastructure and the dissemination method. The ability of the material to stimulate learning is, as always, dependent on the relevance and quality of its content.

More specifically:

- CD-ROM is a powerful method for the dissemination of teaching material, but is an interim technique, due to be replaced by Internet facilities.
- The use of networking is of great potential benefit. However, its effectiveness is dependent on students and academics having a clear idea of how it is to be used and establishing appropriate protocols for interaction. The well-known convergence of telecommunications and computing needs to be merged with cognitive and learning science.
- Telecommunication development is still crucial. Optic fibre will bring the necessary communications capacity, but other essential techniques are data compression and network load balancing. As an aside, a more proactive cost reduction by BT would paradoxically assist its expansion within a growing global market rather than reduce its profitability.

- BPR is essential and underway, but not easily achieved. Its aim involves re-aligning IT to support student-oriented processes, making them more responsive, flexible and efficient. Virtual teams will carry out the work and be dedicated to this aim rather than to a specialism. Course material will decreasingly be distributed by post, increasingly available electronically and more readily updated.

References

AUT (1995) *Higher Education, Preparing for the 21st century*. Association of University Teachers. United House, 9 Pembridge Road, London W11 3JY.

Berge, Z and Collins, M (1995) Computer-mediated communication and the online classroom in distance learning. *Computer-mediated Communication Magazine*, 2(4): April. http://www.december.com/cmc/mag/index.html

CCTA (1994) BPR in the public sector. HM Stationery Office, ISBN 0-11-330-651-2.

Coulson-Thomas, CJ (Ed.) (1994) *Business Process Re-engineering: Myth and Reality*. London: Kogan Page.

Dearing, R. (1997) *National Committee of Inquiry into Higher Education. Higher Education in the Learning Society*. [Commissioned by Gillian Shepherd, Secretary of State for Education, May 1996.]

Hutchison, C (1995) The 'ICP online': jeux sans frontieres on the Cyber Campus. *Journal of Computer-mediated Communication*, 1(1): January. http://www.ascusc.org/jcmc

OU (1996) *Basic Facts and Figures for 1996*. Milton Keynes: Open University.

OU (1997) *Technology Strategy for Academic Advantage*. Milton Keynes: Open University (plus further material available through the Website: http://www.open.ac.uk/OU/Showcase.html).

4 Information Technology as a Tool For Performance Measurement and Auditing

Andrew Williamson and Alfred D. Vella

Abstract

With the development of large, multiproduct companies in the nineteenth century, there has been an interest and a need to find new ways to organise and control companies now too big for an individual to understand and manage. Many new management structures and techniques have been tried, with varying degrees of success, but several have shown that they can offer improved performance and understanding; one of these is the obvious idea of measurement!

Although simple in concept, performance measurement has many other benefits, and presents many dangers and problems if it is not properly understood and applied. It tells the managers, employees and other stakeholders if the company is performing well, and where weaknesses lie. It communicates what is important throughout the company and it can act as an integrative system, ensuring the business processes are achieving the required goals.

Information technology (IT) has many characteristics that make it suitable for contributing to a performance measurement system. It can collect, analyse and present data speedily and inexpensively. It can monitor performance, 'flag' any discrepancies and act as an early warning system for problems. It can also assist in the auditing of company performance. By incorporating measures which can assist an auditor in deciding whether the company is satisfying its requirements and by allowing the auditor to unobtrusively examine the data themselves, the auditing process may be significantly improved.

4.1 Designing a Performance Measurement System

Much has already been said on how the performance measurement system should be designed (Kaplan 1992; Meyer 1994; Neely 1995), but it is worthwhile summarising a few of the salient points. The first is the need to tie the performance measurement system to the company's objectives. These objectives define what the company needs to be good at and what targets should be placed on the company, and the performance measurement system must inform management whether the company is achieving its targets. Measures should be based upon the important activities and targets of the company, not on what is easy to measure.

Deciding how the information generated by the performance measurement system is to be used, must be considered in its design. Unless the information is going to be used, there is no point in collecting it! Measures designed to help managers at a local level will probably be different to those needed by the executive body, and the process of data analysis and reporting will certainly differ. Local managers will need data collected and presented to them speedily, so that they can direct the processes. The executive body may require summary information to monitor the performance of the various business units.

The measures a company uses sends a strong message to the staff on what management believes to be important. Consequently, the measures must be consistent, not only with the objectives but with the strategy and vision of the company. Pronouncements on the importance of quality in a company with a performance measurement system focusing on cost will convince staff that management is serious only about cost.

4.2   Choosing the Performance Measures

Once you have identified what you need to measure, the next step is to select the appropriate measures. Watts (1987) summarised several characteristics of a good measure. *Reliability* is the extent to which a measurement is free from errors. Measurements may have poor reliability because the attribute is difficult to measure, the attribute is highly subjective or because individuals differ in their definition of the attribute. Unreliable measurements are difficult to use, as it is impossible to know whether a particular value is caused by the attribute or the measurement. Measurements also must have *validity*. Measurements are frequently made to imply performance in some activity (such as academic achievement) from another, measured activity (such as IQ tests). Validity is whether the results are appropriate for the use to which they are being put: a measurement may be valid in one context but be invalid in another. Once you have achieved a reliable and valid measurement, it needs to be *accurate*. An accurate measurement is concerned with the absolute level of performance, an accurate measure equalling the true measure.

A measurement is *objective* if it is free from any subjective influence or opinion of the testers. If there are sufficient data for empirically determined measurements from different settings to be compared, the metric may be *standardised*. Once a metric is standardised, a formal system for the classification of results can be established. This enables individuals and companies to be compared. A metric is *comparable* with other metrics if it measures the same attribute. Metrics must be considered in a wider business context and metrics must be *economical* to collect and use. The cost of the collection, calculation and use of the metric should be small compared with the benefits gained. Finally, the measures must be *useful*. Once collected and evaluated, the company must be able to do something constructive with the information. Only if it is useful will any benefit be obtained, so a 'useless' metric is never an economical one.

4.3   Collecting and Presenting the Data

Once the measures have been selected, a system for collecting, analysing and using the data needs to be established. It is here that information technology (IT) can make a significant contribution. To ensure continued and consistent collection of data, it is necessary that the data collection process should become integral to the activities, so that its collection becomes 'second nature'. The process must be easy and quick, otherwise staff will tend to postpone or stop collecting the necessary data. Data collection can be a major annoyance for the staff, so they must be provided with a continuing motivation to collect it and one way of doing this is to make the use of the data visible. Unless the data are used as the basis of management, and seen to be used, the value of the effort in data collection will soon be questioned.

As the data will be used to make decisions, they must be available to, and understood by, all throughout the company. Analysing the data, calculating the measures that are required, writing up the reports and presenting them to management can be time-consuming and expensive tasks. Especially where the data are used for day-to-day management, the speed with which the data can be collected and analysed is vital. Ensuring that the messages in the data are understood requires clear and concise presentation; much work in organisational psychology has shown the problems people have in absorbing data and making correct inferences from them (Kahneman *et al.* 1982).

4.4   Using IT to Assist the Performance Measurement and Auditing Process: An Example From Quality System Auditing

Many of the concerns with data collection and presentation may be addressed by automating the process. The collection can become integral to the process by introducing software that can automatically collect the data whenever and wherever it is generated. This also ensures that the performance measurement system has the most up-to-date data at its disposal, which can be instantly transmitted to whoever needs them. No effort on the part of the staff performing the tasks is needed.

IT can assist in the analysis and presentation of the data. Routines can calculate the results of the measures and undertake some performance analysis, including indicating whether a process value falls outside a predetermined level. Predefined reports, designed with the manager's needs in mind, can present the data in a clear and intuitive manner.

The data collection system can also be the basis of a tool to assist an auditor. The role of an auditor is to be an independent expert making a judgement as to whether the audited party meets a public and agreed standard of behaviour. The judgement should be based upon objective and verifiable evidence. Consequently, an auditor needs to obtain and understand large amounts of data. The data collection system may help in this, if it collects measures appropriate to the audit. These measures may improve the auditing process in several ways. First, it can help the preparation of an audit, by giving an overview of the company's performance, identifying areas where performance may not be satisfactory. This can also be used to plan audits on the basis of need, rather than schedule. The data collected can contribute to at least part of the audit. This will allow the audit to be unobtrusive, not disturbing the normal operations of the company. Finally, by allowing the audit to be done remotely, the auditor can investigate many companies simultaneously, making more effective use of an expensive and rare resource.

In conclusion, the imaginative use of information technology can contribute greatly to the measuring and auditing of company performance. By automating many of the simpler functions that are onerous, potentially making them quicker and more reliable, the process of performance measurement and auditing can be greatly improved.

References

Kahneman, D, Slovic, P and Tversky, A (1982) *Judgement Under Uncertainty: Heuristics and Biases.* Cambridge: Cambridge University Press.

Kaplan, RS and Norton, DP (1992) The balanced scorecard – Measures that drive performance. *Harvard Business Review*, January–February: 71–79.

Meyer, C (1994) How the right measures help teams excel. *Harvard Business Review*, May-June: 95–103.

Neely, A (1995) Getting the measure of your business: A process based approach. In: *Foundation of Manufacturing Industry*, September.

Watts, R (1987) *Measuring Software Quality*. Manchester: NCC Publications.

5 Coordinating Change Through Effective Communication at England's Newest University

Hilary Duckett

Abstract

The management of change is a fashionable yet elusive concept, used to describe initiatives rang-ing from the momentous to the banal, from the corporate to the small scale.

Innumerable strategies have professed to be the panacea for effecting smooth transition. Following a review of management literature, and its bewildering array of ease studies, a reader may be forgiven for concluding that effective change strategies owe as much to luck as judgement. Identifying common themes or shared philosophies appears, at first, illusory. However, once the theories and their respective terminologies are deciphered, a unifying theme of communication emerges. This paper will begin by demonstrating that communication is fundamental to any process of restructuring. The paper will explore the tendency of strategic management approach-es to focus on primarily statistical 'outputs'. For example, staff/student ratios or the number of stu-dent withdrawals as a method for measuring institutional performance. As an alternative, a behavioural methodology will be considered. Within the context of communication, a case study involving the University of Luton (England's newest university) will be discussed. The study illus-trates a strategy successfully used to manage the transition from a College of Higher Education to a University in 7 years. The focus for the study is the effective communication of change. A behav-ioural perspective has been used to interpret the policies applied.

5.1 Introduction

Why is communication central to a programme of change? First, Morgan (1986) describes organisations as "socially constructed realities", exhibiting all the char-acteristics, uncertainties and complexities of social groups. Organisations are fac-tional and consist of amalgamations of groups and sub-groups. Organisations often espouse a central corporate set of beliefs and norms (through mission statements for example) which are invariably re-interpreted by those interest groups enfolded within it. Additionally, the heterogeneity of an organisation frequently launches its composite groups into conflict. Perceived status (academic versus non-academic) or competing objectives (quality versus cost) serve only to perpetuate institutional bar-riers. "Cultural warfare" (Morgan 1986), unless effectively managed, can degenerate into a spiral of retrenchment and hostility. Such highly fragmented environments are charged with tension even before a change programme is announced, therefore, a carefully planned and implemented communication strategy is essential if change is to be accepted by diverse stakeholders.

Secondly, extensive research supports the hypothesis that change will inevitably be resisted by individuals and groups within the organisation. Occupational, social and political allegiances often unite against internally driven changes. Low tolerance for change is often propagated by uncertainty and anxiety. Individuals (or groups) may fear that capabilities and specialisms will become obsolete. Individuals (or groups) may perceive a loss of status or power as a result of restructuring. Such anxieties are symptomatic of a climate in which misunderstanding and distrust dominate. Within such an environment potential resistance may beoffset by effective methods of communication. Failure to mobilise formal communication channels will encourage the informal exchange of information and rumour to prevail.

Thirdly, even an organisation which can claim collective interests and harmonious relations cannot guarantee that once a message of change is communicated it will be understood. Distorted information (accidental or deliberate) may have devastating effects. Strategies for change must be clearly communicated, repeated, reinforced and supported by appropriate opportunities for training and feedback.

Finally, the principle of circularity, (or interdependence) further underpins the importance of communication. All organisations interact with their environment and those in the public sector are not exceptional. For example, recent reductions in the level of higher-education funding will inevitably decrease the number of staff employed and their working practices. Organisations cannot afford to ignore the opportunities and challenges which are externally imposed and all staff must be informed about the changing nature of the market in which their organisation competes. Communicating the origin and impetus for change will enable staff to understand (and possibly accept) the required restructuring.

Having established the centrality of communication to the management of change it is necessary to review these issues in context by considering recent experience at the University of Luton.

In 1987–1988 the institution, then known as Luton College of Higher Education, enrolled 840 full-time students and sandwich higher-education students, mainly onto Higher National Diploma courses. There was one degree course. In 1993, by contrast, the University admitted 7830 full-time and sandwich students, studying on programmes leading to over 100 different awards through the single institution-wide Modular Credit Scheme. This growth of 832% in full-time and sandwich students is the highest of any university or college in the UK.

Despite operating on the lowest unit of funding of any higher-education institution in England, the University has consistently achieved confirmation from external bodies of the quality and breadth of its provision. In 1989 the College acquired corporate status, removing it from the local education authority system. In 1991 the institution was accredited by the Council for National Academic Awards for taught degree courses, and in 1993 the institution successfully applied to the Higher Education Quality Council (HEQC) for research degree awarding powers. As a result, the Privy Council authorised the institution to use the title 'University' in July 1994. Luton was the first institution to have been directly designated a university under the government's new procedures and criteria. Similarly, it was the first university to have achieved Investors in People recognition , a national distinction confirming its commitment to training and development, in April 1994.

The scale of change has therefore been immense, affecting every part of the institution. It has also been rapid. the major part of the change having occurred between

1989 and 1993. From this framework, those tools and techniques which have been used by the University to effectively communicate change will be described. The following factors will be discussed more fully: participation and the need for change; feedback and team building; decentralising power; use of statistical tools; manipulation and cooption; and reward systems.

5.2   Participation and the Need for Change

A guiding principle for effective communication is the avoidance of those strategies which are reliant upon ideological control. A key task of management is to create the conditions under which the direction of development is accepted and policy is owned, often entailing lengthy discussions through the committee structure of the University. This introduces a significant feature of university life: that because it is an intrinsic part of being an academic to be challengeable, academic policies and decisions are made collectively by groups of staff rather than by individuals or imposed top-down without consultation by a board of directors. If the notion of an organisation as a 'socially constructed reality' is accepted it follows that any attempt to communicate a programme of restructuring must recognise and respect the rights of interest groups to express opinions and participate in decision making. Premature closure of debate or discussion may simply conceal deep-rooted tension and dissatisfaction, undercurrents which will inevitably resurface and cause disruption. In addition, attempts to silence or exclude particular groups may be perceived more widely as manipulation, further fuelling mistrust. The importance of intra-organisational participation increases proportionately to the number, complexity and power of interest groups. The University recognised the importance of participation as reflected in the breadth of membership of its central decision-making committees. All categories of staff, all faculties, and representatives of other internal and external groups (Students' Union, local employers, etc.) are represented on one or other of the Academic Board's committees. Such a structure provides the forum for the expression of diverse views and has created a network for information exchange. In addition, new projects are often managed by ad hoc task forces, which have the function of exposing a problem to collective gaze and recommending a course of action which will take account of the legitimate concerns of constituent groups. An existing project group has used wide-ranging expertise (academic and administrative staff, students, and local employers) in its investigation into levels of student literacy. Further, participation by staff students and externals is formally incorporated within the University's quality assurance system, for example the results of annual student-satisfaction surveys influence the central allocation of resources. Such strategies ensure that the process of corporate decision making actively encourages diverse viewpoints. A characteristic of the University's approach is that there is no preconception at the outset about the best solutions, and that the views of each member of staff are equally valuable. Participation is encouraged and the principle of circularity and responsiveness to the interest of sub-groups is endorsed.

Assuring participation in any process of restructuring is dependent upon communicating the need for change. Research conducted by Pugh (1988) demonstrated that external pressures were often accepted more readily by employees than internal ones. In the UK, public sector employees are familiar with the frequency and pace of recent external stimuli. The Patients' Charter and the Students' Charter are prime examples of the movement towards 'user-control' of the public services. Such an external locus of control will inevitably lead to changes in internal systems and structures. Pugh's research suggested that those organisations which attribute new systems, structures and techniques to external pressure are less likely to experience internal resistance. Accordingly, the environmental pressures facing the University have been discussed at all levels of its operation. Training workshops policy documents and briefing notes have characterised a strategy of maximising understanding and participation, and although complete acceptance of the changes cannot be claimed, the need for change is commonly understood. A further technique used by the University has been the establishment of posts with dual accountability, of which the faculty-based Quality Assurance Coordinators are prime examples. These posts, occupied by academic staff, incorporate joint responsibility for teaching and managing the University's quality assurance system at faculty level. Hence, a circular pattern of participation is established which ensures that all faculties: recognise the importance of quality systems; apply consistent standards; monitor their own standards; and centrally report on the effectiveness of these systems.

5.3   Team Building

Building teams between academic and support staff has also been an important feature of the University's strategy. Several short-term cross-University groups have been established dealing with institutional-wide issues such as the development of computerised management information systems (MIS). The aim has been to foster among all staff the conviction that everyone makes a difference to the effectiveness of the University as a place of learning, and that, where there are no preconceptions about the best solutions to the challenges facing the University, the views of each member of staff are equally valuable.

The principles of encouraging participation and team building are inextricably linked to the requirement to build in feedback. The principle of double-loop learning, described by Morgan (1986), is relevant to the design of successful communications systems. The theory suggests that an effective communication strategy is as dependent upon negative feedback as it is positive feedback. The theory is important because as the level of environmental complexity increases so too does the level of organisational uncertainty.

Mechanistic or task-centred structures often lack the flexibility to respond quickly as employees operate within predetermined constraints and exhibit characteristics which conform to operating standards. Refusal to question the relevance or reliability of 'normal' standards may result in a failure to respond to potential weaknesses. Morgan maintains that a process of continuous information exchange is necessary if an organisation is to effectively monitor and respond to its environment. The following principles termed double-loop learning are a prerequisite to effective communication.

Step 1   Systems must have the capacity to sense, monitor and scan significant aspects of their environment.

Step 2   These aspects must be related to the operating norms which guide systems of behaviour.

Step 2a   Systems must be able to question the accuracy of these norms.

Step 3   Systems must be able to initiate corrective action when discrepancies are detected.

The principle of double-loop learning which corrects and questions the relevance of operating norms is illustrated in Figure 5.1. The example provided represents the University's feedback loops in response to the needs for external recognition.

Unless a system of checks and balances accompanies policy making (such as Step 2a) significant environmental threats may remain hidden. Effective feedback loops are dependent upon a climate in which interest groups can communicate information which is contrary or appears to conflict with organisational objectives. Double-looping at the University has ensured that strategies are continuously framed and reframed. It has also fostered a problem-solving approach, avoiding the tendency for interest groups to disguise results which appear to deviate from the norm. Responsiveness to external initiatives, bench marking and incorporation of national good practice are key features of this strategy. The University learns to learn through procedures and systems which are based on progressively accumulated experience and on evaluation.

Support for the decentralisation of power is a further element of the University's communication strategy. Decentralisation has become a recurrent theme in post-classical management theory. Behavioural theories, as developed by authors such as Mayo (1949) and Schien (1965), have emphasised the importance of rewarding those individuals that are willing to challenge preconceptions and are able to recognise external opportunities. Establishing the need for change and developing information channels which allow operating norms to be challenged are only parts of a more holistic communication strategy. Change must be communicated in a manner which

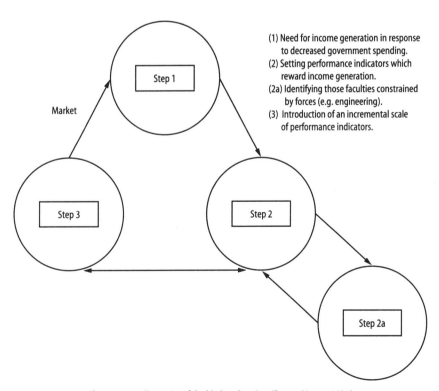

Figure 5.1. An illustration of double-loop learning. (Source: Morgan 1986.)

motivates employees and gains their commitment. The University has consistently decentralised decision making, allowing those staff with responsibility for enacting change the freedom and authority to design and implement requisite strategies. This approach has created a sense of ownership. The University devolves all operating budgets to the faculties, allowing key-resource managers (deans and heads of school) the flexibility to determine optimum resource usage. Whilst this does promote diversity, the central reporting structure ensures that those decisions taken and standards applied are consistent with corporate objectives. Hence, self-regulated autonomy is created which respects the right of individuals (and groups) to express opinions and suggest ideas whilst simultaneously promoting the corporate objectives of the organisation.

5.4 Statistical Tools

The application of statistical tools has been a further feature of the strategic programme at the University. Statistical data are fundamental to the communication strategy and are used to inform decision making. Selected strategies are often justified on the basis of overwhelming statistical evidence. An array of statistical quality indicators have been devised to 'measure performance'. Examples include the student:staff ratios (SSRs) used to 'measure' teaching efficiency, and student withdrawal rates used as a measure of course satisfaction. Table 5.1 provides an example of statistical measures.

A fuller evaluation of the usefulness of such indices does reveal certain limitations. The illustration above is drawn from the University of Derby's statistical record of incremental changes to the SSR in the School of Management. The extent to which such 'quality indicators' are themselves subject to strategic change does diminish their reliability. There are innumerable interpretations of the above data as follows: that 'quality' has halved over a 5-year period (statistical interpretation); that perceptions of quality have changed over the same period (cognitive interpretation); and that teaching and learning methods have changed over the same period (behavioural interpretation). The information produced by statistical techniques is clearly bounded in rationality (Simon 1976) and are subject to the prevailing environmental values, objectives and economic circumstances. However, such techniques remain a powerful communication tool, and are used to influence internal and external perceptions. Internally generated statistical data are necessary to respond to central HEQC quality audits and is used for the subsequent compilation of league tables.

Table 5.1

Year	Student:staff ratio
1980	10:1
1985	15:1
1990	18:1
1995	23:1

Source: University of Derby Senior Management Team.

5.5   Manipulation and Cooption

Any investigation of successful communication strategies would be incomplete without reference to manipulation and cooption. This may appear a surprising element, however all organisations are (at one level) political systems. Failure to predict and manage resistance to change is ill-advised. The influence of interest groups is variable and, is for example, dependent upon stages in a given operating cycle. At the University the cooperation of discrete staffing groups becomes more critical at key points in the academic year. For example, admissions staff perform a critical role during May and September, examinations staff assume priority during February and July. Given this seasonality, the timing and communication of change must be sensitive to the cycle of influence exerted by particular interest groups. The University relays information concerning imminent change selectively and sequences corresponding programmes carefully.

5.6   Reward Systems

Finally, communicating the need for change must extend to publicising organisational support for those individuals (or groups) that are willing to change. During periods of rapid transition skills flexibility is paramount. Organisations which retain rigid job structures actively discourage innovation: whilst rhetoric welcomes change agents the reality often rewards pedestrians. An inflexible organisational structure transmits an inappropriate message to those employees experiencing and adapting to rapid change. Instead, the strategy for communication must extend to the very essence of an organisation and its mission: the belief that communication is simply a process is limited and short-sighted. Communication is integral to and contained within an organisations culture and a commitment to change must, therefore, be reflected in its aims and objectives. Such a progressive approach can be communicated through staff training and development policies, for example. The University has developed and supported a programme of staff development which is characterised by_secondments, practice placements and tailored training workshops. The programme is flexible and responsive to the needs of individual users. In itself this strategy communicates the belief that the University is adapting and responding to its environment by appropriately employing the skills of its staff.

In conclusion, the centrality of communication in effectively managing change has been demonstrated. Communication should not be viewed merely as a process of information exchange as this definition ignores the complexities and realities of organisational life. Rather, communication is all pervasive. It stems from strong corporate leadership which inspires and motivates staff, and visibly displays a common and sustained commitment to corporate transformation. Its success is also dependent upon a climate of openness *and* trust. Effective communication requires the establishment of reliable internal networks, these can be developed by delegating responsibility and setting clear objectives. The importance of effective communication is incontestable: whether the University's experience is generally applicable to other institutions nationally and internationally is, however, more difficult to predict. Luton's particular recent history has raised the collective awareness of staff development systems to a level which may not have found expression in other universities. The University has, however, benefited significantly from its restructuring initiatives, and its success means that, in relation to both its management processes and its standing in the local community, it can face the future with confidence as the sector as a whole consolidates and prepares for a further diminution in the unit of resource.

Acknowledgements

Prepared with information provided by Mr R. Harris – Dean of Quality Assurance, University of Luton and Dr D.J. Smith – Assistant Dean, School of Management, University of Derby.

References

Mayo, E (1949) *The Social Problems of an Industrial Civilisation*. London: Routledge and Kegan Paul.
Morgan, G (1986) *Images of Organisation*. London: Sage Publications.
Pugh, D (1988) Understanding and managing change. In *Planning and Managing Change*. The Open University. London: PCP Ltd.
Schein, EL (1965) *Organizational Psychology*. Englewood Cliffs, NJ: Prentice Hall.
Simon, HA (1976) *Administrative Behavior, A Study of Decision Making Processes In Administrative Organisation*. New York: The Free Press.

6 The Simulation of Taiwan's Power Generation System

Alfred D. Vella and Chuing-Yao Chen

Abstract

A nation's power supply is of vital importance to its future prosperity and the long-term planning of its electricity generating capacity is an important part of its development plans. On the one hand, a lack of power can severely restrict the opportunities for wealth creation causing shortages of items both for home consumption and, possibly more importantly, for export. On the other hand, the ownership costs of production facilities are enormous, tying up capital and using resources even if they are not engaged in production.

One complication of power consumption is the difficulty in forecasting future demand, depending as it does upon weather conditions as well as the prevailing economic climate. Because demand fluctuates a great deal during the day a certain amount of over-capacity is vital if excessive outages are to be avoided.

In this chapter the economic determination of reliability standards for such a supply is described. Use is made of a computer simulation of the whole of Taiwan's generating capacity together with an 'Input–Output' analysis of its economy using the Leontief framework.

Besides the pure economics of power generation the consumer also requires increasing reliability. As consumer groups become more vocal, on the one hand becoming increasingly impatient of electricity shortages and on the other becoming ever more concerned about environmental issues, it is important that the determination of a long-term planning policy is sensitive to extra-economic inputs.

6.1 Introduction

The nature of a power generation system is undoubtedly stochastic. Its behaviour varies depending on demand, unit failures, water inflow, fuel prices and, of course, the weather, as well as many other stochastic variables.

Because of this stochastic nature and the costs of production, capacity shortages are almost unavoidable. When shortages occur they incur costs to both producers and consumers.

Knowing the costs of electricity shortages can help planners in a number of ways. For example, it enables them to set reliability standards for the means of production, transmission and distribution, it gives them information on which to base pricing policies and load management strategies, and it gives them the

49

incentive to develop shortage management strategies, optimum curtailment levels and priorities.

Unfortunately knowing the complex mechanisms that interact to determine the costs of various policies is not enough, one needs a mechanism which can help to evaluate the consequences of planning decisions. It is here that simulation can help. In fact, simulation is almost invariably the only way to make such evaluations meaningful when dealing with very complex systems like this.

A power generation system produces power in order for it to be distributed to satisfy a demand. The simulation described in this chapter ignores all issues relating to the distribution of power and concentrates upon the complex interactions of load (demand) and production (supply). Of course, this has to be related to costs. In a situation where costs are ignored the production planning function is much too simplified. One then merely has to ensure that production capacity exceeds demand and this can be done by including sufficient safety margins in demand prediction models. Therefore, the way that costs vary depending upon the detailed production schedule needs to be modelled and this has been done in some detail in our simulation. We have also tried to quantify the costs of failing to meet demand. These costs include not only opportunity costs of idle resources, costs of spoilt raw material and costs of spoilt product, but also damaged equipment and delayed production.

We also need to take into account the indirect shortage costs that we expend trying to avoid the effects of a shortage, for example by having uninterruptable power supplies as the telecommunications providers and some computer users do.

Although we cannot simulate the entire system in all its detail, we do need to simplify the models so that they can run in a reasonable time on a suitable computer. Also, too detailed a simulation requires much wasted effort and suffers from an increased likelihood of 'being unable to see the wood for the trees'.

To put things into perspective we give some facts about Taipower's operation. In 1992 Taipower employed 26 000 people, generated nearly 100 000 GWh of electricity. The installed capacity was about 30 GW, and its customers generated a peak demand of 17 GW and an average load of 10 GW. It had assets of £1.5 billion, three times its annual revenue.

Difficulties arise from the unpredictability of hourly demand, as well as the way that demand grows as the country's industrial base develops. Although forecasts are available they tend to be a little inaccurate. Table 6.1 illustrates the accuracy of load forecasts for Taiwan, the United States and Japan. As can be seen in Table 6.1, the forecasts have not been very accurate historically. One might be tempted to ask questions such as 'Is it worth spending more effort in producing better forecasts?' or 'How does forecast error affect the economics of power generation?'. These and similar questions can be explored using simulations such as ours.

Table 6.1. Load forecast errors

Five-year forecast errors	Taiwan (%)	USA (%)	Japan (%)
1974	6.8	12.9	26.6
1980	22.3	11.8	22.3
1981	4.9	7.5	20.5
1982	−12.8	3.8	14.8
1983	−9.8	3.3	2.1
1984	−10.0	−1.2	−1.5
1985	−16.7	−1.5	−1.7

6.2 The Simulation Models

Our simulation combines a number of sub-models, the most important of which are the Load Model, the Production Model, the Shortage Cost Model and the Cost Analysis Model. In the following sub-sections we will look at each of these in turn. Unlike many other approaches to generation planning our model does not ignore unit availability, shortage costs and load fluctuations.

6.2.1 The Load Model

The Load Model performs three functions:

- modelling of typical load patterns;
- prediction of future load shapes;
- the simulation of hour by hour loads.

This study uses the long-term forecasts produced by Taipower's Planning Department. These forecasts are based upon forecasts of population growth, per capita income, government development plans, GNP, sectorial industry development plans, rural electrification programmes, etc.

Demand from 'lighting customers' is estimated from 'end-use' models based upon biennial surveys of the saturation rates of 11 major electrical appliances in Taiwan.

'Power customers', on the other hand, are divided into 20 industrial sectors. A regression model is used by Taipower to estimate the growth of such demand by sector.

Our model reads the historical raw load data and calculates a typical weekly load pattern for each month. A load-shaping algorithm ensures that within each week the hourly load is consistent with both the forecasts and the historic records but has a stochastic element to represent factors outside the model.

An important parameter in power generation is the peak load forecast, probably the most important factor controlling this in summer is temperature. This is attributable to the more widespread use of air-conditioning as per capita income has increased in recent years.

Given the peak load and the energy forecast we then need to estimate hourly load. Load-shape curves are normalised curves representing each hour's load as a proportion of the peak load. If such curves can be accurately estimated then all we need to do is to multiply the load ratio by the peak load forecast in order to estimate the hourly load.

Unfortunately, the economic evaluation of a system is very sensitive to the shape of the load demand curve and little previous work has been done on their estimation. In this study we estimate the load curves from historical load data. We are now faced with the problem of predicting the hourly load given: (a) the forecast peak demand; and (b) the forecast total demand at the same time as keeping the load curve approximating historic ones. By modelling the shape curve by the function

$$\text{Load}\,(t) = ct + d - abt$$

and finding values of a, b, c and d we are able to adjust the load shape so that it fits both the historic data and the two independent forecasts (total demand and peak demand), where t represents time and a, b, c and d are constants found by curve fitting.

6.2.2 The Production Model

This model contains the most technical part of our simulation: it includes information on fuel consumption, service times, etc., for each of Taiwan's generating plants. It takes into account pumped storage, thermal and hydro units, their dispatching rules and costs, as well as the technical difficulties of ramping their output up and down.

The model handles the major part of the demand, any shortage in production being passed on to the Shortage Cost Model (see below) to handle.

In generation terms, we classify production units into two types: 'base load' units and 'peaking units'. Base load units are those which produce the major part of the electricity demanded. They are slow to start up, slow to shut down but produce the cheapest power. Base load units include the nuclear capacity. Peaking units have a much faster response to changing conditions than do base units. They can come onstream faster and can also reduce production quickly. However, they tend to be more expensive per unit of power generated. Thus, the rate at which output can be changed varies between different generation units and is described by two 'ramp rates' one for ramping up and the other for ramping down.

A priority list is used to guide loading and unloading of generation units in economic order. The system configuration is built up according to date of commissioning and expected date of decommissioning, and maintenance schedules are included.

The hour by hour simulation takes account of ramping rates and reservoir limitations.

Besides the 'merit order' determined by the economics of operating generating units some technical and reliability constraints have to be met.

First, some generating units need an extended period of start-up. This means that we need to commit certain units well before their full capacity is needed.

Once started, a generator cannot be run below its minimum output without causing undue wear or even damage. This constraint means that certain units are classified as 'base units' which provide the base supply to be augmented by more flexibly peaking units which generally produce electricity at higher cost.

Another constraint (mentioned above), allied to but distinct from start-up, is that of 'ramp rate'. This the rate at which generation can be changed. Different rates apply for increasing and decreasing generation, and each type of generating unit has its own rates. Thus, when planning an increase or decrease in generation, care has to be taken not to exceed the allowed rates for each individual unit involved.

Finally, in order to avoid excessive frequency swings and the risk of instability, the supply and demand have to be constantly balanced. To do this, given uncertainties in both demand and supply (due, for example, to unit failures), provision is made for a 'spinning reserve'.

The spinning reserve is the difference between the anticipated load and the generating capacity ready to produce output at short notice. Both a 'spin up' and a 'spin down' reserve is needed. As the cheaper electricity is often produced by slower base units it is the 'spin down' condition that causes the main problems. It is often necessary to dispatch more expensive peaking units in order to have sufficient spin down capacity.

Given all of these constraints the dispatcher has to decide upon which units to dispatch and when.

The dispatching of hydro units varies according to their type: conventional storage; pumped storage; or run-of-the-river.

Low variable operating costs means that hydro units should be used as much as possible. However, the limited capacity of reservoirs in Taiwan means that they are used for spinning reserve and as peaking units. In the simulation we took into account the interdependencies of units on the same water flow, the inflows being calculated from historical records.

Pumped storage units provide an almost ideal method of absorbing surplus electrical energy from the cheap base load units. They do have the complication that they can be used to store energy in circumstances of low demand so that we can think of such a unit as a combination of a conventional unit with a storage device whose energy must be paid for. Unfortunately, there are also a number of constraints that have to be satisfied. The capacity both as a source and store of energy is limited so that cheap base load electricity generating capacity may not be fully utilised. The pumping–generating cycle is about 80% efficient and this is taken into consideration in the costs of pumped storage.

There are a number of 'run of the river' units in Taiwan. These units do not have reservoirs of any size and so they can either use the energy of the river flow or waste it. Because of this they are treated as base load units.

6.2.3 The Shortage Cost Model

Traditionally 'generation reliability indices' (GRI) provide us with measures of reliability of the generation system which are too coarse grained. Such indices include:

- EENS: the expected energy not served, i.e. total demand not met;
- FLOL: the frequency of loss of load, i.e. the frequency with which demand exceeds supply;
- LOLE: the loss of load expectation, i.e. the number of days in which demand exceeds supply in a year;
- DLOL: duration of loss of load, i.e. the total length of time that demand exceeds supply.

There are many other measures in the literature but the ones above are typical examples.

These indices do not measure the effects of shortage, just the amount of shortage occurring. Although related to these measures, the actual damage to the economy caused by outages cannot be estimated from these measures.

When a shortage occurs, supply needs to be directed to the most beneficial users. The Input–Output or Leontief (1966) Model described below gives us a ranking against which we are to 'distribute' any shortages. As a side effect it also gives us the costs associated with shortages to any industrial sector. Thus, each shortage event can be costed and the total cost over an amount of time can be calculated.

We would like to estimate the financial damage done to the economy by a shortage event. This is not an easy task and has been attempted in a number of ways (Munasinghe 1990), including user surveys (the costs that they claim, their willingness to pay for a better service, etc.) and input–output analysis. It is the latter that we used to produce costs for our simulation.

The idea of input–output analysis is quite simple. In it we try to estimate the effects on a system of changing one of its parameters. In our case we look at the changes in industrial production caused by varying the amount of electricity produced. In order to make such estimates valid one needs to consider knock-on effects as well as direct effects. For example, if less of item A is produced because of a shortage of electricity, then the production of items produced from A and other items used to produce item A may well change.

Our model begins with 'Input–Output' tables produced by the government of Taiwan. These tables divide the economy into 48 sectors and quantify how many units of production of, for example, plastics and plastic products (sector 29) are used in the production of one unit of production of garments (sector 19). Thus, the tables represent the complex interdependencies between sectors as a matrix of 'technical coefficients'. Because of the length of time it takes for tables to be published we used the figures published in 1993 for 1989.

Using these technical coefficients, which we assume are fixed throughout the simulation, we can find relationships between the production of each sector and its supply to the users, final demand and demand that is used for the production of other goods.

By using matrix algebra we can find 'valued added coefficients' for each sector representing its contribution to the economy per unit of production. These coefficients thus tell us the relative importance of each sector to the economy and thus which to give priority in times of electricity shortage. Whether such a strategy could by used in practice will depend upon extra-economic considerations, in other words political considerations.

We thus have a strategy for supply curtailment in times of electricity shortage, as well as an estimate of the resulting economic cost of such curtailment. Our simulation could also be used to test the costs of other proposed curtailment strategies.

6.2.4   The Cost Analysis Model

The aim here is to estimate the costs involved in the realisation of a generation plan so that the economic effects of different plans can be compared objectively. This model combines the variable generation costs calculated in the two previous models with the other costs of ownership, namely capital costs, and then combines these with shortage costs. Of course, we use a system of discounted cash flow for the simulation which can run under different interest rate regimes. Residual values of capital equipment are taken into account using a system of annual equivalent installation costs.

Production costs include both fixed and variable contributions, which are worked out according to the simulation events encountered. Shortage costs, discussed above, are discussed more fully in Chen and Vella (1994).

6.3   Experimental Design

Many factors have been found to determine the economics of electricity generation, in the study reported here five factors were chosen, the effects of which were to be investigated. They were: reserve margin; system composition; load uncertainty; fuel prices; and interest rates. For a discussion of the importance of these and other factors the reader is referred to Elrazaz (1988), Hamound and Billington (1983), Manikki (1991) and Shew (1977).

Because of the uncertain interactions between the five factors a fully factorial experiment was performed. Six values of reserve margin, four of system composition, four of load forecast error, and two each of fuel prices and interest rates were used. Each run lasted for 14 simulated years and was repeated five times. This gave us 1920 runs, enough to be getting on with!

6.3.1 Reserve Margin

This is the difference between 'system capacity' and 'peak load' for the year measured as a percentage of peak load. Care was taken here to use Taipower's definition of reserve margin, where planned outages are not taken into account, rather than the definitions used by some other generators. Values of 8, 12, 16, 20, 24 and 28% were used. This range is consistent with both literature and current practice.

6.3.2 System Composition

Composition here refers to the mix of generator types. Thus, the system could have different percentages of base units, intermediate generating units and peaking units. Although little can be done with existing units, when replacements need to be made some choice is available to the planners. The four compositions were 55–20–25, 50–20–30, 45–20–35 and 40–20–40. When a new unit is needed it is chosen from a set of 'candidate alternatives' which have already been identified by Taipower.

6.3.3 Load Uncertainty

Simulation allows us to include a stochastic element to the study. In any forecast we cannot be certain just how accurate the forecast actually is. Steps can be taken to improve the forecast but as this will add to costs one needs some measure of the cost benefit of forecast accuracy. Both load growth and load variation can be uncertain. In this study we look only at load variation. Based upon Taipower's forecasts new forecasts were produced which were 20% lower, 10% lower, equal and 10% higher.

6.3.4 Fuel Prices

Because of the lead times involved in generation capacity planning it is possible that relative fuel prices can change appreciably during a planning period. It was with this possibility in mind that the effects of such price movements were studied. Standard fuel prices produced by Taipower were used as a starting point. The effects of a doubling of both liquid natural gas and oil prices were investigated.

6.3.5 Interest Rates

For reasons similar to those mentioned under fuel prices, the effects of variable rates of interest prevailing during the planning period need to be examined. Both 7 and 9% were used in this study, values which are in accordance with Taiwan's standard procedures.

The results of the simulation produce six major outputs: installation costs; production costs; shortage costs; total costs; expectation of energy not served; and hourly loss of load expectation.

6.4   Results

6.4.1   Effects of Reserve Margin

As reserve margin rises from zero we expect the installation costs to rise, production costs to remain broadly constant and shortage costs to decrease. The latter should have a beneficial effect upon total costs. However, as shortage costs fall there comes a value of reserve margin at which total costs are a minimum. This occurred at a reserve margin of about 20%.

One might ask why production costs do not fall as reserve margin rises due to the availability of cheaper production units. It was found that this effect, although measurable, was almost balanced by the 'savings' in production costs when an outage occurred!

As would be expected it was also noticeable that high reserve margins were beneficial when load growth is unexpectedly high. Also to be expected was the finding that high reserve margins mean higher reliability. However, we are able to quantify the benefits using this simulation.

6.4.2   Effects of System Composition

The effects of system composition only seem to be pronounced at high or low values of reserve margin. In times of shortage, compositions with high peaking units can help reliability, but at an extra cost. With a 28% reserve margin, a well-mixed system can keep total costs down.

6.4.3   Effects of Load Uncertainty

With an overestimate of load growth, high reserve margins add to costs but only marginally. However, if the load grows unexpectedly quickly then not having a high reserve margin can cost dear. This is due to the rapid increase of shortage costs as demand exceeds supply. Clearly, decisions on target reserve margin need to be taken with this in mind.

6.4.4   Effects of Fuel Prices

This has its biggest effect upon the economics of different system composition. Changes would be expected to favour one or other extreme of composition. However, this makes the system less able to cope with load uncertainties.

6.4.5   Effects of Interest Rates

Although installation and thus total costs are very sensitive to interest rates, they do not have a significant effect upon the choices of other variables. There is, however, the expected shift towards a lower reserve margin as interest rates increase.

6.5   Conclusions

In this chapter we have looked at a use of simulation for modelling a very large electricity generation system in order to evaluate different strategies for growth. The use of such a simulation can play an important role in the planning of new generation facilities by evaluating their impact on the economy given their siting, their type or any other pertinent variable.

It has shown that the optimal reliability, given the assumptions on the economic costs of shortages, is not far from that already chosen by the country's experts. By using it to 'predict' past consumption patterns and costs we were able to give the model a level of credibility beyond that afforded to it by any other means.

One of the weaknesses in the simulation approach, common to all other approaches, is that the quality of the results depend upon the accuracy of the assumptions made. We have talked above of the priority that economic considerations leads us to, but there are always other, sometimes more powerful, considerations to be examined.

The simulation will provide Taipower with objective measures of the impact of planning decisions upon the economy of Taiwan. It is then government's task to consider other extra-economic issues. It is very difficult to estimate the 'cost equivalent' of the feelings of the citizens of an area and so subjective judgements still need to be made.

As Taiwan embarks upon a more free-market approach to the supply of electricity our simulation will enable its government to consider the impact of candidate decisions upon the economy as a whole, and in this way will be able to avoid many of the shortcomings normally associated with the introduction of competition with its duplication of effort and over-supply in the short term.

References

Chen, C-Y & Vella, AD (1994) Estimating the economic costs of electricity shortages using input-output analysis: the case of Taiwan. *Applied Economics*, 26: 1061–1069.

Elrazaz, Z. (1988) Long range forecasting for utilities with dynamic load growth rates. *Canadian Journal of Electrical and Computer Engineering*, 13: 127–131.

Hamound, G & Billington, R (1983) Parameter uncertainty in generating capacity reliability evaluation. *Electrical Power and Energy Systems*, 5: 149–158.

Leontief, W (1966) *Input–Output Economics*. New York: Oxford University Press.

Manikki, P (1991) Electric power capacity planning under uncertain conditions. Third International Conference on Probabilistic Methods Applied to Electric Power Systems. London, 3–5 July 1991: 214–219.

Munasinghe, M (1990) *Electric Power Economics – Selected Works*. Oxford: Butterworths.

Shew, WB (1997) Costs of inadequate capacity in the electric utility industry. *Energy Systems and Policy*, 2: 85–110.

7 Performance Measurement, Goal Setting and Feedback in Engineering Design

J.S. Busby, A. Williamson and G.M. Williams

Abstract

There is much evidence that using performance measures for goal setting and feedback improves performance. But there is also evidence that unassisted human judgement is poor at simultaneously evaluating multiple dimensions of performance, that it tends to attribute too little influence on performance to uncontrollable circumstances, and that it does not dependably infer what behaviours cause good and bad outcomes. We report here on the development of a support tool for the engineering design process which: (1) helps design managers methodically identify appropriate outcome measures of performance; (2) gives performance feedback to design groups in terms of a frontier analysis; and (3) assists goal setting by helping design groups infer which behaviours lead to good outcome performance.

7.1 Introduction

7.1.1 Purpose

The purpose of the work we describe here was to develop a method of systematic and rational performance measurement to serve the processes of goal setting and feedback in engineering design. More specifically, it was to investigate the use of frontier analysis (using data envelopment analysis (DEA)) in the role of data fusion: integrating the different dimensions of outcome performance. Of particular interest to us was how informative frontier analysis would be as a tool for regular, periodic use in the hands of engineers and managers, rather than as a policy tool in the hands of outsiders. Our intended contribution is therefore in investigating the role of an operational research procedure in organisational routines, not in developing the procedure itself.

7.1.2 Context

Our investigation took the form of a participative case study in an engineering firm, and Figure 7.1 shows roughly what this firm does in terms of a process that extends from early development of a product through to supplying it to its users. The

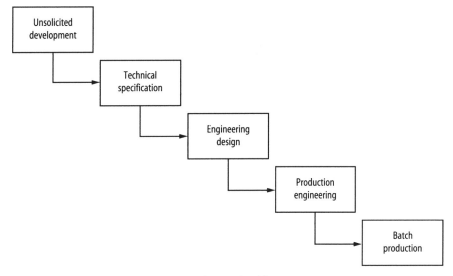

Figure 7.1. The firm's product delivery process.

products are highly complex, expensive items of equipment that are bought and operated exclusively by national governments.

7.1.3 Application

Figure 7.2 shows the engineering design activity conducted by this firm. This covers a wide range of tasks, from the more conceptual and intellectually demanding matters of formulating technical requirements and developing conceptual designs, through to the more routine matters of detail design, described in more detail in Figure 7.3. It was this detail design process that was the subject our work. Figure 7.4 shows for the detail design activity the factors of outcome performance that matter to the world outside detail design, especially the industrial engineering activities (such as jig and fixture design, part programming and process planning) that lie just downstream. The 'co-location' factor refers to the location of design and product operations on the same geographical site: when these are not co-located life is usually a lot harder.

7.2 The Problem Tackled

7.2.1 Why Measurement is Problematic

The figures help illustrate why measuring the performance of even a straightforward task like detail design is problematic.

The products and accomplishments of the task (the outputs) plainly do not have market prices. The point at which outcomes can be measured may be much later than the completion of the design task, and this measurement may confound design performance with the performance of subsequent tasks. For example, the ease with

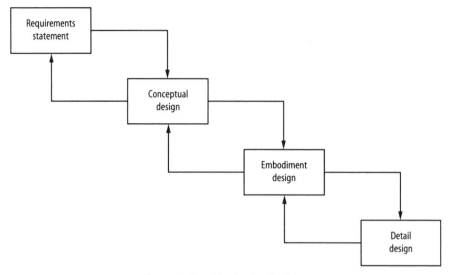

Figure 7.2. The activity of engineering design.

which a product design can be manufactured depends both on intrinsic properties of the design and on the later success of manufacturing engineers in defining suitable production processes and designing good production equipment such as part programmes and fixtures. There are several dimensions of outcome performance which are basically incommensurate, in the sense that there is no functional rule for scaling and combining them. Yet they are empirically associated, in the sense (for instance) that more accomplishment on one dimension tends to produce less on

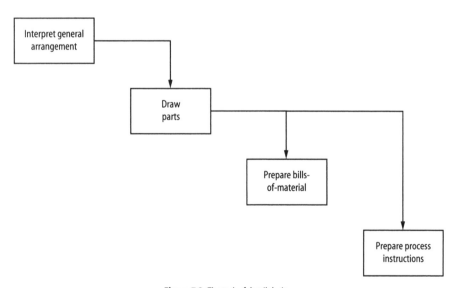

Figure 7.3. The task of detail design.

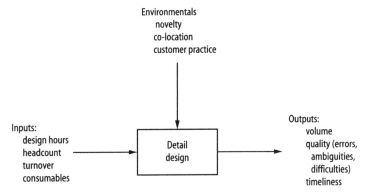

Figure 7.4. Outcome performance factors.

another. Such an association is true, for instance, of the timeliness and freedom from error of drawings. This makes the satisfactory integration of measurements along all of the dimensions hard, whether for the purpose of monitoring, diagnosis or motivation; and there is evidence that human judgement is not very good at this integration (Dawes 1979), in particular being able to pay attention to only two or three cues at once.

There are no absolute standards for these dimensions to provide satisfactory bases for measuring success (although there are norms within the firm, such as drawings taking 40 hours to complete). This suggests that it is comparison between two groups or individuals performing comparable tasks, or between the same groups at different times, that should form the basis of measurement. Unfortunately, as we discuss later, there is resistance amongst individuals to explicit comparison. There is also evidence that unassisted performance rating is subject to attribution biases (Feldman 1981): notably that observers of a process (like managers) attribute too much control over a process to the actors (like designers), while actors attribute too little. This suggests that when managers compare the performance of one designer with another, informally or tacitly, they will be excessively swayed by chance factors in the environment.

The priority that people accord these multiple dimensions of performance varies considerably with their place in the business process. Marketing people want keen prices and so stress the minimisation or at least containment of the hours it takes to complete drawings, while production engineers stress freedom from error. This suggests that one cannot simple-mindedly form a performance index with fixed weights.

Our work attempted to tackle these problems, although the second was tackled only indirectly.

7.3   Background Knowledge

The work is cross-disciplinary and draws on three literatures in the fields of:

- management science, and more specifically DEA (for the formal productivity definition and its associated procedures);
- engineering design (for the application domain);
- organisational behaviour (for the way in which the measurement is best deployed to influence behaviour in the workplace).

In the DEA literature there are a number of engineering applications, some of which are essentially about products like computer printers (Doyle and Green 1991) and testing equipment (Cook and Johnston 1992), some about abstract artefacts such as manufacturing cells (Shafer and Bradford 1995), and some about processes like robotics implementation (Cook *et al.* 1992) and software maintenance (Banker *et al.* 1991). These papers demonstrate the appropriateness of DEA models in the engineering domain, and yield important insights, although they do not discuss in depth how DEA might be used routinely by engineers or their managers for performance feedback. It is perhaps fair to say that DEA is more often conceived as a procedure for use by external specialists in policy decisions, rather than for use by the participants in a process for diagnostic and motivational purposes. It has been tested mostly for its normative strengths in capturing the economic substance of an application: not for the cogency or accessibility of its presentation.

There is, however, some DEA literature that discusses its suitability for managerial tasks. Epstein and Henderson, for instance, provide an extensive evaluation of its suitability for both diagnostic and control tasks supported by experience of its application in a public sector organisation (Epstein and Henderson 1989). They applied three criteria in their evaluation goal congruence, perceived fairness and computational cost, and found from the application that the technique helped to detect relationships amongst performance variables, reveal preferences and stimulate discussion of what performance meant. Dyson *et al.* (1994) also discuss the use of DEA in conjunction with performance measurement for managerial control. They discuss some of the behavioural problems that stem from performance measurement generally and DEA in particular. Belton and Vickers (1993) developed a decision support system that used a revised DEA formulation and an interactive, visual presentation, which was intended to make the technique more acceptable to nontechnical users. This apparently met with favourable responses from such users. On a similar theme, Desai and Walters (1991) propose a device for presenting data visually in multiple dimensions which can also convey the results of a data envelopment analysis. In both these cases the stress was on helping people understand the immediate meaning of a DEA application, rather than on the issues of institutionalising the technique as part of an organisational routine.

In the field of engineering design, performance and productivity measurement has received relatively little attention; there is a much larger literature on product evaluation (typically using programming formulations or expected utilities). However, on the measurement of engineers' performance, specifically, there is some prescriptive work on developing measurement systems in research and development activities (Brown and Gobeli 1992), and on comparing objective measures of individual engineers' performance and subjective ratings by superiors and colleagues (Keller and Holland 1982). There has also been work on determining the attributes that lie behind subjective ratings of engineers' performance (Stahl *et al.* 1984), and on explaining outcome performance by regressing outcome measures against individual behaviours and traits (such as educational level and attending meetings) (Stahl and Koser 1978), and against group characteristics (such as cohesiveness and physical proximity) (Keller 1986).

In the organisational behaviour literature there is a great deal on the processes of goal setting and feedback, an important theme in our work as our purpose was essentially to embed frontier analysis in the organisational routine. Goal setting works by directing people's attention, mobilising effort and increasing persistence in a task (Locke *et al.* 1981). Feedback, it has been suggested, works through cueing and motivational effects (cueing essentially being an error-correcting function)

(Nadler 1979). But the empirical evidence (in one case specifically of engineers working in an organisation – Pritchard 1988) suggests that it is both goal setting and feedback in combination that is most effective in raising performance levels. The most relevant of this literature concerns the characteristics of goal setting and feedback which have the greatest effect on performance in a task. For instance, goals are generally best when they are specific, accepted and demanding (Mento *et al.* 1987). Feedback seems to be best when self-generated (Ivancevich and McMahon 1982), learning-oriented rather than performance-oriented (telling people how they could improve, not how good their results were) (Johnson *et al.* 1993), and when people can choose whether or not to look at it (Ilgen and Moore 1987). Unfortunately, there are many variables which mediate in the effect of these characteristics, related both to individual differences and group structures, making it impossible to develop blanket principles about what makes for good goals or good feedback. As we shall discuss in Section 7.4 the main influence of this literature on our support tool was the link between outcome performance and behaviour and how to detect this link satisfactorily and how to use it to set goals.

7.4   The Solution Developed

Our approach to tackling the problem described in the previous section was to develop a system that would:

- provide a framework for the explicit integration of different dimensions of outcome performance by frontier analysis;
- incorporate environmental variables whose values would otherwise make the work of different groups of detail designers incomparable;
- help people infer from feedback on outcome performance how they should change their behaviours or practices.

The system was to take the form of a computer-based support tool whose elements are shown in Figure 7.5 in terms of the organisational procedures it supports. These

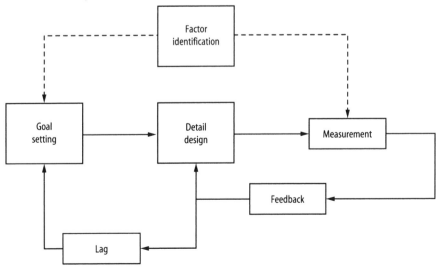

Figure 7.5. The support tool.

fall into three blocks, for the design of the measuring system (principally the identification of appropriate outcome factors), the generation of feedback and the setting of goals. The tool essentially provides a series of forms to prompt and constrain these processes, and processing facilities for carrying out routine calculation and presentation tasks. We have not reproduced the detail of the forms here but only attempted to convey the process in which they are used.

7.5   Designing the Performance Measuring System

The first block of forms, concerned with designing the measuring system, itself had three main facilities.

In the first a process model is used to assist the direct identification of outcome factors of performance (outputs, to be maximised, inputs, to be minimised, and environmental variables which affect the ability of the participants to convert inputs into outputs). The process model, basically a more detailed version of Figures 7.1–7.3, is prepared in a proprietary modelling tool and is imported in skeletal form into our support tool. It contains a decomposition of the firm's basic business process into its primary activities (of which detail design is one at the second stage of decomposition). There is then a further decomposition of the activities into their constituent tasks. The result is a picture of what other activities an activity such as detail design affects, and how it affects them. This then, we have assumed, is the picture one needs in order to identify the outcome factors of performance.

The second facility (illustrated in Figure 7.6) provides an indirect but more concrete way of identifying some of the outcome factors, and is similar in essence to devices sometimes used to improve subjective ratings. It calls on the user to identify the products of the detail design activity (such as detail drawings and bills of material) and to identify their recipients. These recipients are then asked to locate good and bad examples of the product. It is the characteristics that distinguish good

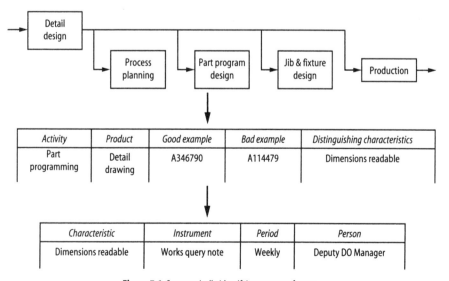

Activity	Product	Good example	Bad example	Distinguishing characteristics
Part programming	Detail drawing	A346790	A114479	Dimensions readable

Characteristic	Instrument	Period	Person
Dimensions readable	Works query note	Weekly	Deputy DO Manager

Figure 7.6. Systematically identifying outcome factors.

and bad examples that are identified as outcome performance factors. For instance, process planners use product drawings to compile a detailed sequence of production operations at the shop floor. If a characteristic that distinguishes good from bad drawings is the legibility of annotations (such as dimensions or process instructions) then legibility, or perhaps a generalisation of it such as freedom from ambiguity, becomes prima facie an outcome factor.

The third facility helps economise on outcome factors in two basic ways. The first is to reveal empirical associations between factors, which can then be combined or eliminated on the basis of redundancy. This simply calculates pairwise correlation coefficients. It is perhaps naive not to use a more holistic approach, like factor analysis, to do this, but in many cases even the use of simple correlations is pushing the limits of some users' understanding. It is important to remember at this low level of measurement (much more detailed than the company level) cause–effect relationships are often fairly obvious, making statistical analysis heavy-handed and uninformative. For example, the relationship (amongst the inputs) between the size of the design team and the number of hours they use up, given a project of fixed duration, is qualitatively straightforward, even if people cannot estimate quantitatively how close the two dimensions are.

The second way of economising on outcome factors is to find semantic rather than empirical associations. Some factors are related in particular ways by definition, and may even amount to the same thing (given a scaling factor) with different names. Given that performance measures are usually introduced to an organisation one-by-one, for ad hoc reasons, the existence of such associations is plausible. For instance, it is common to have several measures of cost, such as design hours, expenses and consumables, and total direct costs (costs traceable to a project). To have both design hours and total costs as distinct outcome factors would be a mistake as there is no sense of one being capable of substituting for the other: one is in fact subsumed in the other by definition.

7.6 Delivering Performance Feedback

The next block of facilities gives performance feedback.

The first element is outcome feedback of the type provided by the basic DEA formulation (an example of which is shown in Figure 7.7). A decision-making unit (in this case most likely to be a section in the firm's design office) can see the value of its performance index, and the gap between its current performance and the efficient frontier. It can also see its reference peers defining the relevant facet of the efficient frontier, and the extent to which each is represented in its performance index. In other words, the outcome feedback takes the form of a summary number, the improvement potential in each dimension and a suggestion of who to emulate in order to improve performance. There is latitude in the selection of factors that are used in the analysis so that one can test the impact on one's feedback of altering the performance criteria applied to one's activity.

The second element is simply a record of current performance in relation to the last recorded goals for the unit in question: both outcome goals and behaviour goals (described in the next section).

One point that was mentioned to us by a practitioner in this field was the importance of getting the decision-making unit, or its representative or manager, to accept the numbers before being told who the reference peers are. It was the experience of

Outcome performance for	Section RJ
Index	85%
Reference peers	Section OL, Section OU, Section RF
Improvement gaps	
(constant input)	12% errors, 17% ambiguities
(constant output)	20% design hours, 2% headcount

Figure 7.7. Outcome performance feedback.

this practitioner that otherwise people would too readily find reasons why they were not comparable with these peers. There is, therefore, in the support tool, a rather gratuitous constraint that the numbers have to be 'signed off' before the reference peers are identified.

7.7   Setting Performance Goals

The first way of setting a goal is simply to base it on the gaps in outcome performance displayed by the feedback facility. In practice, one would not adopt a gap as a goal automatically, but instead use it as an anchor for a process of negotiation between, say, a section leader in the design office and the design office manager.

The second way is to set behaviour goals, the rationale for which is the finding discussed in Section 3 that feedback that tells people how to improve is more effective than feedback that only tells them the inadequacy of their results. By setting behaviour goals one can give behavioural feedback by comparing actual and goal behaviours. The basic procedure here is that a decision-making unit should look at its reference peers and identify those behaviours that lead to the reference peers' success. To do this directly, however, leaves the procedure open, potentially, to a good deal of bias. For a start, one has to look for correlation between behaviours and good outcome performance, which, when dealing with a handful of reference peers, is unlikely to be statistically dependable. To go a further step and infer causation one has also, of course, to get temporal precedence and ceteris paribus. In most real settings both are very hard to come by: people and organisations rarely change just one aspect of behaviour or one practice at a time in a systematic way, and it is often unclear as to whether a change in behaviour happens before a change in results or whether the change in results occured first. The upshot is that there is no objective way of making this inference between outcome performance and behaviour in most real settings. It is therefore important to assist as much as possible the subjective inference of this potential causation.

The support tool therefore provides an indirect, but again simple and concrete, procedure (illustrated in Figure 7.8). Once the reference peers are obtained, the process model is used to identify systematically the main tasks involved in the detail design activity. For each task a critical incident (or if necessary a small number of critical incidents) are identified such that it is performance in this incident that defines the outcome of the task. For example, the simple process of issuing a drawing hinges on the critical decision of when to issue it, perhaps before the designer

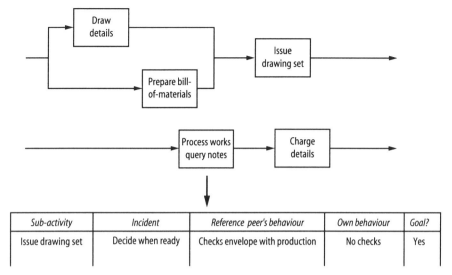

Sub-activity	Incident	Reference peer's behaviour	Own behaviour	Goal?
Issue drawing set	Decide when ready	Checks envelope with production	No checks	Yes

Figure 7.8. Inferring effective behaviours.

has discussed production issues with a production engineer, or perhaps afterwards. One then asks whether the behaviour of any reference peer differs from oneself in the critical incident. If it does then it becomes prima facie a behaviour goal.

The procedure is, of course, imperfect and ultimately does not detect whether the peer's behaviour in fact contributes towards its efficiency. Before it is accepted as a goal the manager and section leader (in an application such as this) must agree on whether this contribution does exist.

7.8   Observations on the Application

7.8.1   The State of the Underlying Data

An initial exercise was undertaken in the company with which we are collaborating to apply frontier analysis (without the support tool described in the last section) to performance measures that were already being gathered by the organisation. The purpose was to test the availability, validity and reliability of raw performance data as they then existed. Essentially the unit of analysis was not an organisational unit but a work unit: that is, a project and, at a lower level of decomposition, a work package. This, of course, is problematic from the standpoint of goal setting and feedback as a given person or group does not receive knowledge of results consistently over time. But it was the only practicable approach we could take that was acceptable to the company with which we were working.

Figure 7.9 shows the data that could eventually be obtained and analysed. The instrument is the specific quantity counted, the factor the underlying dimension of outcome performance it stands for. The object shows the unit of measurement: either a discrete project or (at a lower level) a work package.

Gathering these data was a protracted and involved process, and meant consulting several people in different parts of the organisation. Thus, hitherto, engineers

Instrument	Underlying factor	Object
Hours booked	Design hours	Project (partly)
Estimated hours to complete	Design hours	Work package (partly)
Works queries	Drawing quality	Project and work package (indirectly)
Drawings issued	Drawing volume	Project and work package
Percent lateness	Timeliness	Project and work package
Average lateness	Timeliness	Project and work package
Changes needed	Novelty	Project and work package ie changes to previous product
Drawings	Unanticipated volume	Project and work package ie drawings not in budget

Figure 7.9. Available performance data.

and managers had simply been unable to get a comprehensive picture of performance. We had originally envisaged the problem to be data integration in the definitional sense: the use of trade-offs and priorities to produce an overall statement of performance. But the problem, at least in part, turned out to be data integration in a more procedural sense, setting the raw measures to the same place at the same time in order to process and observe them.

A second problem was that the definition of certain measures suited an accounting process, but not goal setting and feedback. For instance, the hours taken to complete engineering drawings were recorded against particular work packages, each representing a major module of the product. But the hours spent dealing with queries raised against these drawings (for instance because production people could not understand them) were recorded against a separate work package which acted as a bucket for all hours spent dealing with queries. This makes the cost incurred on different work packages incapable of comparison. One really needs to see all the costs associated with a package to be sure that the performance measure is not an artefact of the way engineers divide their efforts between designing things thoroughly in the first place and rectifying hastily completed drawings afterwards.

Third, some of the measures shown on Figure 7.9 had to be worked out laboriously. For instance, to find the number of queries on the drawings in each work package meant finding out which drawings were associated with the work package and then how many queries were recorded against the drawings. The performance measures, in other words, were not recorded against the same objects.

We are unable to present the data that went into this analysis, and the outcome, as the collaborating organisation insisted that it be kept confidential.

7.8.2   The Reaction of Engineering Designers

We mentioned earlier the resistance of people in the company to performance measurement by comparison. The nature of work in perhaps any organisation makes this understandable. There are always circumstances that make someone's work incomparable with another's; some element of outcome performance is always random, yet there is the danger managers will jump to conclusions on excessively small samples; people usually disagree in some way about goals and priorities even with others doing the same jobs; and there may be strong fears that explicit data make redundancy more likely by strengthening the hand of managers who need a pretext to lay people off. This resistance to comparison does not necessarily run counter to the interest of the company as a commercial whole. For if performance comparisons fail to consider environmental variables, or fail to capture the full array of goals that apply to a task, they will lead to bad decisions and poor morale. Set against this is the virtual inevitability of comparison with one's peers or one's past performance if there is no well-defined norm of good performance, or if there is commercial pressure always to improve performance.

The best course of action is to ameliorate the defects of performance measurement and comparison as far as possible, which is partly what the support tool was meant to do. The systematic attention to identifying the factors of outcome performance (based on how the detail design task affected the outside world) was meant to limit the myopia of some performance measurements. The incorporation of environmental variables and assistance in inferring good behaviours from good outcomes was meant to make comparison more objective and thereby fairer. In addition, it is important to tell the potential audience that this tool of explicit performance feedback and goal setting replaces a much more tacit system in which the subjective ratings of managers take the place of objective measures, and feedback is imbalanced, patchy and hard to interpret. The choice is not between comparison and no comparison: it is between comparison on explicit and as far as possible equitable grounds, and comparison on the basis of managers' judgement, something we know is swayed by personal likes and dislikes.

7.9   Conclusion

7.91   A Summary

We have described the development of a support system that was intended to assist people in designing performance measures, setting goals and providing feedback in the engineering design process. The technical core of this support tool was frontier analysis (in the form of DEA), and to this were added several forms to prompt and constrain the way this was applied. These prompts and constraints were essentially designed to address problems of organisational behaviour, such as the difficulties of inferring effective patterns of behaviour from outcome performance.

7.9.2   Limitations of the Work

There are several technical simplifications which limit the validity of this work.

First, the basic model in which there are trade-offs amongst accomplishments might be wrong. One of the points on which Japanese-style organisation and the traditional Western style are said to differ is that in the former quantities such as cost and quality are seen as complementary. The idea of the 'cost of quality' is that inadequate attention to the repeatability and accuracy of the production process cause one to incur costs: the costs of inspection, rectification and so forth. Thus, more accomplishment in reducing cost should not be associated with less accomplishment in reducing quality. One could argue that the issue is resolved by looking at the empirical evidence and testing whether two dimensions of accomplishments in fact covary inversely. But the idea is that historical evidence of a trade-off does not establish that it is inevitable, only a reflection of outdated practices (like allowing product defects because their eradication is assumed to be too expensive).

A second limitation is that we used the basic formulation of DEA in conditions where some of the enhancements formulated in the literature would have been more appropriate for the job in hand. Performance is not always comensatory, for instance, in the different variables, in the sense that more of one does not always make up for less of another. There are limits to the tolerability of mistakes in drawings, whatever the speed with which the drawings are delivered. This suggests a model of the type suggested by Dyson and Thanassoulis (1988) in which weight flexibility is reduced, although the difficulty of interpreting weights in intuitive, operational terms makes the assignment of weight restrictions problematic. Doyle and Green (1994) suggest the use of cross-efficiencies as a less arbitrary way of discouraging over-specialisation on one dimension of performance alone. Some of the environmental variables are really categorical, such as whether or not computer-aided design equipment was available to the unit in question, and again this should in principle have been reflected in the use of a model like that suggested by Banker and Morey (1986). Finally, the performance data are partly stochastic, in the sense that they do not have perfect validity (the number of queries is an imperfect proxy for the badness of drawings) and human performance has imperfect reliability (doing one or two drawings badly amongst 20 or 30 because of personal problems is perhaps a natural consequence of human activity and should not be penalised). This suggests a model of the type proposed by Banker *et al.* (1991). But whether the audience could interpret the output of such a model is doubtful (we rather struggled, in fact).

A third limitation concerns the question of what is an outcome variable and what an environmental variable. For instance, when a production operator on the shop floor fails to make something exactly to the drawing he must obtain a concession if he or she is not to have to rework the part in question. Dealing with concessions is a costly business for design engineers who have to evaluate the seriousness of the deviation. On face value, it is important to count concessions and apply this as an environmental variable to explain some of the cost (an input) incurred by the design engineer through no fault of his or her own. However, it is quite plausible that in some cases the production operator fails to make to drawing because the part has not been designed in a way that assists the production operation. The issue of 'design-for-manufacture' is an important one in engineering design. Therefore, to a very uncertain degree, the design engineer has influence over what seemed at first to be an environmental variable. This is a case of a more general theme, that the complexity and bidirectionality of causal relationships between tasks in engineering activities sometimes makes the business of distinguishing exogenous and endogenous factors (to a particular task) quite hard.

A fourth, and related, limitation is our failure to capture all the circumstances that vary between projects as environmental variables. There are too many, their effects are too uncertain and their objective measurement is too impractical. Really the only sensible course of action is to use one's judgement and attempt to get the agreement of those involved before the results of using a particular subset of the environmentals in the performance measurement are known.

7.9.3   Further Developments

Perhaps the most obvious development is to apply the same approach to tasks that lie upstream of detail design, notably concept and embodiment design. These are more interesting in the sense that they involve more fundamental decisions and have a greater influence on the goodness of the product and the ease with which later processes can be carried out.

Here, however, the most critical goal of the engineering designer is probably to do with satisfying the user or customer of the product. This makes the problems of confounding and delay more profound. The quality of the product, both in terms of what it does and how well it does it, is not just a function of its concept and functionality but the detail of its construction and the appropriateness of its materials and components; and not just a function of design generally but of its manufacture. Thus, the user's satisfaction, as a performance measure, confounds the sucess of all these processes; and, of course, products can come into use several years after the design took place: so feedback to the designer can take as long to be available. Both these properties make performance feedback of this kind highly unsatisfactory.

One way of tackling this would be to use predictive indices, of the kind used to assess the cost of a product (Li *et al.* 1993). If it were possible to predict adequately the main outcome measures of performance in terms of design characteristics that were measurable at the time of design, by regressing historical outcomes against these characteristics, the designer would have immediate feedback. This would be feedback that is not confounded by the performance of downstream processes (whose performance variation is captured in the non-systematic variance in the predictive model). It is an open question as to whether such an approach is feasible, but it appears to be worth investigating.

But even predictive indices only go part of the way, of course. Ultimately, the preferences and values of users are formed or changed by their use of a product, so the prediction of a product's satisfactoriness becomes indeterminate.

Acknowledgements

The authors would like to acknowledge the support of the EPSRC under grant GR/J 95300. The authors used, at the time of writing, the DEA software supplied by the Warwick Business School for all DEA processing.

References

Banker, RD, Datar, SM and Kemerer, CF (1991) A model to evaluate variables impacting the productivity of software maintenance projects. *Management Science*, 37(1): 1–17.

Banker, RD and Morey, RC (1986) The use of categorical variables in data envelopment analysis. *Management Science*, 32(12): 1613–1627.

Belton, V and Vickers, SP (1993) Demystifying DEA a visual interactive approach based on multiple criteria analysis. *Journal of the Operational Research Society*, 44(9): 883–896.

Brown, WB and Gobeli, D (1992) Observations on the measurement of R&D productivity: a case study. *IEEE Transactions on Engineering Management*, 39(4): 325–331.

Cook, WD and Johnston, DA (1992) Evaluating suppliers of complex systems: a multiple criteria approach. *Journal of the Operational Research Society*, 43(11): 1055–1061.

Cook, WD, Johnston, DA and McCutcheon, D (1992) Implementations of robotics: identifying efficient implementors. *OMEGA*, 20(2): 227–239.

Dawes, RM (1979) The robust beauty of improper linear models in decision making. *American Psychologist*, 34: 571–582. Reprinted in Kahneman D, Slovic, P and Tversky, A (1982) *Judgment Under Uncertainty: Heuristics and Biases.* Cambridge: Cambridge University Press.

Desai, A and Walters, LC (1991) Graphical presentations of data envelopment analyses: management implications from parallel axes representations. *Decision Sciences*, 22: 335–353.

Doyle, J and Green, R (1994) Efficiency and cross-efficiency in DEA: derivations, meanings and uses. *Journal of the Operational Research Society*, 45(5): 567–578.

Doyle, JR and Green, RH (1991) Comparing products using data envelopment analysis. *OMEGA*, 19(6): 631–638.

Dyson, RG, Athanassopoulos, AD and Thanassoulis, E (1994) *Performance measurement systems, managerial control and data envelopment analysis.* Warwick Business School Research Paper No. 117.

Dyson, RG and Thanassoulis, E (1988) Reducing weight flexibility in data envelopment analysis. *Journal of the Operational Research Society*, 39(6): 563–576.

Epstein, MK and Henderson, JC (1989) Data envelopment analysis for managerial control and diagnosis. *Decision Sciences*, 20: 90–119.

Feldman, JM (1981) Beyond attribution theory: cognitive processes in performance appraisal. *Journal of Applied Psychology*, 66(2): 127–148.

Ilgen, DR and Moore, CF (1987) Types and choices of performance feedback. *Journal of Applied Psychology*, 72(3): 401–406.

Ivancevich, JM and McMahon, JT (1982) The effects of goal setting, external feedback and self-generated feedback on outcome variables: a field experiment. *Academy of Management Journal*, 25(2): 359–372.

Johnson, D, Perlow, R and Pieper, K (1993) Differences in task performance as a function of type of feedback: learning-oriented versus performance-oriented feedback. *Journal of Applied Social Psychology*, 23(4): 303–320.

Keller, RT (1986) Predictors of the performance of project groups in R&D organisations. *Academy of Management Journal*, 29(4): 715–726.

Keller, RT and Holland, WE (1982) The measurement of performance among research and development professional employees: a longtitudinal analysis. *IEEE Transactions on Engineering Management*, 29(2): 54–58.

Li, M, Stokes, CA, French, MJ and Widden, MB (1993) Function costing: recent developments. In *Proceedings of the International Conference on Engineering Design ICED93*, 17–19 August 1993, The Hague: 1123–1129.

Locke, EA, Shaw, KN, Saari, LM and Latham, GP (1981) Goal setting and task performance: 1969–1980. *Psychological Bulletin*, 90(1): 125–152.

Mento, AJ, Steel, RP and Karren, RJ (1987) A meta-analytic study of the effects of goal setting on task performance: 1966–1984. *Organizational Behavior and Human Decision Processes*, 39: 52–83.

Nadler, DA (1979) The effects of feedback on task group behaviour: a review of the experimental research. *Organizational Behavior and Human Performance*, 23: 309–338.

Pritchard, RD, Jones, SD, Roth, PL, Stuebing, KK and Ekeberg, SE (1988) Effects of group feedback, goal setting and incentives on organizational productivity. *Journal of Applied Psychology*, 73(2): 337–358.

Shafer, SM and Bradford, JW (1995) Efficiency measurement of alternative machine component grouping solutions via data envelopment analysis. *IEEE Transactions on Engineering Management*, 42(2): 159–165.

Stahl, MJ and Koser, MC (1978) Weighted productivity in R&D: some associated individual and organisational variables. *IEEE Transactions on Engineering Management*, 25(1): 20–24.

Stahl, MJ, Zimmerer, TW and Gulati, A (1984) Measuring innovation, productivity and job performance of professionals: a decision modelling approach. *IEEE Transactions on Engineering Management*, 31(1): 25–29.

8 Using Information Technology to Manage the Change Process in Organisations

Alfred D. Vella and Andrew Williamson

Abstract

A great deal of information is held within the quality management systems (QMS) of many companies. This information is collected and stored primarily to aid the quality system in its task of monitoring the companies performance and in allowing third party auditors access to the information that they need to make judgements on the health of the QMS. In general auditors have little time to access more than just a small sample of this information and it is an aim of the project described in this paper to make the information that companies have much more easily accessible to auditors and management alike both in its raw form and in its summary form. The project shows how, by using intelligent systems that can access a company's QMS the change process can be eased. At present the quality of the automated information processes that we can build is far below that of an experienced auditor. However because of the speed and costs of on-line computing, much more information can be used in forming a view of the workings of the QMS. It is expected that this tool will aid the auditor make much better informed judgements leading to many benefits to both the company and the auditor.

8.1   Introduction

The ability of organisations to improve their products and business processes, and manage change effectively has become a key factor for industrial success. However, successful management requires information on goals, processes and performance to be shared amongst the staff, suppliers, customers and other interested parties of the company.

This chapter describes the use of a prototype information technology (IT) system which would assist the measurement and management of business processes. It has been developed by Cranfield University, British Standards Institution QA (BSI QA) and ICL Computers Ltd. The system collects relevant quality information, calculates selected performance metrics that provide insight into the quality processes in the organisation, and can communicate this information to managers and stakeholders in the company. Providing knowledge of this type in a consistent and timely manner is necessary for the change process to be successful.

A system such as this may have many potential uses in the measurement and management of change. It could assist outside parties, such as certification bodies or customers to monitor the 'state of health' of their clients. It may allow senior managers to monitor the performance of far-flung business units and provide a more focused and inconspicuous means for regulatory bodies to monitor the performance of selected companies.

8.2 Measuring Change in an Organisation

Many management disciplines, from the systems analysis to business process re-engineering to total quality management, have stressed the need to monitor the implementation of change. Unless the change process is accurately and consistently monitored, they argue, you cannot determine whether the processes are effective, focused on the goals, and mentor the staff on what new processes and methods need to be introduced to ensure continued business success.

Unfortunately, measuring processes is not necessarily straightforward. Problems that have been encountered include the difficulty of identifying correct measures for a process (as opposed to measuring what is easily measurable), designing and operating a consistent, cost-effective measurement system, and using the measures to improve individual and group performance. Sadly, in many companies measurement is seen, possibly unfairly, as a coercive tool, rather than a means to educate and improve. Once these problems have been addressed, there is still the matter of obtaining the information, analysing and presenting it to managers. It is here that information technology has, potentially, much to offer. The ability to unobtrusively gather information, analyse it, and present it in an understandable and timely manner may make business process measurement easier and more powerful.

A particular example of this problem, and one which the partners concentrated upon, was concerned with monitoring the quality management system by external assessors. Used properly, quality management is a powerful mechanism to change and improve the business processes in a company. By concentrating upon the factors that satisfy the customer, and continually improving the service and value offered, a company should gain better business processes and financial performance.

Quality management system assessors are faced by problems typically encountered by managers. They need to assess large amounts of possible incomplete information speedily. They must look for signs of change and improvement. Finally, they must make decisions based upon this information on the health of the company's quality management system

8.3 The Quality Management System Audit Process

The basis of an audit is to compare the company's activities with an external standard, and to state whether the company has satisfactorily met the requirements of that standard. For quality management systems, the ISO 9000 series of standards are widely accepted as describing a complete and competent quality management system, and quite a large industry has developed to register companies against these standards. This registration illustrates that the company concerned has achieved a high level of operation of its quality management system.

Usually, an audit has an experienced assessor visiting the company. They review the managerial and technical processes, and collect evidence to decide whether the supplier meets the agreed standard of performance. In so doing they are faced with much information, and from that information they need to determine if the company has the systems in place to ensure that the standards are being met. It is important to realise that they are making a judgement about the competence of the system, not trying to find isolated non-conformances – it is the assessors task to decide if the non-conformances show that the overall system is not effective.

Although the audit process has operated satisfactorily for some time, there are some improvements which the project partners believed information technology could make. Audits are not very frequent, certification bodies usually audit two or three times a year. So the assessors have only a brief view of the company's processes, and need to spend much time in routine data collection which does not add value to the company nor make best use of the assessors' skills. Audits are usually scheduled in advance, so a company with a stable and successful quality system may be audited almost as frequently as a company with severe quality problems. They may resent the cost and inconvenience of what they consider unnecessary visits – certification bodies are certainly aware of this issue. Finally, frequently the assessors need to find the areas of interest while they are auditing and may only be able to spend a short time tackling the areas of concern. If they had an up-to-date picture of the company prior to visiting, they can use their time more effectively.

Information technology may allow some of these issues to be tackled. An IT-based system may have constant, but unobtrusive access to the company's data, ensuring a continuous and accurate portrayal of the quality management system. This will allow assessors, and the company's own management, to have a better understanding of the performance of their processes, without labour-consuming and slow data collection, analysis and presentation. Using this continuous picture of the company, the assessor may be able to identify some of the company's problems before the visit, allowing them to schedule vists more appropriately and making them better prepared when they arrive. As the data collection is automated, the assessor and managers can concentrate upon added-value actions rather than be tied up with routine tasks.

8.4 An IT System For Continuous Measurement of Business Processes

The main role of the IT system, primarily developed by ICL Computers Ltd, was to investigate the technical and business issues raised, and to provide an example of a working system for demonstration and research. The system, more fully described by Vella and Williamson (1994), consists of three main parts (Figure 8.1). An

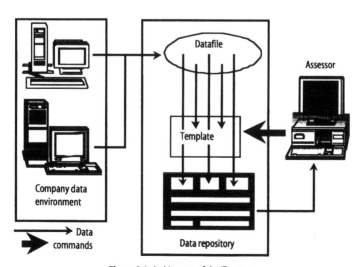

Figure 8.1. Architecture of the IT system.

external IT system in the company provides data to the 'MOLE engine' (the project was named MOLE), where it is stored in a datafile on a database (on an ICL mainframe computer). Originally, it was planned to have the software 'seek' the records it needs in the company's IT system. However, this proved to be technically complex and raised the issue of data security for the company providing the data. In particular, companies would be concerned about commercially sensitive material being accessed outside of their control. Consequently, it was decided to identify the data the assessor needs on a regular basis and have these data stored on the datafile accessable to the auditor. Although this restricts the investigation the auditor can undertake, later work in the project showed that the assessor can learn much from a few measures, and can investigate more fully when visiting the company.

The assessor accesses these data using a PC, connected to the data via a modem link. The graphical user interface (written in Visual Basic) supports a range of queries that have been predetermined by the assessors. These queries are written in SQL, and these commands can be sent down the modem link to the datafile. The data repository contains a standard data definition, and the data repository transfers and converts the data from the datafile into this definition. A template is used to match the data in the datafile to the data repository. Various templates were available, depending on the level of access permitted to the user. This definition is interrogated by the VB screen interface which can locate the data it requires in this definition. Once the necessary data have been loaded into the data repository, the VB screen interface does most of the analysis and formatting of the data for presentation to the auditor, including the calculation and display of the metrics discussed next.

The assessor will still be presented with much information they will need to analyse. Consequently, the project investigated using performance metrics to analyse and condense the data to a meaningful and manageable form. As well as this major advantage, it was hoped that these metrics could provide a continuing and invisible monitoring of the company, and if a process was not meeting the required performance, management could be made aware and action promptly taken.

The project found that certain metrics were very effective for this assessment. In particular, those that monitor continuing, discrete activities could be useful to an assessor. As these activities occur on a regular basis they can provide a reasonably up-to-date picture of the company (as opposed to 'one-off' events, like registration to ISO 9000, which tells the assessor little once it has happened). ISO 9000 stresses the importance of a system of internal audit, management review and corrective/preventative action to improve the business processes within the company. If this cycle of activities is being carried out, the assessor can have some confidence in the operation of the quality system (partly because any deficiencies should be noted and addressed by this process). The metrics used by the project concentrated on measuring these activities, examples being:

- percentage of audits carried out to plan;
- percentage of corrective actions completed on time;
- percentage of documents/processes reviewed.

Although, for example, performing an audit on time does not guarantee quality problems will be uncovered it does provide some indication that the company takes its responsibilities to quality seriously.

The IT system cannot replace the assessment visit: only limited, preselected data and measures are available, and the depth of any enquiry is restricted to what the data can support. The biggest issue in developing a product, however, was the small number of companies with significant amounts of data on computers accessible to the IT system. When more have updated the processes and systems using information technology, it will be worthwhile to develop the system as a commercial product.

8.5   Managing and Measuring Change in Organisations

Where systems of the type described above may help managers and other stakeholders is in providing timely, relevant and understandable information. Timely because the IT system can monitor the processes as they are being carried out and report on problems and variances immediately. Relevant because the information needed for decision making can be collected and understandable because the metrics condense and summarise the information.

This will allow the company, and external stakeholders, to react promptly to change, to ensure that the change processes are achieving the expected results, and target and improve the operations and activities of the company.

Acknowledgements

The authors would like to acknowledge the contributions and suggestions of Frank Ibbotson and Alan Mountford at ICL Computers Ltd, and Richard Jones and John Souter at BSI QA.

Reference

Vella, A and Williamson, A (1994) Data exchange in quality management. *Revue Internationale de CFAO et d'Infographie*, **9**(3): 293–304.

Theme II

Modelling for Information Systems

9 Issues in Information Systems Development Models

Ray J. Paul and Robert D. Macredie

Abstract

This paper will briefly introduce the kinds of approaches that are used in developing information systems, ranging from those arising out of engineering disciplines and those which bring a 'softer' perspective to bear on the development of information systems (IS). The general benefits and limitations of different classes of development/modelling approach will be introduced. This will help place the chapters in this theme in perspective and will provide broad background information to the reader.

9.1   Introduction

Much research and development effort has been expended in proposing, exploring and refining models for developing information systems (IS). This chapter will provide a brief overview of the dominant themes in the area through a review of traditional, 'hard' models and the 'soft' socio-technical approaches which aim to address the limitations of hard models. We will also briefly consider the directions which the field seems to be following and offer our perspective on the difficulties which are faced by research and developers looking for appropriate and successful models for IS development.

9.2   Traditional Development Models

The traditional basic model for the development of information systems is the 'waterfall' life-cycle model (Figure 9.1) which comes straight from product-oriented engineering. As Figure 9.1 shows, the characteristics of this model are that it takes a sequential and highly structured view of development (there are obviously a number of variations on the model shown in Figure 9.1, but they display the same underlying structured and sequential approach).

This type of traditional development models tends to succeed in providing some sort of high-level 'plan' which aims to guide the development. This is achieved through the division of the development process into stages, giving the impression

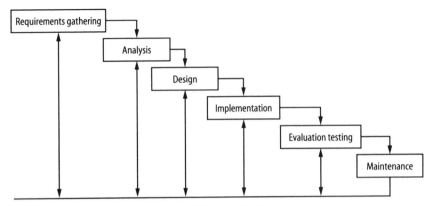

Figure 9.1. The traditional waterfall life-cycle model.

that development is somehow more 'manageable'. Even if the resulting system fails to deliver what it is supposed to upon completion, this approach at least gives the stakeholders involved a feeling of being in control by following a plan.

Many variants of the basic waterfall model have been developed , although most tend to reflect the steps of the waterfall model, with very little differences between them (Davis 1974). It has been argued that as a framework for the development of modern systems, this model is inadequate. In the development of computer systems, the model dates back to the necessarily reductionist approach of scientists involved in World War II computing projects. The problems addressed by such projects were highly deterministic. The solutions were also strongly linked to the (limited) hardware capabilities of the time (Agresti 1986). In contrast, modern information systems are fundamentally 'soft' human activity systems (Checkland and Scholes 1990) and yet we are trying to develop them by using a 'hard' product-oriented approach embedded in methodologies. This dichotomy might constitute a major cause of systems development failure.

The kinds of 'soft' problems that are prevalent in developing today's information systems for use in complex organisational settings are the fluid nature of requirements, and the complex and dynamic social nature of the organisational environments in which systems have to operate.

Models which aim to address this have been developed and applied with varying degrees of success. A key field of development has been the increasing emphasis placed on the use of prototypes of systems, to explore aspects of systems development, such as requirements gathering and analysis, and their embodiment into small-scale versions of the system for critical appraisal. Whilst Brooks (1975) and others since recommend that prototypes be regarded as throw-away exercises which inform systems development, there is a tendency for the effort invested in them to be seen as wasted unless the prototype goes on to form part of the final system. This can lead to developers becoming too closely attached to prototypes to the detriment of the final system.

If used wisely, prototyping can offer some alleviation of the difficulties associated with the rigid, waterfall-inspired models of development. Furthermore, prototyping has been taken on as a central principle in broader development models. Perhaps the most famous of these, and the one which gave rise to a shift in emphasis which has been widely adopted, was the proposal by Boehm (1988) of a Spiral

Model of development. This model builds on aspects of both the classic waterfall model and prototyping approaches, and considers the importance of risk analysis in the development. The Spiral Model can be thought of as an evolutionary model, as it views the development of systems in an emerging and changing way, responding to the dynamics of the environment and the changing understanding of that environment on the part of the developers.

There are also models within the object-oriented paradigm which are gaining popularity, as are environments for supporting and helping manage the development process (notably the refinement of computer-aided software engineering (CASE) tools supporting structured systems development methodologies).

There are, of course, also many other information systems development models which draw on aspects of those briefly reviewed here, but the IS literature shows that system development models, and the information systems produced by them, have been the subject of much criticism (Avgerou and Cornford 1993; Beath and Orlikowski 1994; Fitzgerald 1995, 1996).

This perhaps explains why there is also an extensive body of research dedicated to finding new directions for information systems development approaches, including new development models. This has been exemplified by the studies of Mumford (1983) and Avison and Wood-Harper (1990), to name but two.

9.3   The Move to Socio-technical Models

As we have suggested, there has been a realisation over the past 15–20 years that the models of development which have been inherited from traditional product engineering have weaknesses when applied to socio-technical systems such as those which commonly form an integral part of many organisational processes. This had led to a range of models being proposed to address shortcomings with existing models. These new models tend to focus much more closely on the whole system, addressing the lack of focus on the human element and their contribution to the system of previous models (see, for example, Suchman 1987; Winograd and Flores 1986). This may take a multitude of forms, but often offers insight into the soft, social processes which any proposed information system is likely to have to support, or at least work with. Socio-technical models can be thought of as falling into two broad categories, although this is clearly a crude distinction.

The first category focuses not on providing models for the development of information systems, but instead looks at models to help us gain an understanding of the environment in which the system will be situated. The classic example of such an approach is Checkland and Scholes' (1990) Soft System Methodology (SSM) (see also Checkland 1981). SSM aims to develop a 'rich picture' of the environment through interaction with the stakeholders, using this to provide definitions of key elements of the system, or systems within the environment (called root definitions). These root definitions are used to inform the production of abstract representations of the system in the form of conceptual models. Modelling the system will expose problem areas, such as where understanding amongst stakeholders may vary, which can be addressed by iteration until a suitable set of root definitions are formed. These models are then compared with the earlier expression of the environment/situation to highlight areas where changes might be appropriate and/or feasible. This might highlight areas where actions can be taken – such as helping to define the scope of a possible information system.

The second category of model produces methods which provide wider support for the actual development of systems. A strong example of such a socio-technical approach is Avison and Wood-Harper's (1990) Multiview, which aims to define a staged methodology which supports the development of information systems. Multiview suggests that designers/developers undertake detailed analyses of human activity within the development environment, leading to descriptions of aspects of the environment, or system, being considered. These might include the stakeholders involved in the system, the purpose of the system and the different perspectives of the parties involved. These descriptions form what Avison and Wood-Harper call the primary task model (PTM). The PTM acts as input to Multiview's second stage, which undertakes an analysis of information captured in the PTM leading to conceptual modelling of information flows and structure (through entity relationship modelling and data modelling) within the system/environment. This provides a functional model, from which tasks and roles in the new system are defined. Only when this has been completed are technical aspects of the system considered. Multiview supports designers by providing them with design direction and support, but the rigidity of the order in which stages are undertaken and the set activities which must be completed can make it difficult to apply Multiview in certain design situations.

9.4   A Living Perspective

The criticism that Multiview, like most other models, imposes a structural framework is one which should be taken seriously yet which raises far-reaching issues for information systems development. The use of any prescriptive development model is bound by its nature to create significant – we would argue implicit and insoluble – problems for developers and ultimately users of information systems. Paul (1994) has argued that alternative ways of thinking about systems, and their development and use, are needed if we are to move away from systems which are problematic and which are perceived as failures.

A central point is questioning the nature of requirements, and their centrality to design models and systems design methods. The notion of requirements capture and the problems that this causes in developing systems for dynamic business environments has already been noted, yet development models seem to persist in giving this area central importance. Even if requirements could be accurately captured, and a system designed and developed to meet them, the system would only be successful for as long as the requirements held. In many business environments this is unlikely to be far past the requirement capture phase, let alone long into the operation of the system. Approaches such as prototyping and the socio-technical approaches tend to recognise the broad difficulty in requirements capture and analysis, but offer solutions based around refinement of requirements, rather than recognising their volatility and temporal constraints.

Alternative ways of thinking about development (such as those outlined in Paul 1994) may help address these difficulties, but this is still an area which requires much research and, most probably, a mind-set which will be completely alien to most developers and outside the scope of the mechanisms which fund information systems development.

Many of the issues which we have briefly discussed – the distinction between hard and soft models and methods; the development of socio-technical approaches; the use of mixed methods – are explored in the chapters in this theme. It is hoped that after reading them, the complexities of information systems development are more clearly illustrated and that it becomes evident that a definitive solution to providing models for information systems development is unattainable.

References

Agresti, W (1986) The conventional software life-cycle model: its evolution and assumptions. In *New Paradigms for Software Development, Tutorial.* Agresti, W (Ed.). Washington, DC: IEEE Computer Society Press: 2–5.

Avgerou, C and Cornford, T (1993) A review of the methodologies movement. *Journal of Information Technology,* 8(4): 277–286.

Avison, DE and Wood-Harper, AT (1990). *Multiview: An Exploration in Information Systems Development.* Oxford: Blackwell Scientific Publications.

Beath, CM and Orlikowski, WJ (1994) The contradictory structure of systems development methodologies: deconstructing the IS-user relationship in information engineering. *Information Systems Research,* 5(4): 350–377.

Boehm, B (1988) A spiral model for software development and enhancement. *Computer,* 21(5): 61–72.

Brooks, F (1975) *The Mythical Man Month.* Reading, MA: Addison Wesley.

Checkland, PB (1981) *Systems Thinking, Systems Practice.* Chichester: John Wiley.

Checkland, PB and Scholes, J (1990) *Soft Systems Methodology in Action.* Chichester: John Wiley.

Davis, GB (1974) *Management Information Systems: Conceptual Foundations, Structure, and Development.* Tokyo: McGraw-Hill.

Fitzgerald, B (1995) *The Use of Systems Development Methods: A Survey.* ESRC, Research and Discussion Papers, Reference 9/95, University College Cork, Ireland.

Fitzgerald, B (1996) Formalized systems development methodologies: a critical perspective. *Information Systems Journal,* 6(1): 3–23.

Mumford, E (1983) *Designing Participatively.* Manchester: Manchester Business School.

Paul, RJ (1994) Why users cannot get what they want. *International Journal of Manufacturing System Design,* 1(4): 389–394.

Suchman, LA (1987) *Plans and Situated Action: The Problem of Human Machine Communication.* Cambridge: Cambridge University Press.

Winograd, T and Flores, F (1986) *Understanding Computers and Cognition: A New Foundation in Design.* Norwood, NJ: Ablex.

10 The Metaphysical Foundations of Soft and Hard Information Systems Methodologies

Stephen K. Probert

Abstract

The purpose of this chapter is to examine the basic epistemological and ontological foundations of soft and hard information systems (IS) methodologies. A number of writers have discussed the philosophical underpinnings of Soft Systems Methodology (SSM); the general conclusion being that SSM embodies the philosophical assumptions of (some form of) subjectivism. It will be argued that whilst the advocates of SSM subscribe to a subjective mode of enquiry, such a mode has its history – and its rationale – firmly grounded in the early modern philosophies of the natural sciences. In contemporary epistemological terms, this approach can be characterised as a variant of foundationalism. Lewis has recently studied the epistemological foundations of hard IS methodologies. Although these methodologies are generally committed to an approach based on objectivist assumptions, they are also based on a variant of foundationalism. The overlaps between hard and soft IS methodologies' metaphysical foundations will be explored, and it will be argued that, whilst there may be epistemological overlaps between the two broad approaches, there are problems reconciling the ontological assumptions of these two broad approaches. It will be concluded that these problems (whilst causing some difficulties) are not insurmountable.

10.1   Soft Systems Methodology (SSM) and Subjectivism

It has been claimed that SSM should be considered as an epistemology:

> [T]he essence of soft systems thinking ... [is] that it provides a coherent intellectual framework ... as *an epistemology* which can be used to try to understand and intervene usefully in the rich and surprising flux of everyday situations.
>
> *Checkland and Scholes 1990, p. 24*

In recent years a number of writers have discussed the philosophical underpinnings of Soft Systems Methodology (SSM); the general conclusion being that SSM embodies the philosophical assumptions of (some form of) subjectivism (e.g. Mingers 1984). In recent years, two sorts of accounts of epistemology have been propounded by the (main) SSM advocates. Although these two accounts are ultimately contradictory they are similar in that they are both highly psychologistical accounts of epistemology; they both focus on the *process* of enquiry. These two accounts will be termed *the so-called Kantian account* and *the Lockean account*, and these will now be characterised. A fuller study of the issues surrounding these two accounts is given elsewhere (Probert 1994a). The main features of these accounts are summarised below.

10.2   The So-called Kantian Account

In the most recent and detailed account of the developed form of SSM, Checkland and Scholes (1990) see their epistemological tradition as stemming from Immanuel Kant (1724–1804):

> When the Spanish conquistadors arrived in what is now Mexico, the indigenous people, unfamiliar with horse riding and seeing riders dismount from horses, thought that creatures had arrived on their shores who could divide themselves in two at will. This story provides a good illustration of the way in which we have in our heads stocks of ideas by means of which we interpret the world outside ourselves. Philosophically the story supports the view of Kant, that we *structure* the world by means of already-present, innate ideas, rather than the view of Locke [John Locke, 1632-1704] that our minds are blank screens upon which the world writes its impressions. But it seems clear that the supposedly 'innate' ideas may have two sources. They may indeed be part of the genetic inheritance of mankind, truly innate; or they may be built up as a result of our experience of the world... What is being argued is that we perceive the world through the filter of – or using the framework of – the ideas internal to us; but that the source of many (most?) of those ideas is the perceived world outside ... As human beings we enact this process everyday, usually unconsciously.
>
> *Checkland and Scholes 1990, pp. 19–20*

(It should be noted immediately that Locke's theory of perception is not as vacuous as the SSM advocates suggest in this quotation, as will become clear shortly.) The essence of this account is that perception is representational, but representations are only possible via the mediation of ideas pre-possessed by the perceiving subject. As ideas are the necessary prerequisites of coherent perceptions some ideas must be *innate* – they are 'born with us' as part of our genetic inheritance.

Kant's transcendental idealism is far too complex to be explored in this work, so suffice it to point out that Checkland and Scholes' (1990) account of epistemology should not be construed as Kantian:

> No name can do justice to this profound and complex philosophy which arose out of the two most important philosophical theories of his time: the rationalism of Descartes and Leibnitz and the empiricism of Locke, Berkeley, and Hume ... *Kant agreed with the empiricists that there cannot be innate ideas in the sense of anything known prior to any sense experience, but he was not prepared to say that therefore all knowledge must be derived from experience* ... Kant's procedure differed significantly from the generally psychological empiricist method, for rather than seeking for the impressions upon which certain ideas are based, he investigated the relationship that exist between the fundamental concepts related to a subject's having experience of objects. He was concerned with theoretical questions of a sort he calls 'transcendental', such as 'under what conditions is experience of an objective world possible?'
>
> *Flew 1979, pp. 175–176* [emphases added]

Kant was not really interested in the processes of perception – he was primarily interested in what must be necessary for a subject to be capable of having *any* perception; not how it is that one has a perception *of* things like a horse and rider.

There are two main aspects to the so-called Kantian account. First, the observer is seen as 'trying to make sense of' his or her perceptions of the world by applying ideas to his or her *raw* perceptions; some of these ideas are innate. The claim that observers try to make sense of the world in this way most closely resembles accounts put forward in the tradition of the Cartesian project of pure enquiry – first articulated by Descartes (1596-1650) around 1640. There are three related features of Descartes's account of epistemology (all of which are central features of the of the SSM advocates' so-called Kantian account). These are: (1) the doctrine of innate ideas; (2) the subjective representation of reality; and (3) the intellectual construction of models. These features will now be discussed.

10.2.1 The Doctrine of Innate Ideas

The notion, advanced by Checkland and Scholes, that our thinking is 'structured' by innate ideas also hails from Descartes's rationalism (rather than from Kant's transcendental idealism):

> Another controversial tenet of Descartes's position is that some of our ideas are innate... [One reason] for the necessity of innate ideas is that we can apprehend the specific quality of our experience only if we possess ideas with which to interpret it.
>
> *Aune 1970, pp. 28–29*

Descartes himself argued:

> I cannot doubt but that there is in me a certain passive faculty of perception, that is of receiving and taking knowledge of the ideas of sensible [physical] things; but this would be useless to me, if there did not also exist in me, or in some other thing, another active faculty capable of forming and producing those ideas.
>
> *Descartes 1912, p. 133*

Checkland and Scholes clearly root the "active faculty" both in "our genetic inheritance" and in the psychological processes of the individual subject. Descartes also argued that this "active faculty" does not just arbitrarily make up these ideas:

> [And] what I here find of most importance is ... that I discover in my mind innumerable ideas of certain objects, although perhaps they possess no reality beyond my thought, and which are not framed by me though it may be in my power to think them, but possess true and immutable natures of their own. As, for example, when I imagine a triangle, although there is not perhaps and never was in the universe apart from my thought one such figure, it remains true nevertheless that this figure possesses a certain determinate nature, form, or essence, which is immutable and eternal, and not framed by me, nor in any degree dependent on my thought ... and which accordingly cannot be said to have been invented by me.
>
> *Descartes 1912, p. 121*

It should be noted that Descartes ultimately argued that these innate ideas are transferred to us from the mind of God, whereas Checkland and Scholes' account is entirely secular, and is generally expressed in terms of "our genetic inheritance".

10.2.2 The Subjective Representation of Reality

For both Checkland (and Scholes) and Descartes, knowledge is to be produced or created *in the mind of an individual subject*; the basic epistemological notion is of an attempted representation (or interpretation) of the world by a subject, and this is clearly a Cartesian legacy:

> Descartes's account ... is expressed in terms of a representational theory of perception. We are given a picture of the mind in direct contact only with its own experiences or ideas, *outside* which there are objects, causing these experiences and imperfectly represented by them. Descartes thinks that, strictly speaking, the purely mental ideas involved in perception do not *resemble* the world at all, and even with regard to the corporeal representations of the world in the brain, which he believes to occur as part of the perceptual process, he emphasises that the important point is that they should be capable of conveying the required complexity of information about external things, not that they should resemble them (*Dioptric vi* 113).
>
> *Williams 1978, pp. 239–240*

Checkland's account of the purpose of building the conceptual models (used extensively in SSM) is strikingly similar in important respects:

> The important point is that, in using SSM, we must never lose sight of the fact that the models are *not* would-be descriptions of parts of the world. They are abstract logical machines for pursuing a purpose ... which can generate insightful debate when set against actual would-be purposeful action in the real-world.
>
> *Checkland 1990, p. 311*

For both Descartes and the SSM advocates, the same implications are drawn from this *subjective representation* approach to human enquiry: the need for *models* of reality. Of course, the SSM advocates are primarily concerned with modelling *social reality*, which they believe to be (strictly-speaking) 'unmodellable' owing to the free-will that they attribute to actors in the real-world (Probert 1994b), and this aspect of SSM will be returned to later in the discussion concerning ontology.

10.2.3   The Intellectual Construction of Models

Bernard Williams has recently summed up Descartes's contribution to epistemology in the following manner:

> Descartes is, rightly, said to be a rationalist philosopher ... But it's sometimes supposed that he was such a strong rationalist that he thought the whole of science was to be deduced from metaphysics by purely mathematical or logical reasoning ... He thought no such thing. In fact, he is absolutely consistent in saying that experiments are necessary to distinguish between some ways of explaining nature and others. You can build different models. This is a very modern aspect of his thought. You can build or construct different intellectual models of the world within his laws, and experiment is needed to discover which truly represent nature.
>
> *Williams 1987, p. 90*

(Note that this account is only related to the natural world, and not the social world.) Checkland's philosophy of (natural) science is quite definitely of this sort:

> Natural scientists cannot fail to be aware of two fundamental considerations: first, that in the professional talk concerning the work, words are used as carefully defined technical terms ... second, that the words so carefully defined refer to models, to intellectual constructs rather than supposed physical reality. The natural scientist is well aware that he or she is playing a game against nature in which the intellectual constructions are used to predict physical happenings which can be checked experimentally.
>
> *Checkland 1988, p. 235*

Just how Cartesian the SSM advocates' so-called Kantian account of epistemology is can be shown by the following observation:

[M]any passages showed that he accorded a crucial role to experiment. Descartes's actual conception of scientific method often resembles ... the model where a hypothesis is advanced, and the results logically deduced from it are then compared with actual observation.

Flew 1979, p. 86

The conclusion to be drawn is that the epistemological assumptions of the proponents of the so-called Kantian account of epistemology are those of *Cartesian rationalism*.

10.3   Cartesian Reductionism

Before exploring these possible objections fully it will be necessary to briefly examine the SSM advocates' use of the term 'reductionism'. Checkland's use of the term 'reductionism' is non-standard in contemporary epistemological terms, but standard in the (looser) general philosophical sense and this can be (potentially) misleading. Flew defines 'reductionism' as follows:

REDUCTIONISM (or Reductivism). 1. The belief that human behaviour can be reduced to or interpreted in terms of that of lower animals; and that, ultimately, can itself be reduced to physical laws ... 2. More generally, any doctrine that claims to reduce the apparently more sophisticated and complex to the less so.

Flew 1979, p. 279

It is the latter, philosophically looser, sense that the SSM advocates seem to intend. However, in contemporary epistemology, a more usual definition would be:

REDUCTIONISM: the belief that each meaningful statement is equivalent to some logical construct upon terms which refer to immediate experience.

Quine 1980, p. 20

Note that "meaningful" (above) means, basically, *grammatical and intelligible*, e.g. "Barking dogs bark" is meaningful (but vacuous), as is "Paris is the capital city of Antarctica" (this is meaningful, but false).

Quine's argument is that statements, and not exclusively scientific statements, do not refer to particular sensory experiences in isolation. Consequently, particular experiences will not always give rise to particular statements:

The totality of our so-called knowledge or beliefs, from the most casual matters of geography and history to the profoundest laws of atomic physics or even of pure mathematics and logic, is a man-made fabric which impinges on experience only along the edges. Or, to change the figure, total science is like a field of force whose boundary conditions are experience. A conflict with experience at the periphery occasions readjustments in the interior of the field... But the total field is so underdetermined by its boundary conditions, experience, that there is much latitude of choice as to what statements to reevaluate in the light of any single contrary experience.

Quine 1980, pp. 42–43

An example may help here. Prior to conducting chemical experiments we may be told that if sulphur is present on a splint then a bright yellow flame will be present if the splint is immersed in a Bunsen burner flame. If we were to do such an experiment and a bright yellow flame did not appear (although there was good reason to believe that sulphur was present on the splint) we might conclude that there was something wrong with the whole of chemical theory, but *pragmatically* we would probably search for a simpler explanation – say that some other chemical was present which inhibited the experiment from working properly, or that there was an insufficient amount of sulphur for the experiment to work properly, and so on. We would not immediately rush to the conclusion that we had *falsified* the chemical theory that gave rise to the periodic table of elements. As such Quine's *epistemological holism* stands as a rebuttal to Popper's *critical rationalism*. Somewhat ironically Checkland (claims to) support a Popperian philosophy of science, which is ultimately dependent on the validity of *epistemological reductionism*, and which (for example) Quine explicitly rejects:

> If a hypothesis implies observations at all, we may stand ready to drop the hypothesis as false as soon as an observation that it predicts fails to occur. In fact, however, the refutation of hypothesis is not that simple ... there is the matter of the supporting chorus. It is not the contemplated hypothesis alone that does the implying, but rather that hypothesis and a supporting chorus of background beliefs.
>
> *Quine and Ullian 1978, pp. 102–103*

Popper was fully aware of the need for the acceptability of epistemological reductionism for his philosophy of science to be satisfactory:

> [T]hough every one of our assumptions may be challenged, it is quite impractical to challenge all of them at the same time ... Quine formulates (with reference to Duhem) [a view that] ... our statements about the external world face the tribunal of sense experience not individually but only as a corporate body ... it should be said that the [Quine's] holistic argument goes much too far. It is possible in quite a few cases to find which hypothesis is responsible for the refutation.
>
> *Popper 1972, pp. 238–239*

It is important to note that Checkland (1981) supports Popper's reductionist view of epistemology.

10.4   The Lockean Accounts

These accounts of epistemology are entirely Lockean in character, and appear both before, after and simultaneously with the publication of Checkland and Scholes' (1990) account (the so-called Kantian account). Their main difference lies in the outright denial of the possibility of innate ideas:

> I shall drastically summarise the development of systems thinking ... a human observer tries to make sense of his or her perceived reality ... by means of some intellectual concepts used in some mental process or methodology ... 'System' is one of the concepts used in this process, but considerable confusion is caused by the fact the word is used not only as the name of an abstract concept which the observer tries to map onto perceived reality, but also as a label word for things in the world – as when we refer to 'the education system' or 'the legal system'. The confusion is of course not helped by the fact that the ultimate source of 'concepts' ... is (can only be) perceived reality; that is the ultimate source of the concepts through which we try to make sense of perceived reality in a never-ending cyclic process of learning ... Perceived reality and the intellectual concepts steadily create each other.
>
> *Checkland 1990, pp. 305–306*

A similar account has been propounded in a more recent article:

> [W]e may note that in the end the ultimate source of abstract notions ... is the perceived world itself ... the world as we perceive it yields concepts by means of which we perceive the world; there are no absolutes, only a continuous process in which the concepts create the perceived world which creates the concepts.
>
> *Checkland 1991a, p. 27*

These are Lockean accounts because Checkland quite explicitly states that the only source of ideas (or concepts) is perceived reality – and therefore ideas (or concepts) cannot be innate – and this is one of Locke's most important and influential theses:

> Locke argues in detail in book 2 [of Locke, 1977 (original 1706)], we can account for all of the ideas in our minds by experience. Experience is of two sorts. There are ideas of sensation, derived from the outer senses, and ideas of reflection, which are those ideas of which we become aware by introspection.
>
> *Flew 1979, p. 190*

In Locke's own words:

> Whatever idea is in the mind is either an actual perception or else, having been an actual perception, is so in the mind that by memory it can be made an actual perception again ... ideas are no more born with us than arts and sciences.
>
> *Locke 1977, pp. 27–29*

However, it will be worthwhile to indicate the full extent of the Lockean nature of the epistemological assumptions of the SSM advocates (as propounded in the non-Cartesian accounts). The main difference between the Lockean and the so-called Kantian accounts is their denial of innate ideas, however it has been noted that there are considerable similarities between Descartes's and Locke's accounts of epistemology:

> Locke's theory of thought and knowledge, too, can look superficially like Descartes's. He takes thought to involve a series of ideas which exist 'in the mind', or 'before the mind', and which represent things outside the mind. Reasoning is a sort of mental operation on ideas which leads to knowledge or belief.
>
> *Ayers 1987, p. 121*

Put this way it may seem that the SSM advocates' account of the relationship between ontology and epistemology is more sceptical than Locke's – that mental ideas do not strictly represent the natural world:

> [T]he world is taken to be very puzzling: there is no reason why we should have evolved brains beyond those needed to survive on the planet's surface; there is no reason to suppose our senses and brains can tell us what reality is really like.
>
> *Checkland 1983, p. 672*

But Locke's argument was that our senses only give knowledge that there are some things outside ourselves (which is clearly assumed above). Locke did not argue that our senses can tell us what those things are really like:

> Locke developed a ... line of thought ... Although the senses give us knowledge, they give us limited knowledge – knowledge of the existence of things, not knowledge of their nature or essence. And because all our thought is restricted to the concepts that we have acquired through our senses, even our speculations about the world are restricted. He thought that there was no method by which scientists could expect to arrive at the underlying nature of things. So, despite his rejection of absolute scepticism about the external world, he was himself a sort of modified sceptic. We know that the world is there, but we don't know what it's really like.
>
> *Ayers 1987, p. 123*

The SSM advocates are (sometimes, but not always!) also 'sort of modified sceptics', as can be seen when they are articulating their ideas that holons (*systems* in everyday parlance) somehow 'reside' in the enquiring subject, rather than being *in the world*. For the SSM advocates, systems modelling is a mental activity; its validity is therefore something *internal* to us – something constructed by the enquirer. We can apply systems thinking to "perceived reality", in an unfolding flux of events and ideas. This notion is entirely Lockean in character:

> His [Locke's] explanation of the possibility of mathematical science, and geometry in particular, is importantly different from Descartes's. For ... Locke it's an abstract science which is created by us. We so to speak pick geometrical properties of things, and we can go on to construct such properties *ad lib* beyond the limits of our experience. In this way we can create the subject matter of a sort of non-empirical science. Such a science is possible because it's not really concerned with the nature of things at all. It's simply concerned, as Locke puts it, with our own ideas.
>
> *Ayers 1987, p. 130*

Although at no point do the SSM advocates involve themselves in discussions about primary and secondary qualities (these are Lockean notions); the conclusion I draw is that, broadly speaking, the epistemological assumptions of Checkland's 1990 and 1991(a) accounts are those of *Lockean empiricism*. It should be noted that such accounts were precisely the sort of accounts that Kant was keen to deny:

> The illustrious Locke ... meeting with pure concepts of the understanding in experience deduced them also from experience, and yet proceeded so *inconsequently* that he attempted with their aid to obtain knowledge which far transcends all limits of experience.
>
> *Kant 1933, p. 127*

Kant's argument is that Locke's ultimate mistake was to conduct his analysis by reflecting on the *process* of perception, rather than on *the conditions of its possibility*. It is *not* argued here that Locke's or Kant's accounts of epistemology are superior or inferior to other accounts of epistemology, this is a question for philosophical discussion that lies outside the scope of this work.

10.5 Hard Systems Approaches

Hard systems approaches are generally assumed to be based on an 'objectivist' paradigm of epistemology (i.e. that of the natural sciences). But, according to Lewis (1994), there are ineliminably 'subjective' elements to judgements inherent in any hard systems analysis:

> [T]heir vision of what constitutes a problem partly arises from the 'hard systems approaches' emphasis on providing not only a *rational* but also an *objective* analysis ... In practice though the hard systems approaches can never be genuinely objective or politically neutral. For example, the choice of criteria which can be used to evaluate the effectiveness of various alternatives must always mean acceptance of *some* group's values judgements about what is important. Their inherent but un-admitted subjectivity also become clear with respect to the requirement to obtain clear objectives as the starting point of analysis. First, many different objectives can be identified for a complex entity such as a business organisation and attempts to explain their behaviour in terms of the pursuit of a single objective do not stand up to close examination ... Secondly, human organisations do not themselves have objectives. Objectives are attributed to them by the observer and, clearly, different observers may attribute different objectives.
>
> *Lewis 1994, p. 30*

Lewis analyses the process of data analysis – often assumed to be a paradigmatic example of an enquiry based on objectivist assumptions. Here, too, Lewis concludes that in this process some subjective assumptions are ineliminable:

> [I]n practice, data analysis must include a large degree of subjective choice. This subjectivity exists whether or not the philosophy of the data-focused approaches uses the concept 'entity' (or 'object') to be an ontological device ... however well researched and rigorous are the techniques for manipulation and refinement of the conceptual data model, they ultimately rely on upon a subjective and interpretative identification of entities or objects ... The subjective content of data analysis has been admitted by the more thoughtful writers on the subject.
>
> *Lewis 1994, p. 150*

Lewis's study comprehensively examines many of the writings of the advocates of the hard systems tradition of IS analysis. There are some differences between these writers, but Lewis's claim to have found ineliminable subjective elements in the various writers' epistemological frameworks is a kind of *second-order* judgement by Lewis. Although 'work in progress' by the author suggests that Lewis's procedure may not be entirely adequate (for reasons that lie beyond the scope of this work), it can be generally concluded that Lewis's arguments are sound enough for the analysis herein to proceed. Consequently, it can be concluded at this stage that:

1. The epistemological assumptions of the SSM advocates are similar to those of the early modern philosophies of the natural sciences.
2. Hard systems approaches contain ineliminable elements of 'subjectivity'.

10.6 Contemporary Epistemology

In order to dimensionalise the findings so far, recourse will be made to the concepts of contemporary epistemology. This work will use as its source Haack (1993). In contemporary epistemology, a distinction is usually made between *foundationalist* and *coherentist* accounts of epistemology. In essence, the distinction is concerned with the question as to whether any beliefs are privileged over others. It will be argued that both hard and soft approaches adopt predominantly foundationalist strategies. It is doubtful whether coherentist approaches could be sensibly employed within systems analysis, as such approaches are not intended to explain the acquisition of 'piecemeal' knowledge:

> The characteristic theses of coherentist theories of justification are that justification is exclusively a matter of relations among beliefs, and that it is the coherence of beliefs within a set which justifies the member beliefs.
>
> *Haack 1993, p. 17*

The closest thing to an example of a coherentist strategy in IS analysis might be the prescriptions to carry out 'cross-referencing' between different products, as should be done when using structured systems analysis and design method (SSADM), for example. If anomalies are generated during the cross-referencing process then this would require some further analysis to be carried out to rectify the situation. However, no methodology (of which the author is presently aware) relies entirely on the procedure of cross-referencing to generate the 'true' requirements. Such faith in this procedure would imply that because cross-referencing between different products can be successfully carried out, it follows that the products resulting from the analysis of the information system are entirely correct. What happens in such approaches would seem to be that the 'elementary' elements of analysis (data-flow diagrams (DFDs), entity models, etc.) are seen to be epistemologically foundational – but fallible. Cross-referencing exposes some of the errors made during 'elementary' (i.e. foundational) analysis.

Foundationalist epistemologies assume that some beliefs are more 'privileged' (fundamental or more basic) than others:

> [A] theory qualifies as foundationalist which subscribes to the theses:
> (FD1) Some justified beliefs are basic; a basic belief is justified independently of the support of any other belief;
> and:
> (FD2) All other justified beliefs are derived; a derived belief is justified via the support, direct or indirect, of a basic belief or beliefs.
>
> *Haack 1993, p. 14*

Both IS approaches (hard and soft) subscribe to this thesis; it is in which type of beliefs that they privilege that their real differences lie. Haack finds that there are many variants of foundationalism. The two which are of most importance in this analysis are (what she characterises as):

1. The experientialist version of empirical foundationalism.
2. The extrinsic version of empirical foundationalism.

As was argued in the discussion concerning Lockean empiricism 'empiricist' should not be assumed to be 'objectivist':

> 'Empirical', here, should be understood as roughly equivalent to 'factual', not as necessarily restricted to beliefs about the external world... one style of empirical foundationalism [the experientialist version] takes beliefs about the subject's own, current, conscious states as basic, another [the extrinsic version] takes simple beliefs about the external world as basic.
>
> *Haack 1993, p. 15*

It can now be concluded that, broadly speaking, soft approaches assume the experientialist version to be the case, whilst the hard approaches assume the extrinsic version to be the case:

> [A]ccording to the experientialist version of empirical foundationalism, basic beliefs are justified, not by the support of other beliefs, but by the support of the subject's (sensory and/or introspective) experience; according to the extrinsic version of empirical foundationalism, basic beliefs are justified because of the existence of a causal or law-like connection between the subject's having the belief and the state of affairs which makes it true.
>
> *Haack 1993, p. 15*

Now, what is one to make of statement such as this:

> With regard to epistemology we may identify two extreme positions of positivism and interpretivism. Positivism is characterised by a belief in the existence of causal relationships and general laws that may be identified and investigated through rational action. In contrast, interpretivism allows that no individual account of reality can ever be proven as more correct than another since we are unable to compare them against any objective knowledge of a 'true' reality.
>
> *Lewis 1994, p. 138*

The "extreme" called "positivism" may be identified with the extrinsic version of empirical foundationalism, and the "extreme" called "interpretivism" may be identified with the experientialist version of empirical foundationalism. However, these positions should not be presented as being in binary opposition to each other; both are variants of foundationalism. Furthermore, the more general distinction between foundationalism and coherentism does not even get a mention in such accounts. Moreover, there are many 'variations on these themes' within contemporary epistemology, and Haack finds that within foundationalism there are four basic variants of both coherentism and foundationalism (some of which are further sub-divided). However, these variants need not be discussed further in this work.

10.7 Ontological Issues

To begin with, it will be worth clarifying the ontological position inherent in Soft Systems Methodology (as there is little doubt that hard approaches assume that there is a real world 'out there', and that this world can be known about). Mingers (1984) notes that Checkland offers us the following assertion:

> [W]e have no access to what the world *is*, to ontology, only to descriptions of the world ... that is to say, epistemology ... We should never say of something in the world: 'it is a system', only: 'it may be described as a system'.
>
> *Checkland 1983, p. 671*

Discussing this notion of subjectivism, Mingers states:

> Two things are worth noting. Firstly the statement itself is epistemological rather than ontological. It neither asserts nor denies what might exist but directs itself solely to our knowledge. This is as it must be. The view that we cannot know what exists logically precludes any such assertions or denials. Secondly the statement applies to the whole of reality – the physical, as well as the social world – and so equally applies to natural science.
>
> *Mingers 1984, p. 90*

So it appears to follow from the subjectivist epistemological assumptions embraced by the SSM advocates that, in a sense, epistemology (and not ontology) is the *only* field about which definite assertions can be made.

10.8 The Basic Ontological Assumptions of the SSM Advocates

In this respect, and despite Mingers' succinct remarks, it should be noted that SSM advocates generally appear to hold that there are crucial *ontological* differences between the *subject matters* of the natural and social sciences (*natural phenomena* and *human activity*, respectively):

> Any approach to rational intervention in human affairs has to accept that in studying purposeful human action and in trying to bring about change in human situations, it is not simply a matter of setting to work to discover 'laws' governing the phenomena in question. Autonomous human beings could, in principle, deliberately act in a way which could either confirm or refute any supposed 'laws' of human affairs.
>
> *Checkland 1991b, p. 59*

The argument that autonomy is an emergent property of human beings can be described as *ontological holism*. Put simply SSM advocates hold that the *natural* world consists of a rule-obeying domain and that the world of *human activity* consists of a self-determining domain. That different domains of explanation are possible is explained by this idea of *ontological holism*:

'The whole is more than the sum of its parts'. My student had understood the idea exactly when I heard her say to a fellow student: 'You are certainly more than the sum of your parts, you're an idiot!'. She was saying that the description 'idiot' has no meaning at any level below that of her companion regarded as a single entity.

Checkland 1983, p. 669

Now it could be argued that SSM advocates in fact believe that the concept of ontological holism is merely part of their *epistemology* – which 'might be relevant' to aiding understanding and so on. However, they do consider it to be a *plausible* ontological account. In any case it should be pointed out that the metaphysical assumptions of the SSM advocates *as propounded by those advocates* contain definite ontological commitments:

Perceiving the systems movement as a whole ... and examining the work that goes on within it, draws attention to the fundamentally different types of entity (things, phenomena or situations) which the researcher or practitioner may deem to be 'systems'. Three fundamentally different types may be discerned ... *Type 3*: situations in which interconnections are cultural, situations dominated by *the meanings attributed to their perceptions by autonomous observers*. Most real-world situations are of this type.

Checkland 1983, p. 670

The interesting point here is not that there are things which the researcher may be deeming to be systems but that there are *autonomous observers* in the description. This is an ontological statement. The SSM advocates do not seem willing to advocate solipsism as a plausible philosophy; there are other autonomous observers in the world besides themselves (or, strictly speaking, besides *themself*!). For the SSM advocates, autonomous observers are fundamental ontological *givens*: i.e. they exist – and this is made explicit in the metaphysical assumptions embedded in *Type 3* of the proposed taxonomy of systems enquiry (provided in Checkland 1983, p. 670). This is stated more baldly thus:

Situations of type 3 derive from the autonomy of the human observer, from his or her freedom to attribute meaning to perceptions.

Checkland 1983, p. 670

So, despite the SSM advocates' occasional assertions to the effect that statements about ontology are unjustifiable, it is reasonable to argue that SSM advocates in fact hold ontological holism to be the case. In fact, this position is both a sine qua non for SSM to be considered as 'an epistemology', and – many might consider – the *raison d'être* of SSM.

10.9   The Data Manipulation/Meaning Attribution Gap

According to the SSM advocates, data manipulation is something machines can do; meaning attribution is 'uniquely human'. Although SSM is a methodology which can help us to understand the 'rich' world of human 'meaning attribution', the problem of designing the data manipulation systems still remains outstanding. If an accommodation between various people's 'meaning attributions' can be achieved *and* a suitable data manipulation system can be constructed *then, and only then*, might we have an adequate information system. On this view, SSM-type conceptual models are only items which 'might be relevant' to 'making sense of' human activities – i.e. the meanings people supposedly attribute to their actions. On this view a conceptual model is only a model which might be relevant to informing someone as to the data that need to be manipulated – even if it is 'a system to make the changes':

Data with attributed meaning in context we may define as 'information'. It seems most appropriate to assume that the purpose of creating an organised IS is to serve real-world action. Organised provision of information in organisations is always linkable in principle to action: to deciding to do things, doing them, [etc] ... From these considerations (that 'information' is data to which meaning has been attributed in a particular context, and that information systems serve action) two consequences flow. Firstly, the boundary of an IS, if we are using that phrase seriously, will always have to include the attribution of meaning, which is a uniquely human act ... Secondly, designing an IS will require explicit attention to the purposeful action which the IS serves, and hence to the particular actions meaningful and relevant to particular groups of actors in a particular situation.

Checkland and Scholes 1990, pp. 54–55

Such a view sounds quite reasonable at first glance, but an ontological problem can be discerned. The problem, in fact, ultimately concerns the notion of human freewill. Supposing a conceptual model (even one 'thought up' at random) was an *exact match* of some organised human activity (at least in the mind of the person who 'thought it up') – for how long would it remain so? On this view the answer must be *indeterminate*:

Of course the designers of the data manipulating machine will have in mind a particular set of meaning attributions and will hope that the manipulated data will always be interpreted as particular information – but they cannot guarantee that, since users are ultimately autonomous.

Checkland and Scholes 1990, pp. 54–55

An example may help here. Suppose Joe (a home owner) is told that the mortgage rate is to be increased. Joe may decide to cut his expenditure (e.g. cancel his holiday). After a few weeks, suppose Joe is told that, once again, the mortgage rate is to be increased. Joe may again decide to cut his expenditure (e.g. sell his car). If the mortgage rate is increased again, Joe may decide to cut his expenditure further – but he *might* decide to sell his house and spend the money on a long holiday (or just leave the country and forget about the house). The SSM advocates assume that Joe is free to decide such things *arbitrarily*. Consequently, no one can say exactly when Joe will make the decision to 'shift' the meaning attributed to the data. As meaning attribution is, on this view, an essential element of information, any 'model' of an *information system* (so defined) is inherently unstable.

Although I have not encountered much tangible evidence to suggest that the advocates of structured approaches subscribe to the philosophical thesis of determinism, they do seem to subscribe to a philosophy of 'bounded' or restricted human freedom. A pejorative example may help to clarify this issue. Assume a physical DFD for an existing system is placed in front of you. It has processes such as "calculate VAT" on it (assume that this is currently done manually). It would be reasonable for you to conclude that some person(s) calculates VAT in the way indicated on the DFD, i.e. that some organised human activity follows this regular pattern. Of course, the actor(s) could decide *not* to "calculate VAT" (etc.), and decide to "eat the invoice" – but it would surely be reasonable to assume that in reality they might end up in some trouble if they did. In all probability, the advocates of structured approaches assume, the actor(s) would calculate the VAT in the way suggested on the DFD. It also seems reasonable to conjecture that the advocates of structured approaches believe that there are sufficient concrete instruments of power in organisations to ensure that most recalcitrant actors do the things that management wish them to do most of the time. This seems to be reasonable prima facie.

10.10 Human Free-will as an Ontological Non-problem

Conceptual models and DFDs may be similar enough in linguistic usage and figurative structure to be compatible. What is needed in order to make progress is a theory of the problem of human 'free-will'. Quine makes the following observations:

> Clearly we have free will. The supposed problem comes of a confusion, indeed a confusing turn of phrase. Freedom of the will means that *we* are free to *do* as we will; not that our will is free to will as it will, which would be nonsense. We *are* free to do as we will, unless someone holds us back, or unless we will something beyond our strength or talent. Our actions count as free insofar as our will is a cause of them. Certainly the will has its causes in turn; no one could wish otherwise. If we thought wills could not be caused we would not try to train our children ... we would not try to sell things, or to deter criminals.
>
> *Quine 1977, p. 173*

Such a view implies that modelling of human activities is possible. However, anyone who believes in *absolute* human freedom (of action) is inevitably bound to a view that the modelling of information systems (given the definition above) is, strictly speaking, a futile activity. The model could always be 'out of date before it is written' because of (the possibility of) 'autonomous real-world behaviour' on the part of the actors in the study:

> [W]hen a model of a human activity system does not match observed human activity the fault might be the model builder's but it might also be due to the autonomous real-world behaviour of human beings. *We cannot expect a match between model and reality* ... both because of the multitude of autonomous perceptions and because these perceptions will continually change, perhaps erratically.
>
> *Checkland 1981, p. 249* [emphasis added]

SSM-type conceptual models cannot be models in the true sense, because of the *indeterminacy* problem outlined earlier, and it is the ontological assumption of absolute human free-will (and not epistemological differences) that generates the apparent gulf between hard and soft methodologies for IS analysis.

Any academic or practitioner who intends to use conceptual models as a basis for information system design will have to contend *not* (or at least *not only*) with the technical problems but with the philosophical issue of human free-will. But any academic or practitioner who adopts a position which embraces the idea that the human will is restricted in any way whatsoever will always run the risk of accusation that what he or she is doing is "not proper SSM", moreover they may even be accused of subscribing to the philosophical thesis of determinism, a view which however unpalatable still has its adherents – for example Skinner, who says of attempts to explain behaviour as arising from some *autonomous* "inner man" in the "soul" of the person:

> The function of inner man is to provide an explanation which will not be explained in turn. Explanation stops with him. He is not a mediator between past history and current behaviour, he is a *centre* from which behaviour emanates. He initiates, originates, creates, and in doing so he remains, as he was for the Greeks, divine. We say that he is autonomous – and, so far as a science of behaviour is concerned, that means miraculous.
>
> *Skinner 1973, p. 19*

However, as has been mentioned previously, another view may be more plausible:

The notion that determinism precludes freedom is easily accounted for. If one's choices are determined by prior events, and ultimately by forces outside oneself, then how can choose? Very well, one cannot. But freedom to do otherwise than one likes or sees fit would be a sordid boon.

Quine 1987, p. 70

In order to adopt this view it would, though, be necessary to make some changes to the ontological stance currently embodied (although not always explicitly stated) within SSM. These changes might attune with many people's experiences of actually using IS methodologies in a 'mixed mode', e.g. Gammack:

[M]y experience in a number of expert system developments for which I did the knowledge elicitation ... [was that] Theoretically I believed the purist view that knowledge acquisition was impossible ... But practically I just went out and did it! What's more – it worked, just as many practitioners could have told me it would.

Gammack 1995, p. 163

Accepting that the human will is free, but that the human being nevertheless often pursues 'patterned', apparently rule-governed, behaviour towards clear objectives would be one way of explaining Gammack's (and most likely many other people's) experiences. Of course, this is *not* to say either that:

1. Human beings are automatons.
2. Objectives do not change.

10.11   Conclusion – Contemporary Epistemology Revisited

It has been argued that there is more 'overlap' between the epistemology underlying hard and soft approaches to IS analysis (i.e. foundationalism) than is generally assumed. Adopting a mid-position between the extrinsic and experientialist versions of foundationalism is quite possible. Haack argues:

[T]he epistemologist can be neither an uncritical participant in, nor a completely detached observer of, our pre-analytic standards of epistemic justification, but a reflective, and potentially a revisionary, participant. The epistemologist can't be a completely detached observer, because to do epistemology at all (or to undertake any kind of enquiry) one must employ some standards of evidence, of what counts as a reason for or against a belief – standards which one takes to be an indication of truth. But the epistemologist can't be a completely uncritical participant, because one has to allow for the possibility that what pre-analytic intuition judges strong, or flimsy, evidence, and what really is an indication of truth, may fail to correspond. In fact, however, I don't think this possibility is realised; I think pre-analytic intuition conforms, at least approximately, to criteria which are, at least in a weak sense, ratifiable as genuinely truth-indicative.

Haack 1993, p. 13

In straightforward terms, Haack is arguing that objective judgements always call for the uncritical acceptance of certain standards as to what is – and what is not – to *count* as evidence. Correspondingly, subjective judgements about what is the case – whilst lacking standards for their complete acceptance – give indications as to what *might* be the case (i.e. they are truth-indicative). There may be several possible explanations as to what a library is there to provide, but it is not there to put a man on the moon or to shine my shoes in the morning! However, Haack also argues that powerful elements of the coherentist thesis should also be included in a reconstructed epistemology (she calls this "foundherentism"). Such an approach as Haack suggests would both advocate and enhance the value of any cross-referencing procedures that could be developed between the two approaches to IS analysis (hard and soft). Whilst further discussion lies outside the scope of the present work it can be concluded that, providing that one can accept an ontological 'middle ground' on the issue of free-will (as Quine argues for), the epistemological issues can sensibly be reconciled by admitting:

1. The truth-indicative nature of *bona fide* subjective judgements about what appears to be the case.
2. The ineliminably subjective nature of objective judgements about what is the case.

Such a view would, at any rate, appear to be endorsed by some of those reflectively engaged in IS practice, such as Gammack – who concludes that:

> [S]ubjectivity and objectivity exist as extremes on a continuum where the difference between them is one of degree rather than of kind.
>
> *Gammack 1995, p. 181*

This should not, now, be a surprising conclusion.

References

Aune, B (1970) *Rationalism, Empiricism, and Pragmatism*. New York: Random House.
Ayers, M (1987) Locke and Berkeley. In *The Great Philosophers*. Magee, B (Ed.). Oxford: Oxford University Press: 118–143.
Checkland, PB (1981) *Systems Thinking, Systems Practice*. Chichester: John Wiley.
Checkland, PB (1983) O.R. and the systems movement: mappings and conflicts. *Journal of the Operational Research Society*, 34(8): 661–675.
Checkland, PB (1988) The case for 'holon'. *Systems Practice*, 1(3): 235–238.
Checkland, PB (1990) Information systems and systems thinking: time to unite? In *Soft Systems Methodology in Action*. Checkland, PB and Scholes, J. Chichester: John Wiley: 303–315.
Checkland, PB (1991a) Towards the coherent expression of systems ideas. *Journal of Applied Systems Analysis*, 16: 25–28.
Checkland, PB (1991b) From optimizing to learning: a development of systems thinking for the 1990s. In *Critical Systems Thinking: Directed Readings*. Flood, RL and Jackson, MC (Eds). Chichester: John Wiley: 59–75.
Checkland, PB and Scholes, J (1990) *Soft Systems Methodology in Action*. Chichester: John Wiley.
Descartes, R (1912) *A Discourse on Method; Meditations on the First Philosophy; Principles of Philosophy*. London: Dent.
Flew, A (1979) *A Dictionary of Philosophy*. London: Pan.
Gammack, J (1995) Modelling subjective requirements objectively. In *Information Systems Provision*. Stowell , FA (Ed.). London: McGraw-Hill: 159–185.
Haack, S (1993) *Evidence and Enquiry*. Oxford: Basil Blackwell.
Kant, I (1933) *Critique of Pure Reason* (2nd edition). London: Macmillan.
Lewis, P (1994) *Information-Systems Development*. London: Pitman.
Locke, J (1977) *An Essay Concerning Human Understanding* (5th edition). London: Dent.
Mingers, J (1984) Subjectivism and Soft Systems Methodology – a critique. *Journal of Applied Systems Analysis*, 11: 85–103.
Popper, KR (1972) *Conjectures and Refutations* (4th edition). London: Routledge and Kegan Paul.
Probert, SK (1994a) The epistemological assumptions of the (main) Soft Systems Methodology advocates. In *Proceedings of the International Systems Dynamics Conference*. Stirling: The Systems Dynamics Society: 170–180.

Probert, SK (1994b) On the models of the meanings (and the meanings of the models) in Soft Systems Methodology. In *Proceedings of the Second Conference on Information Systems Methodologies 1994*. Swindon: BCS Publications: 185-194.

Quine, WV (1977) The ideas of Quine. In *Men of Ideas*. Magee, B (Ed.). London: BBC Publications: 168-179.

Quine, WV (1980) *From a Logical Point of View* (2nd edition). Cambridge, MA.: Harvard University Press.

Quine, WV (1987) *Quiddities: An Intermittently Philosophical Dictionary*. London: Penguin.

Quine, WV and Ullian, JS (1978) *The Web of Belief* (2nd edition). New York: Random House.

Skinner, BF (1973) *Beyond Freedom and Dignity*. Harmondsworth: Penguin.

Williams, B (1978) *Descartes: The Project of Pure Enquiry*. Harmondsworth: Penguin.

Williams, B (1987) Descartes. In *The Great Philosophers*. Magee, B (Ed.). Oxford: Oxford University Press: 76-95.

11 Information Systems Intervention: A Total Systems View

Steve Clarke and Brian Lehaney

Abstract

Computer information systems development has grown out of the functionalist traditions of natural science. Whilst the structured or 'hard' approaches resulting from this have undoubtedly given rise to successful developments, increasingly in the last 20 years or so concentration has been on those problem contexts in which a functionalist, problem-solving method has proved least effective; contexts categorised primarily by the 'soft' issues of human activity.

Unfortunately, rather than this giving rise to a conciliation between the two approaches, with each being seen as valuable in its own context, what has happened has been an increasing divergence, with 'hard' and 'soft' methodologies competing for pre-eminence.

The intervention on which this chapter is based involves the surfacing of both 'hard' and 'soft' issues, and initially not only was a choice between a 'hard' or 'soft' methodology found to be inadequate, but even the nature of the problem context was not clear.

What was found to be needed went beyond selection of methodology, and demanded a complementarist approach in a systemic framework to control the intervention and ultimately arrive at a 'solution' which met the consensus view of all parties.

The course of action undertaken takes a 'total systems view' of the problem context.

An appraisal of the value of such an approach in this case, and the possible applicability to similar interventions, is the focus of this chapter.

11.1 Introduction

In 1992 the University of Luton piloted an undergraduate modular scheme of study, prior to the transfer of the entire undergraduate programme to modular provision from 1993 on.

Details of how this change affected the University and the manner in which it has been managed are documented elsewhere (see Clarke 1994; Clarke and Lehaney 1995, 1997).

The purpose of this chapter is to review, at a critical time in its development, the information system designed to support the new modular programme, when the objective is to move from a largely centralised management information system (MIS) to a more distributed system giving greater end-user access and control.

Throughout the intervention the need to find out about the problem situation by discussion and debate has been more important than the design of solutions. Indeed, the type of problem definition needed as the focus of an information system design effort has proved elusive.

This chapter begins by outlining the problem situation, and then continues with a consideration of the possible approaches. The process of creative thinking leading to choice of methodologies, and the proposals for implementation of that choice, are outlined.

Conclusions and recommendations are given which it is felt will give guidance for future interventions.

11.2   The Problem Situation

The University of Luton Higher Education Management Information System (HEMIS) is computer software designed to control student records under a modular framework, and provide management information from those records.

It is a mini-computer-based (Digital VAX) system, written in Oracle (a proprietary database). The driving force for its development was the move to modular schemes of study by the new universities following the Education Reform Act. At the end of 1991 some 10 Higher Education (H/E) institutions combined to determine what was needed, and HEMIS was the result.

HEMIS was initially taken up by two H/E institutions (Luton and Nene). Implementation at Luton was completed for the academic year 1993–1994. so that it is now in its third full year of operation.

Development of HEMIS to date has taken a structured approach (Clarke 1994). The development has been expert driven, under the control of The University of Luton Management Services and EMIS Ltd, the system developers. The user has been seen as The University of Luton central administration, and concentration has been on supplying accurate and timely management information.

This development has largely succeeded in providing the information envisaged in the initial implementation phases. However, in early 1994, it became clear that more benefit could be derived from the system in terms of what it offered to end users, particularly at the Faculty level, and that a greater concentration on such end-user issues would serve to improve the quality of information provided by the system in a number of areas.

A study was undertaken at that time (Clarke 1994) from which can be elicited a number of key findings relevant to this chapter.

Primary among these is an opportunity to improve the timeliness and quality of information provided by the system, in which key factors are seen to be a reduced reliance on printed output, and increased on-line input facilities. Further, there is a belief that HEMIS could do more to reduce operational workloads, much of which are still served by personal information systems outside central control.

In early 1995 improved HEMIS access at Faculty level was discussed by the MIS Quality Group (a group formed in 1994 to advise on MIS at University level). It soon became clear that, whilst there is an ongoing need to address the quality of existing systems, the expansion of user access opens up issues of how best to serve the different user groups in the University.

11.3   System Definition

The way in which a system such as this is perceived is a key factor in the selection of any approach to improving it.

Previous approaches adopted by the University have been dominated by structured systems development life-cycle (SDLC)-based methods, and may be categorised as methodologically isolationist (Jackson 1987), although this has been implicit rather than explicit.

This structured approach forces focus on to a definable problem, locating the analysis in a functionalist paradigm (Burrell and Morgan 1979, p. 25) – see Figure 11.1.

In the functionalist, or partial systems, view concentration on the 'hard' systems issues forces a partial view of the system of study which is technologically focused. System design is the main objective (inputs, outputs, files, records and fields being the goal), with user input to the process being subsumed within the main study, effectively annexed to the main SDLC methodology and supporting the design process from outside the system.

Such a view can be contrasted with the 'total systems view' shown in Figure 11.2.

The system must be perceived not as a clearly defined technical or organisational problem to which a solution is to be found; not as a 'student record system' in the functional sense; but as a complex interaction of all the issues involved in recording and monitoring student enrolment, attendance and performance: a system of 'student recording and monitoring'.

The focus in such a 'total systems view' shifts from technology or organisational functions to the views and ideals of the stakeholder groups involved in the system.

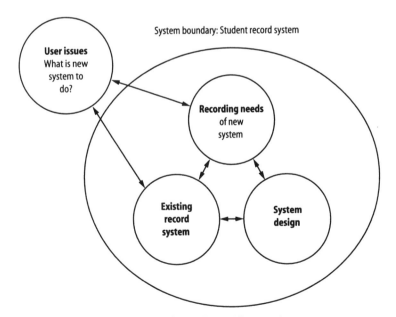

Figure 11.1. The functionalist (partial) systems view.

System boundary: Student record system

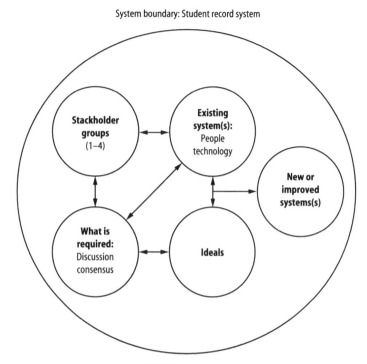

Figure 11.2. The total systems view.

The task becomes not one of how to engineer a solution to a known and agreed problem, but how to study and improve a problem situation made up of complex interacting issues.

People not only become part of the system, they are the primary focus of study.

11.4   The Approach: A Consideration and Decision

So, what do these alternative systems views indicate in terms of the approach needed to the problem situation at The University of Luton?

With a centralised information system (IS) aiming to provide accurate management information, structured methods have been seen as valid. In addition, when working to tight time scales, the use of such 'problem-solving' techniques is understandable.

But the difficulties which may result from insufficient attention to social issues should not be ignored:

> [A] neglect of the subtleties of the social context of an information system is likely to have negative consequences in terms of human needs and aspirations, and from a more managerial perspective, to lack of motivation, poor productivity and resistance to change.
>
> *Walsham 1993, p. 30*

With the now clear objective to give access to Faculties, the approach is in need of reconsideration. The development of the MIS can no longer be turned into a 'problem to be solved', expressible in terms of problem–means–solution. It must instead be viewed as a system of human activity supported by a computerised information system (CIS) and enabled by information technology (IT). Whilst it may be possible to 'engineer' IT, or even the programs and procedures which may be seen as part of it, the human activity system (HAS) is not susceptible to an engineered solution.

In the last 20 years or so, much of the debate in this field has focused on the so-called 'hard' versus 'soft' approaches. It is my contention that, whilst this debate has much to offer the information systems community, there is a need to move beyond it, and look at the issues involved in attempting to combine both hard and soft methods in a single intervention.

The position reached in these discussions, and its relevance to the development of information systems, may be summarised in the following way.

A possible solution to the problem situation faced by The University of Luton is choice of a soft method, with Soft Systems Methodology (SSM) perhaps being preferred as a means of achieving consensus and determining improvements to be made. But there are problems with this approach (see Mingers 1984; Petheram 1991; Probert 1994; Romm 1994 for further detail and references), from which Jackson's (1990) concerns summarise well the factors which have led to the detailed considerations of approach adopted in this intervention.

Jackson (1990) begins his critique with an analysis of Checkland's views on hard systems thinking, categorising them as being:

> Guided by functionalist assumptions. The world is seen as made up of systems which can be studied 'objectively' and which have clearly identifiable purposes.

These functionalist roots of hard systems thinking severely limit its domain of applicability, but equally soft systems thinking suffers from its own limitations:

> The recommendations of soft systems thinking remain 'regulative' because no attempt is made to ensure that the conditions for 'genuine' debate are provided. The kind of open participative debate which is essential for the success of the soft systems approach, and is the only justification for the results obtained, is impossible to obtain in problem situations in which there is conflict between interest groups, each of which is able to mobilise differential power resources. Soft systems thinking either has to walk away from these problem situations, or it has to fly in the face of its own philosophical principles and acquiesce in proposed changes emerging from limited debates, characterised by 'distorted' communication.
>
> *Jackson 1990, p. 663*

There is a further justification for believing in the need for development beyond the hard/soft issues:

> No single methodology has been or will ever be developed that is sufficient to deal with the wide variety of issues that we are confronted with in contemporary society.
>
> *Jackson and Keys 1984, p. 477*

> Openness and conciliation between theoretical paradigms is necessary, but methodologies can do no more that legitimately contribute in areas of specific context.
>
> *Flood 1990, p. 69*

In the typical hard/soft debate, discussion takes place at a methodological level; but this debate is essentially of a paradigmatic nature.

Hard approaches are philosophically functionalist, whilst soft are interpretivist. Adherents to the hard school see problems, and seek to arrange the entities within systems systematically to derive solutions to those problems. Soft thinkers see problem situations which exist in the interpretation of the observer, and seek to address the situation as a whole.

Flood and Ulrich (1990) categorise these hard and soft methods, respectively, as "non-reflective positivistic and non-reflective interpretivistic".

A consequence of this is that the hard school is predominantly pragmatic, dominated by technique with limited reference to underlying theory at any level. Functionalist methods prevail, giving rise to frequent challenges when applied within social contexts.

The soft school, similarly, mostly operates at a methodological level. Adherents to the most widely used methodology, Soft Systems Methodology, will often apply its constitutive and strategic rules with no reference to underlying theory.

The point to which this argument leads is one where: a view of only the functionalist elements of the problem situation is inadequate; adherence to a single methodology or paradigm cannot meet all the needs of the problem situation; an approach is needed which can combine methodologies from different paradigms in a wider systems context; human rather than technical issues are prime; the concentration is on dealing continuously with interacting issues rather than a succession of one-off problem-solving exercises.

Thus, we have developed a need for a continuous, iterative process, rather than a start–end problem–solution approach; for the incorporation of different methods, possibly with conflicting paradigmatic assumptions; for dealing systemically with both technical and human activities; for achieving meaningful participation.

One approach to information systems intervention best satisfies these criteria – Total Systems Intervention (TSI).

Although developed as an aid to interventions in management science in general, it is my contention that the domain of information systems has much to gain from the application of TSI.

11.5   The Process of TSI Applied to the Problem Situation

It is not the purpose of this paper to detail the workings of TSI (for more information see Flood 1995; Flood and Jackson 1991a, 1991b, 1991c, pp. 331–337), but rather to describe and critique its application to the current case.

By way of a brief description for those unfamiliar with TSI, it breaks down 'problem solving' into the three phases of creativity, choice and implementation, each of which is described in more detail below through the current intervention.

TSI further operates in three modes: problem solving; critical review; and critical reflection. Problem solving can be seen by viewing Figure 11.3 in a clockwise direction, progressing through creativity, choice of method and implementation of method. Critical review applies the process of TSI to reviewing the available methods and their relevance to the intervention. Critical reflection follows Figure 11.3 in an anti-clockwise direction, reflecting at each phase on the outcome of the previous phase(s).

The current intervention at The University of Luton is ongoing, and activity only up to and including choice is covered in this chapter.

TSI is not a methodology as such, but rather is an approach to dealing with unstructured problem situations which aims to apply relevant methodologies where they can make a legitimate contribution. Its thrust is complementarist, enabling methodologies from competing paradigms to be used together (Jackson 1990; Jackson and Keys 1984 are good starting points for more information on this).

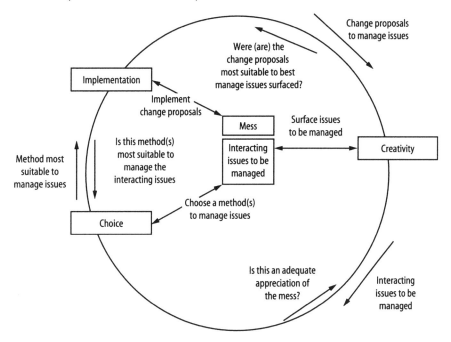

Figure 11.3. The process of Total Systems Inervention (Flood 1995).

11.5.1 Creativity

The objective of the creativity phase is to generate views of the problem situation which will inform choice of methodology.

A recommended (Flood 1995) output may be in the form of dominant and dependent metaphors through which the problem situation may be viewed, and this was the approach adopted in this case.

The aim was to get participants to see the situation from different viewpoints, and for this a brainstorming session was set up to encourage lateral thinking (de Bono 1977, pp. 131–146).

Key user groups were identified as being management, Faculty administration, academics and students, and of these it was decided initially to focus on Faculty administration.

Each of the University's six faculties was invited to send two representatives to a meeting held on 10 August 1995. In the event there were 15 participants.

The brainstorming session followed guidelines of de Bono (1977, pp. 131–146), and were further informed by recommendations of Flood (1995).

Participants were invited to form two self-selected groups, each nominating its own chair and note-taker, with the consultant acting as a facilitator and explicitly not taking on the role of expert.

The central issue was stated as:

How can monitoring and recording of students at Faculty level be better facilitated by information systems?.

The only additional guidance given by the facilitator was in the form of questions to elicit how participants viewed the problem situation. In particular, participants

were encouraged to consider, in terms of the past, present and future of the organisation, whether student monitoring and recording would be best perceived as a
repetitive process which could be mechanised to improve efficiency, a collaborative
'social' process or a process subject to determination by those in positions of power
(corresponding to mechanistic, socio-cultural and socio-political metaphors).

The session was limited to 30 minutes, at which point the meeting closed.
Participants were invited to send any further thoughts to the facilitator before the
next meeting, set for 31 August 1995.

11.5.2   Findings

Following discussions held in the second meeting, these findings are presented as
the views of the participants, to be used in informing choice of methodology.

The objective of the second session was given as:

To be agreed on the approach to be taken for the next stage of development.

The issues raised were:

- a need for flexible systems;
- a need for consultation;
- that problems stem from a bureaucratic, stable past sitting uneasily with a
  socio-cultural future in a period of continuous change. The present is seen as an
  uncomfortable transition, exhibiting a mix of bureaucratic, socio-cultural and
  socio-political.

So, the organisation is changing from mechanistic to socio-cultural, with socio-
political influences. In fact, the question of Faculty access to MIS was articulated by
one participant as "how to improve the system to give a more flexible, socio-cultural
view".

The outcome of the creativity phase was therefore a dominant socio-cultural
metaphor, with dependent mechanistic and socio-political metaphors.

This suggests that the main concern is the question of what should be done
(debate), with a lesser consideration of how to do things (design) and why they
should be done or whose interests will be served (liberate or 'disimprison').

The conclusion to be drawn from this is that the main requirement is that of debating the key human and technical issues, and deciding what to do about them.
Subsidiary to this is a need to design effective processes, and to a lesser extent to
liberate from dominating designs and outcomes.

There was extensive discussion at this stage owing to the key nature of these outcomes. The result was the interesting conclusion shown in Figure 11.4.

Figure 11.4 expresses the views of the brainstorming group.

The perception of a desired future was clearly expressed, and the idea was put forward that two futures might reasonably be assessed: one rooted in maintaining past
views (undesired) and one taken from future views (desired), with the latter having
clear strategic importance.

11.5.3   Choice

The choice phase prioritises the issues surfaced by creativity, and guides the choice
of method(s). The aim is to manage interacting issues, and the choice of method
must reflect this.

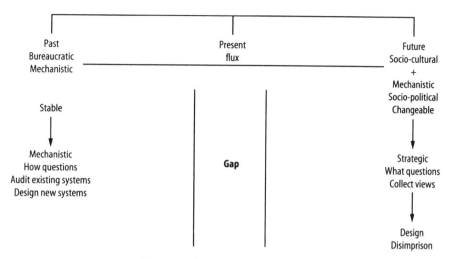

Figure 11.4. Informing choice through creativity.

The "Complementarist Framework" (Flood 1993) is used as a guide to tackling the technical and human issues surfaced by the creativity phase.

Choice of method is assisted by reference to 9 11.1.

As the need for debate is prime, the choice is between Strategic Assumption Surfacing and Testing (SAST) (Mason and Mitroff 1981), Soft Systems Methodology (SSM) (Checkland 1989) and Interactive Planning (IP) (Ackoff 1981).

Much of SSM is concerned with finding out about problem situations, and certainly stages 1–5 were considered for the creativity phase. Choice, however, informs the methodology(s) to be used in implementation, and SSM was judged ill-suited to this task. In particular, it was hard to envisage how the generation of conceptual models, and of desirable and feasible improvements, would prove helpful in this process.

SAST addresses simple/pluralistic issues, being particularly suited to adversarial debate. It is possible that its strengths will be of value as the intervention progresses, but at this stage SAST does not address present concerns.

IP has much to offer. The ideas of means and ends planning, and of idealised design, are directly relevant to the view developed of the system.

For these reasons, IP has been chosen as the dominant methodology.

However, the need to address the mechanistic and socio-political dimensions must not be forgotten.

SDLC approaches will be used for the former, commencing with an audit of existing information systems to be conducted concurrently with the IP investigation. Finally, the political dimension will be monitored, and elements of Critical Systems Heuristics (Ulrich 1983) applied where needed (for example, to open up issues of power and expertise).

The problem-solving mode of TSI has now been used up to the choice phase, and critical review has been employed to determine the relevant methodologies.

Before progressing to implementation it is now important to critically reflect on the position reached thus far.

11.6   Critical Reflection

Critical reflection may be achieved by asking the question at the choice phase:

Is this an adequate appreciation of the organisation?

Flood 1995

A useful exercise here is to check the outcome of the choice phase against the common and distinguishing principles in Table 11.1.

It seems reasonable to see the perceptions of the problem situation as predominantly concerned with participation, learning and understanding, with consensual rather than adversarial debate as pre-eminent. Communication, control, design and structure are clearly important to those issues surfaced as applicable to SDLC methodologies, whilst the exercise of power appears as an issue of less concern.

Additionally, the outcomes may be checked against those TSI principles (Flood and Jackson 1991a, p. 50) seen as most relevant to the intervention.

In particular: organisational complexity is such that a quick fix is not possible, but a range of methods used in a complementarist fashion are required; the need to appreciate the strengths and weaknesses of different methodologies; the systemic, iterative cycle of enquiry; and the involvement at all stages of the intervention of the facilitator(s), client and others.

In all, the outcome of creativity and choice does seem to give a view of the organisation on which future development may be based.

11.7   Critique of the Intervention

In any intervention it is important that:

The system remains critical of itself

Flood 1995

In the spirit of TSI, any intervention must be incomplete unless the approach itself is subjected to critique.

It is important to reflect on whether TSI has enabled the intervention to be better controlled than would have been the case with the perceived alternatives.

11.8   Systems Development Life-cycle

Adoption of such a methodology clearly generates positive results where the problem can be defined as relatively simple (few interactions, few parts, little human activity) and there is agreement on what is required.

It seems clear in the present intervention that the situation is not expressible as a problem at all, but rather, in Ackoff's terminology, as a "mess"; or what Flood would call "a set of interacting issues to be managed". Further, as the success of the intervention relies on a number of views to be satisfied, the single, unitary nature of problems so necessary to SDLC is not in evidence.

Table 1. Methodological choice matrix (Flood 1995)

Methodology	Designing		Debating		Disimprisoning	
	SDLC	VSD	SAST	IP	SSM	CSH
Common principles	Communication Control Efficiency Effectiveness Emphasis on location and elimination of error		Participation Learning Understanding			Identify whose interests are served Link organisational power structures to biases in society Identify how biases are mobilised in the organisation Identify experts and their position in the power structure
Distinguishing principles	Design control Structure prime	Process control Environmental analysis Organisation prime	Attenuating Adversarial debate	Diversifying Consensual debate		Identify source of: motivation control expertise legitimisation

Key:
SDLC, Systems Development Life-cycle (Wetherbe and Vitalari 1994).
VSD, Viable Systems Diagnosis (Beer 1981, 1984).
SAST, Strategic Assumption Surfacing and Testing (Mason and Mitroff 1981).
IP, Interactive Planning (Ackoff 1981).
SSM, Soft Systems Methodology (Checkland 1989).
CSH, Critical Systems Heuristics (Ulrich 1983).

11.9   Soft Methods

Although soft methods can be seen as clearly beneficial in the present intervention, the issue is rather one of whether any specific choice of soft method could have been made.

Certainly, the creativity exercise has enabled a much more informed choice in this respect, and it is difficult to see how this could have been achieved without some prior analysis.

SSM demonstrates this problem admirably. It undoubtedly better fits the problem situation in its ability to address the pluralistic views of the participants. But had a choice to progress with SSM been made at the outset, many shortcomings of the methodology would have prejudiced the intervention; shortcomings which led to it not being chosen after the creativity phase of TSI.

11.10   Total Systems Intervention

The value of TSI lies, in my view, in it not being a methodology as such.

In this type of intervention, adherence to one methodology would be inadequate, whereas the informed choice leading from TSI allows the use of different (often seen by many as competing) methodologies where each has a legitimate contribution to make.

In addition, the use of TSI promotes a view of problems as ongoing 'messes' to be improved, and within the iterative process the need for continued critical reflection keeps creativity, choice and implementation under review at all times.

11.11   Conclusions and Recommendations

Information systems development is a field dominated by isolationist or imperialist (Jackson 1987) adherence to SDLC-based methodologies, which, whilst adequate for solving simple/unitary problems, fall down when faced with increased complexity and/or pluralistic views.

Soft methods such as SSM have much to offer, but there seems little justification for a choice based on the merits of the method ahead of any analysis of the problem situation.

Use of either structured or soft methodologies generates only a partial view of the system of study which is inadequate in complex interactive problem contexts.

In such contexts the information systems community has much to gain from TSI, which can be used to guide an intervention in a complementarist, critical framework, generating a 'total systems view'.

We would recommend TSI to anyone undertaking development or improvement of information systems in such situations.

References

Ackoff, RL (1981) *Creating the Corporate Future*. New York: John Wiley.

Beer, S (1981) *Brain of the Firm*. Chichester: John Wiley.

Beer, S (1984) The viable system model: its provenance, development, methodology and pathology. *Journal of the Operational Research Society*, **35**: 7–25.

Burrell, G and Morgan, G (1979) *Sociological Paradigms and Organisational Analysis*. London: Heinemann.

Checkland, PB (1989) Soft Systems Methodology. *Human Systems Management*, **8**(4): 273–289.

Clarke, SA (1994) *A Strategic Framework for Optimising the Performance of Computerised Information Systems in Higher Education*. Faculty of Management, University of Luton (Masters dissertation).

Clarke, SA and Lehaney, B (1995) The problems of change to a semester-based modular teaching scheme. *Innovation and Learning in Education*, **1**(2): 39–45.

Clarke, SA and Lehaney, B (1997) Information systems strategic planning: a model for implementation in changing organisations. *Systems Research and Behavioral Science*, **14**(2): 129–136.

de Bono, E (1977). *Lateral Thinking*. Aylesbury: Pelican Books, Hazell Watson & Viney Ltd.

Flood, RL (1990) Liberating systems theory: toward critical systems thinking. *Human Relations*, **43**(1): 49–75.

Flood, RL (1993) Practising freedom: designing, debating, and disemprisoning. *OMEGA*, **21**(1): 7–16.

Flood, RL (1995) Total Systems Intervention (TSI): a reconstitution. *Journal of the Operational Research Society*, **46**: 174–191.

Flood, RL and Jackson, MC (1991a) *Creative Problem Solving: Total Systems Intervention*. Chichester: John Wiley.

Flood, RL and Jackson, MC (Eds) (1991b) *Critical Systems Thinking: Directed Readings*. Chichester: John Wiley.

Flood, RL and Jackson, MC (1991c) Total Systems Intervention: a practical face to critical systems thinking. In *Critical Systems Thinking: Directed Readings*. Flood, RL and Jackson, MC (Eds). Chichester: John Wiley.

Flood, RL and Ulrich, W (1990) Testament to conversations on critical systems thinking between two systems practitioners. *Systems Practice*, **3**(1): 7–27.

Jackson, MC (1987) Present positions and future prospects in management science. *OMEGA*, **15**(6): 455–466.

Jackson, MC (1990) Beyond a system of systems methodologies. *Journal of the Operational Research Society*, **41**(8): 657–668.

Jackson, MC and Keys, P (1984) Towards a system of systems methodologies. *Journal of the Operational Research Society*, **35**(6): 473–486.

Mason, RO and Mitroff, II (1981) *Challenging Strategic Planning Assumptions: Theory, Cases and Techniques*. New York: John Wiley.

Mingers, J (1984) Subjectivism and Soft Systems Methodology: a critique. *Journal of Applied Systems Analysis*, **11**: 85–104.

Petheram, B (1991) Grafting a "soft front end" onto a hard methodology – some questionable assumptions. In *Proceedings of Systems Thinking in Europe, Huddersfield*. New York: Plenum.

Probert, SK (1994) The epistemological assumptions of the (main) Soft System Methodology advocates. In *International Conference of Systems Dynamics, Stirling, Scotland*. Chichester: John Wiley.

Romm, N (1994) Continuing tensions between Soft Systems Methodology and Critical Systems Heuristics. *University of Hull Working Papers* (5), 1–38.

Ulrich, W (1983) *Critical Heuristics of Social Planning: A New Approach to Practical Philosophy*. Berne: Haupt.

Walsham, G (1993) *Interpreting Information Systems in Organisations*. Chichester: John Wiley.

Wetherbe, JC and Vitalari, NP (1994) *Systems Analysis and Design: Best Practices*. St. Paul, MN: West.

12 Why Mixed Methods are Necessary to Derive Enterprise-wide Solutions

D. (Rajan) Anketell

Abstract

The high costs and failures of many information systems projects have attracted severe criticism, analysis and recommendations. Unfortunately these appear to have done little to stem the flow of such incidents. Consequently the general level of dissatisfaction with the use of information technology, and the gulf between expectations and reality, does not appear to have significantly diminished. Fortunately, there have been some successes. In this chapter the author draws upon his experience of over 30 years in the development and implementation of effective low-cost enterprise-wide information systems. A number of case histories are used to derive some useful lessons, and a mixed method is described which has proved to be both effective and durable in the face of rapid advances in technology.

12.1 Introduction

Operational research practitioners, information systems developers and other specialists have identified many classes of problems, and have developed methods and techniques for their solution. Early successes stimulated further research which in turn encouraged an increasing degree of specialisation. Unfortunately, the latter appears to have fostered a tendency to focus on a favoured method or technology irrespective of the nature of the business problem. Consequently, despite the explosive advances in information technology, the overall record of actual achievement in business application has fallen far short of the expectation. However, there have been some cases of real accomplishment. Does this mean that success in this field is a hit and miss affair? Or are there lessons to be learned and principles to be discovered that can serve as a guide to those working in operational research, information systems, business process re-engineering and senior management?

This chapter will attempt to provide a positive response to this question and will suggest that the solution lies in the adoption of a strategy based on a holistic approach and the use of mixed methods. It will present a number of case histories which highlight some of the drawbacks of conventional methods, and trace the formulation of a strategy for the successful development and implementation of effective low-cost enterprise-wide information systems and business processes that can respond rapidly to change. This strategy, which is independent of changing technology or management theory, is based on two complementary methodologies (Anketell 1993,1994) that have been developed by the author over a period of 30 years. The central concepts of 'Simple Architectures and Models' (SAM) and 'Mixed Open Methods' (MOM) are described together with a framework for their application.

The cumulative evidence of these case histories suggests that the development and implementation of corporate strategies require the use, in whole or part, of many methods and should therefore be controlled not by specialists, but by generalists wielding the baton of a poor, determined, questioning, thinking, simple, selective mixer.

12.2   Case Histories

The case histories that are described span a period of 30 years from 1964 to the present. They include a number of business situations that had failed to respond to traditional methods. The simple mixed methods that were applied successfully are discussed together with the main lessons that were learned. Some examples are discussed in depth, whereas the treatment of others is very brief. The latter with their place in the time frame are included in order to demonstrate that the methods described can be successfully applied in a variety of organisations and are independent of advances in technology.

12.2.1   Production Planning and Control (1965)

A manufacturer of a very wide range of electrical products was experiencing problems with its deliveries despite the very high level of central stocks and work in progress. At one end of their range the company manufactured large quantities of small standard items such as aircraft altimeters costing in the region of £100. At the other end of the range were a few custom-built large and complex airport radar installations costing millions of pounds. Deliveries of most products and in particular those of high value were often seriously delayed due to the lack of a few small items required during the various stages of production. To help solve the problem the company engaged the services of a senior production control consultant who recommended the implementation of a computer inventory control system. Unfortunately, the new system failed to solve the problem and the internal O & M department was asked to conduct an independent examination. This was carried out by an operational research postgraduate, who was a new recruit to the department.

The first task was to seek the cooperation of all levels of staff in all departments. They were questioned at great length about their objectives, specific tasks and actions; and their behaviour and actual performance in the field was closely observed. These investigations revealed that the system followed by the company was to allocate job numbers to orders and to follow a system of back scheduling from delivery dates. Jobs were assigned to progress chasers whose task was to ensure that all the various parts, raw materials, sub-assemblies, etc., in the bill of materials were available to meet the requirements of the production schedule. The main problem, which was not identified by the initial study, was caused by the action of the progress chasers whose objective was to maximise their performance. They always acted independently and at times in competition with one another. In order to avoid any delays to their jobs due to a shortage of materials they would inform central stores of their requirements as soon as they received the job orders. The required items would be immediately extracted from the central stores and placed in 'private' work in progress bins even though they may not have been needed for a considerable period. Once removed from the stores there was no central record of the location of the items and consequently no overall control of materials or production. The result was that large expensive jobs were delayed while waiting for a few small parts to be received at central stores. Their requirement could often have been obtained immediately from the bin of another job which did not have an urgent need for the particular parts. Once the main problem had been identified it was clear that the solution lay in the adoption of a holistic approach to production. Progress chasers were encouraged to adopt a more helpful and cooperative attitude. Their objectives and tasks were redefined, and they were to be helped by the implementation of an integrated production scheduling and stock control system. The new system would indicate the location of all items whether they were in central stores or in work in progress bins; and the latter were no longer to be regarded as the private province of particular progress chasers.

If any lessons are to be learned from this example some reasons are required to explain why such a simple solution proved so elusive to a number of experienced practitioners. At least three factors appeared to have had particular significance. The first was that the focus of attention was on the use of preferred methods and techniques, and not on the business problem. The second was that experience without wisdom can be a constraint because it limits the ability to question established beliefs and customs. Any tendency for the experience of maturity to displace the curiosity of youth needs to be guarded against. Thirdly, it would appear that solutions based on partial processes are unlikely to solve corporate problems. They require holistic solutions.

12.2.2   A Leading Unit Trust Company (1968)

Save and Prosper, one of the largest unit trust management companies in the UK, had recently begun to sell life insurance policies linked to some of its unit trusts. Senior management wished to examine the effects of alternative strategies on their business. The problem was that the actuarial department using the techniques that had served so well in the past took many months to produce the results of only a few alternatives. The highly trained specialists in that department tended to focus on their conventional methods and techniques, and were having difficulty in addressing the new business requirement. The company, therefore, sought advice from an external source. During the course of this investigation all related objectives and procedures were rigorously questioned and examined. As a result a simple but effective model of the unit-linked insurance operations was proposed. The initial reaction from the specialists was one of scepticism and dismay at the apparent lack of rigour. However, as the estimated cost was low and anticipated benefits significant the project was approved by the board. The model was developed, programmed in FORTRAN, tested using historical data and implemented on the recently introduced IBM 360/30 mainframe. The result was a reduction in the time taken to evaluate alternative strategies from a period of months to 24 hours. The model enabled various alternatives to be specified and the data punched onto cards during the day for processing overnight. The decision makers received the results the following morning and after evaluation were able to specify further alternatives if they so desired. Soon after implementation the model was used by the company to evaluate alternative strategies during a successful takeover operation of a rival group called Ebor Securities.

At that time the model broke new ground and was a success despite the initial misgivings of some specialists. Since then other models, which share similar features, have been developed elsewhere. Some of them form the basis of the very popular personal computer spreadsheet packages that are now readily available.

A new lesson was learned during this project. This was that the commercial need for speed and economy often overrides the pursuit of unnecessary perfection. Another was the importance of lateral thinking, and the use of methods and techniques picked from fields outside the particular domain of the problem.

12.2.3   A Small Life Assurance Company (1972)

Nation Life, a small life assurance company offering almost as wide a variety of products as some of the large Life Companies, had built up a large backlog of work in most of the departments and the administration costs were getting out of control. The level of customer satisfaction had fallen to a very low level, and as the company wished to develop new products and to expand it needed to significantly improve the existing manually based operations. Because the company lacked the necessary expertise to solve the problem, it sought assistance from a number of external specialist organisations.

All the subsequent investigations, which were based on various conventional methods, recommended the introduction of computer systems. Unfortunately, the cost of implementing any of the recommendations was prohibitive. At that time the few application packages that were available failed to meet all the requirements. They were also very expensive, as were the mandatory mainframe computers. Estimates for developing the required application software to run on the recently available cheaper 'mini-computers' were also well out of reach. All the proposed systems were based on the automation of existing manual processes in accordance with the traditional functions of an insurance organisation. However, the managing director, who was aware of the successful application of unorthodox methods (he was, in fact, the actuary in the previous case history), decided to try them out within his new organisation. The objective was to devise and implement, within a short period and at low cost, a system which would reduce the backlog of work and create a platform for growth.

The project was carried out by one consultant and was in four parts. The first part was to gather detailed information on the business processes and requirements of the whole organisation. The second was to introduce immediate improvements to the manual processes and systems. The third was to develop an effective integrated computer data processing and management information system that could be implemented at very low cost within 1 year. The fourth part was to manage the implementation.

Once the focus was shifted away from methodologies to the business problem it was possible to make progress and the first two stages were completed within 6 months. During this period a detailed investigation into the company's objectives, strategy and business processes was carried out. Basic activity and data-flow diagrams were prepared, analysed and discussed with representatives at varying levels of seniority from the different departments within the organisation. As a result a simple unified model of the whole organisation was developed. It used a client's policy as the link between all the main functional departments. This was a very significant development because it showed that many of the existing problems were at the boundaries between the functional departments. A further advantage was that the model showed how immediate improvements in the manual systems could be implemented without the need for expensive restructuring of the company, which seems to be a requirement of many of the advocates of business process re-engineering methods. The new procedures enabled the processing backlog to be reduced from over 3 months to an average of under 2 weeks, and this great improvement in customer service was achieved with the added bonus of a reduction in staff levels.

The third part of the project took about 3 months to complete. It included the search for alternatives because even though the structure of the system had been greatly simplified the estimated costs of using conventional methods for the design and implementation of a computer system were still beyond the reach of the company. Many discussions took place with hardware and software specialists regarding the various systems design and software generation methods that were available. Hierarchical databases were beginning to be implemented. However, the time and cost required to develop such a system was prohibitive. Fortunately, one of the specialists drew attention to a concept outlined in an early paper by Codd (1971) on the relational database methods, which are now in widespread use. This information helped to provide the solution because it became apparent (even with our limited knowledge at the time) that there was a good correspondence between the simple holistic cross-functional model that had been constructed and the relational method. Time and cost constraints prevented the adoption of all the normal forms of the relational method, but a system was designed with the client's policy number (seven digits) as the main key and the master files were to be updated using the index sequential processing method. Sub-keys were allocated to codes for the type of cover, type of fund, etc. Programming time and costs were to be kept low by the frequent use of sub-routines and by the choice of RPG 11 as the programming language. The principle of reuse was selected from object technology as it appeared to be the only inherent concept that was capable of practical application at that time. An IBM System 3 model 10 mini-computer was selected as the hardware platform. A local computer bureau was selected to carry out the programming task and the initial processing until the company took delivery of its own hardware.

This study shows how the concepts outlined in Sections 12.4–12.7 were used to focus on the business problem and derive a solution which conventional methods appeared to have been unable to solve. It shows how the principles incorporated in SAM and MOM enabled a client-based life insurance application system (including policy underwriting, administration, premium and commission accounting, and claims processing) to be designed, programmed and implemented within 1 year at a fraction of the cost of systems developed and implemented by conventional methods.

New lessons were learned during this project. One of these was that a lack of funds (i.e. being poor) does not have to be an insuperable barrier. Instead it can provide a great incentive to seek new methods and to investigate the use of old ideas in new areas. Another lesson was the importance of the involvement of the chief executive officer (CEO) and his determination to achieve the objective. His enthusiasm was contagious and his support vital in the resolution of potential areas of conflicting interests within the organisation. A further lesson was that the use of established methods and processes with new technology is restrictive. The full benefits of new technology can only be obtained through the use of new processes. The study also provided a clear indication of the best way to combine and utilise the respective skills of generalists and specialists.

12.2.4   A Lloyds Insurance Intermediary (1979–Present)

Burgoyne Alford (now C.E. Heath Insurance Services Ltd. after a series of mergers) was a Lloyds intermediary offering mainly comprehensive household insurance. The BA Group also owned a contact lens insurance company. The BA Group were about to embark on a big expansion programme and wished to obtain the benefits of moving from a manual to a computer-based operation. They selected the author to assist them with this task. The result was the development and implementation of an enterprise-wide data processing and information system at an initial cost of under £15 000 (excluding the mini-computer hardware). This corporate system, from inception, included many of the essential features of those systems and concepts that have been given names such as management information systems, executive information systems, work group computing, data mining and the data warehouse. All these benefits were gained with the use of dumb terminals and a mini-computer, and without the use of the client server and advanced personal computer technology, which is now being widely promoted as essential.

The experience gained with the life company and other projects enabled the whole analysis and development process to be undertaken at a very much quicker rate even though the type of company, its culture and class of products were very different. One of the main lessons that had been learned was that some of the work could be carried out in parallel. This enabled program deliveries to be commenced at a very early stage in the development process. It introduced a form of prototyping which helped to avoid the higher costs that are incurred when changes are requested at a later date. These improvements enabled program deliveries to be commenced within 3 weeks and to be completed within 3 months even with some substantial changes that resulted from use of the prototype.

The company has grown almost beyond recognition since that time in terms of size and product range. During this period the original application software was subject to continuous and, at times, sudden and considerable modification and enhancement as the business environment and requirements changed. However, the application of the concepts and methods outlined below in Sections 12.4–12.7 enabled these enhancements to be implemented rapidly at relatively low cost, and the system continues to service the company to this day.

12.2.5   An Intermediary Offering Extended Warranty Schemes (1980)

The methods described in this chapter were used to develop an information technology strategy closely linked to the business strategy, and to supply customised application software to Multiguarantee Limited, an insurance intermediary which offered extended warranty policies on motor vehicles. The business model was conceived, processes redesigned, and application software developed and implemented within a few months at a cost below £10 000. Soon afterwards the company reappraised its objectives and strategy in order to enter the domestic appliance warranty market. During the next 2 years, as the company expanded into the new market and sales grew explosively from 10 000 to nearly 1 000 000 policies, the business needs and practices were in a state of almost continuous change. The methods described below in Sections 12.4–12.7 enabled the system to respond rapidly at low cost to these changes and provided a firm base for the expansion.

12.2.6   A General Insurance Company (1985)

Use of the methods outlined in this chapter enabled a household system to be customised for the London & Edinburgh Insurance Company Limited, and for implementation to be completed within a few months. Subsequently there was a requirement for an enhancement to include the processing of personal health and accident insurance. This was a very different class of insurance with new requirements. However, the methodologies described earlier enabled the necessary enhancements to be implemented within the existing household system within a few weeks at very low cost.

12.2.7   Hard or Soft (1988)

A number of enhancements were made to the application software and new faster hardware systems were introduced. However, many of the users complained of poor response times. Advocates of the hard school favoured responding to the demand for improved performance through the purchase hardware upgrades. However, the cost proved unacceptable. During a brainstorming session a suggestion was made to alter the screen message displayed on enquiry from "please wait" to "searching for your requested policy". Only one line of coding required to be changed. This not only satisfied the users but also appeared to increase productivity. The initial message appeared to arouse emotions of annoyance and resentment because users felt that their time was being wasted while having to wait. However, the subsequent message appeared to be satisfactory because users felt that their needs were being attended to and they were able to focus their attention on what they had to do next.

The lesson learned was that spending large sums purely on technological enhancements is often neither necessary nor the sole solution, and that the human element should never be ignored.

12.3   Some Limitations of Conventional Methodologies and Techniques

A variety of reasons for the high costs incurred in the design, construction and implementation of information systems and technology have been put forward, and numerous methodologies and techniques have been developed and advocated as panaceas. These have included the use of case tools, client server systems, databases (various types), complex and elaborate architectures and models, fourth-generation languages, object-oriented systems, open systems, outsourcing, prototyping, structured design and analysis methods, various project management techniques, software quality management, etc. Each has almost as many advocates as it has detractors, and their popularity rises and falls like the hemline in ladies' fashions.

When properly used, some of these methodologies and techniques have made significant contributions to the development of information systems. But, as the foregoing case histories have shown, many of the pure methods have failed to achieve their promise. It is suggested that one of the main reasons for this is a misalignment of the usually beneficial filter and focus mechanisms. The latter have evolved over millions of years to enable life-forms to focus only on what is essential for survival and to filter out unnecessary information (noise). Unfortunately it appears that pure specialisms tend to foster a focus on the methodology itself at the expense of the overall problem. The perception of their advocates is consequently limited by the filter effect and any information that is irrelevant to the method is ignored. Such behaviour adds strength to the view that there are none so blind as those that will not see. Other reasons for the limited success of pure methods appear to include one or more of the following:

- A failure to adopt a global corporate approach.
- A cumbersome, complex and rigid structure which costly to learn and implement.
- A strict adherence to the rules which discourages criticism, limits understanding and restricts progress.
- An inability to respond rapidly to change.
- An emphasis on technology with a tendency to ignore the needs of the people who will use it.
- Lack of understanding of the economic value of time.
- The focus of attention at the wrong stage of the development cycle, i.e. at efficient software production prior to the acquisition of adequate information on objectives, strategy and the environment: this has led to rapid progress down the wrong track.

12.4   The Strategy

Many of the above limitations can be overcome very simply by the adoption of a strategy which emphasises four important basic concepts, namely analysis, simplicity, openness and integration. The importance of these concepts appear to be widely acknowledged but often neglected in practice. Thus, there appears to be a need for a methodology which not only incorporates these features, but also actively encourages their use. As Dr Johnson is reputed to have said, "All men need to be reminded. Few to be informed".

12.4.1   Analysis

The initial aim is to pursue a wide-ranging programme of enquiry in order to obtain a thorough understanding of:

- The objectives, which initially may lack clarity and be incompatible with each other.
- The business processes.
- The tools, i.e. the available methodologies and techniques.

The importance of information gathering prior to execution is illustrated by the old proverbs "look before you leap" and "measure twice cut once".

The writer Rudyard Kipling had this to say on the subject:

> I keep six honest serving men
> They taught me all I knew
> There names are HOW and WHY and WHEN
> And WHAT and WHERE and WHO.

A proper analysis depends not only on the ability to pose questions but also on the capacity to listen carefully to the response. It can sometimes be hindered by a fear of asking or answering questions, failure to listen or by the adoption of an adversarial attitude. These have to be overcome because it is essential to gain a thorough understanding of the whole problem and the information requirements prior to construction of the business model, system development and software generation.

12.4.2 Simplicity

Understanding is a prerequisite of the simplification process which is necessary to break down large complex projects into smaller manageable structures prior to reassembly. Simple architectures, models and systems have a number of advantages:

- In most cases they will provide good results very quickly at low cost.
- They are much easier to understand, and therefore are easier to manage, maintain quality and implement.
- They have low development, implementation, training and maintenance costs.
- In general they are more flexible than large complex structures and are therefore much easier to modify quickly at low cost as the business environment changes.
- It is easier to incorporate the Pareto (80/20) principle which indicates that the major part of the requirements account for a relatively small proportion of the total cost.

The concept of simplicity helps to focus on the economic value of time and the practicality of commercial applications. It is often more important to do things simply and quickly than to try to do them in the best or in an ideal way. The importance of this concept is also emphasised by some old proverbs which include "make hay while the sun shines", "a stitch in time saves nine" and "strike while the iron is hot". More recent distinguished advocates include Sir John Harvey-Jones (also known as the Trouble Shooter in the television series on improving business performance). According to Sir John, "To run a business everything has to be simple. If it is not simple people make mistakes". Furthermore, in this era of rapid change any organisation that takes too long to introduce improvements will find itself being rapidly overtaken by its more nimble competitors.

12.4.3 Openness

Many of the methods and techniques in use appear to be closed and bound by rigid rules They have a number of serious disadvantages:

- The focus of attention is often on the methodology itself and not the business problem that needs a solution.
- Difficulty in interpretation. Much time and energy is wasted on alternative definitions of the 'true faith', e.g. client server, open systems, etc. This only serves to confuse and irritate the customer, who is interested in the solution to his or her problem and not in the niceties of definition.
- Inflexibility and the inability to respond to change.

These disadvantages can be avoided by a methodology which is open, i.e. one which is not constrained by narrow definitions and can incorporate new ideas, methods and techniques as these become available. An open methodology encourages the focus on the business problem and not on itself. It also encourages enquiry, thought and innovation.

12.4.4 Integration

It is important to adopt a holistic approach particularly in the early stages. The information requirements and business processes of the whole organisation need to be examined prior to design and implementation. Most conventional methods of information systems development adopt a functional approach often with an emphasis on technology. This has led to considerable duplication of data, and to the cumbersome, inefficient and expensive systems formed by the need to maintain interfaces between the functional sub-systems themselves; and also between those that have been added later in the form of management information systems, executive information systems, etc.

12.5   Simple Architectures and Models

The principles of simplicity and integration form the basis of the alternative approach used in SAM, which through a process of detailed questioning seeks to determine the information requirements of the whole organisation and a common factor linking all functions. Once this has been done it is possible to build a suitable model and an architectural framework. The Pareto principle can then be used to develop an implementation plan whereby some of the requirements at each level within each function can be provided for in the initial stage. This enables organisations to obtain quick benefits and to fund further stages of development from the benefits gained in the earlier stages. As the systems developed by this method are enterprise-wide systems from the outset they do not suffer from the 'add on' effect mentioned in Section12.4.4, and they have been found to be easy to use, easy to enhance and quick to respond to change at low cost.

12.6   Mixed Open Method

Many conventional methods are constrained by rigid rules and suffer from the limitations outlined in Section 12.3. These disadvantages can be avoided by a methodology which is open and can incorporate new ideas, methods and techniques as these become available. This concept of openness is adopted in MOM, where the aim is to examine many ideas, techniques and methods borrowed if necessary from many sciences, to make an appropriate selection in whole, or in part, and finally to amalgamate these into a suitable hybrid solution, i.e. pick and mix. This is a lesson which can learned from other professions. A carpenter understands the need for many tools to do his job; so does the surgeon who can now use electronic, mechanical and sonar equipment to complement his skills and sharp knife.

12.7   The Procedural Framework

SAM and MOM complement one another and should be used in conjunction. The aim is to create and maintain a focus on the business requirements in order to find the best possible overall solution within the cost and time that is available, preferably at the least cost and shortest time. The procedure is as follows.

1. Gather initial information to establish objectives including costs and time scales.
2. Gather further information on detailed requirements and business processes.
3. Break down complexity and simplify.
4. Build the initial model in accordance with the concepts outlined in Sections 12.4 and 12.5.

5. Examine the current armoury of techniques and methods in a variety of disciplines.
6. Select the most suitable parts of the most appropriate methods, etc., and prepare a suitable mix which will provide a solution.
7. Examine the cost and time scales for the result of Step 6.
8. If outside the initial target range and is unacceptable consider the 80/20 principle and repeat steps 1–8 with redefinitions, alternative parameters, other recipes, etc., until an acceptable solution is obtained.

It is a cyclical process, which facilitates implementation in stages with allowance for continuous modification to reflect changes in business requirements; and within each step of the framework there are no rules to act as constraints.

This procedure encourages open discussion and active participation at all levels within all functions of the organisation and this makes a great contribution to the successful outcome because it:

- enables the IT strategy to be closely linked to the overall business strategy.
- allows the ownership of the strategy and the system to be claimed by all.
- results in the implementation and maintenance of a fully integrated system.

This is much more effective than the complex systems developed by traditional methods which automate existing processes independently by function which then need to be linked with each other, and with yet other bolt-on systems made necessary by the (spurious) segmentation of information systems into management information systems, executive information systems, etc.

12.8   Some General Observations and Conclusions

Use of the mixed methods described in this chapter enabled effective models and software architectures of a wide variety of classes of insurance (life, general, motor, health, pets, reinsurance, etc.) to be implemented within very short periods. This contrasts with systems developed by other methods which have taken hundreds of man-years to build and cost hundreds of millions of pounds.

Information technology will continue to make rapid advances. New hardware, new theories and methods will be developed, and these will make some of their predecessors obsolete. Systems that have relied on them have required and will continue to require extensive modifications, or expensive and time-consuming redesign. However, unlike most of the pure methodologies the mixed methods employed by SAM and MOM can absorb new ideas, etc., without difficulty, and their systems have been shown to possess the desirable features of adaptability and durability.

The activities of an organisation are diverse involving many interactions between humans, humans and computer systems, and between different computer systems in both local and global arenas. The information needs of an organisation reflect this diversity. This factor together with others discussed in this chapter make it very difficult, if not impossible, to derive enterprise-wide solutions through the use of a pure method. Instead, the requirement is for mixed methods such as SAM and MOM, which can be used to create a variety of new systems made up from a harmonious selection of themes from hard and soft methods, while control is maintained by the baton of a poor, determined, questioning, thinking, simple, selective mixer.

Finally, it is worth remembering that it is better use of technology, and not the fashionable use of better technology, which provides organisations with a competitive edge and success.

References

Anketell, D (1993) *How to Design, Implement and Change Information Systems at Low Cost.* Unpublished paper presented at the seminar of the Management Division of the IBM Computer Users' Association in September 1993, Eastleigh, UK.

Anketell, D (1994). In search of a strategy for the successful *implementation of information* technology at low cost. *Proceedings of The Second European Conference on Information Systems,* **3**: 503–511

Codd, EF (1971) A database sublanguage founded on the relational calculus. In *Proceedings of the Association for Computing Machinery SIGFIDET Workshop Data Description, Access and Control.* New York: ACM, 1971.

13 Tailorable Information Systems Add Value to Organisations in Changing Environments

Nandish V. Patel

Abstract

A plausible theoretical framework is proposed for researching and developing tailorable information systems which move beyond the mock fixed-point theorem of information systems development. The mock fixed-point theorem of information systems is a paradigm currently used for analysing, designing and developing information systems, but it has not been successful in delivering viable information systems which meet business users' changing information requirements. Such requirements can be addressed by researching the development of tailorable information systems. Tailorable information systems research is concerned with both the development and subsequent usage of computer-based business information systems.

13.1 Introduction

Information systems in business organisations are normally developed on the basis of managerial information requirements which have been determined at a temporally fixed point relative to the dynamic life of a business. The success of these information systems has been questioned by researchers and practitioners. Some spectacular failures such as Taurus, the London Stock Exchange's paperless shares transactions systems, have occurred (Watts 1992). In all cases, huge expenditures of time, labour and monies have been wasted. In this chapter it is argued that such systems have failed because of a fundamental lack of understanding of business systems as living (human) systems. This lack of understanding has given way to viewing organisations as largely static entities, and has consequently led to systems development methodologies which reflect this view of organisations. Consequently, business information systems are designed on the fallacious fixed-point theorem of information systems development (Paul 1994).

In accordance with the theme of adding value in a changing world, it is argued in this chapter that information systems which support changing businesses also need to be changeable to be able to add value to an organisation. Such change is here characterised as the ability of all the stakeholders in an information system to be able to tailor that system to meet changing information needs – referred to as tailorable information systems. The concept of tailorability is equally applicable to systems' developers, maintainers and users, although this chapter specifically addresses end-user tailorability.

Tailorable information systems and computer systems, jointly referred to as tailorable systems, which are compatible with living systems exist in real business organisations but are few in number, whereas business dynamics dictate that there should be a greater prevalence of them. The Rank Xerox EuroPARC Research Centre have developed a mainframe-based tailorable system using Buttons object-oriented technology (Maclean *et al.* 1990). Tailorable systems have been designed for workstation environments, as have developers' tools for designing such systems (Hesketh 1992). Other developed systems referred to as adaptable systems exhibit characteristics of tailorability and may also fall into this category (Dewan and Choudhary 1991). Other systems are described as adaptable, but these cannot be classified as tailorable because they remove control over the systems operations from the user. Often such systems use expert systems technology to achieve their aims. Rather than encourage a greater use of a system, automatically adapting systems remove control from a user. This may lead a user into dysfunctional behaviours such as disguising personal goals and preferences when using the system. The purpose of tailorable systems is diametrically opposite, it is to provide control over systems to a user.

The anomaly in business is that there is a lack of prevalence of tailorable information systems. Business users require such systems to aid them in their ever-changing work environment, where change and the ability to adapt to it is a major contemporary business issue. Tailorable systems alluded to above lack a theoretical base. In terms of tailorable information systems, a theory is vital in order to be able to explain how and why systems work, to predict outcomes and thereby control their operation. If the theory is apt at explaining tailorable systems, then it can be used to successfully replicate such systems. The present research is concerned both with understanding the pragmatics – how to build tailorable systems – and with the theory informing tailorable systems design.

In this chapter research is introduced into the design of *tailorable information systems*, systems that can adapt to a user's changing requirements. The research is conducted within the larger framework of living information systems thinking (LIST), which is the argument that information systems should be compatible with living (human) business systems. Such systems can only be fully understood when first viewed from a conceptual perspective.

In the next section an exposition of the fixed-point theorem of information systems will be presented, which is based on the notion that everyone involved in a system design can agree on what they want, which further assumes they know what they want from the system to be designed – something that is not certain (Paul 1993). Then a rationale for researching and building tailorable systems, and their benefits to businesses, will be discussed. The concepts of tailorability and customisation will then be juxtaposed to enable differentiation and definition, and some empirical work as part of the research into tailorable information systems will be cited. Penultimately, the concept of tailorability will be analysed, its theoretical basis and its constituent parts will be discussed. Ultimately, the future directions of the present research and its benefits will be summarily stated.

13.1.1 The Mock Fixed-point Theorem of Information Systems Development

In a dynamic business environment, information systems have historically been developed on mainframe platforms and more recently on distributed workstation solutions, to meet a set of predetermined business information requirements of managers. These requirements have been determined at a given point in time in the business's life by using any number of systems design and development methodologies. For example, one such method is Structured Systems Analysis and Design Method (SSADM). The resultant systems have proved to be rigid and inflexible to changes in business information needs for decision making. This temporally static approach of systems design methodologies to determine information requirements and systems development has been eloquently critiqued by Paul (1993) in the form of the Fixed-point Theorem of Information Systems Development. Information systems developed on the basis of the fixed-point theorem invariably subsequently require huge monetary and labour expenditure in the form of programming maintenance to be kept current and valid as the business and its environment change. Such expenditure is necessary because users of these systems require new or different variations of functionality, which arise because the information required has changed in business processes that are dynamic.

The mock fixed-point theorem of information systems is that:

> There exists some point in time when everyone involved in the system knows what they want and agrees with everyone else.
>
> *Paul 1993*

This approach is typical of systems development methodologies used for designing and developing information systems, which assume that user requirements can be known and agreed before the development of a system begins. To know what is required for a given system is a complex process in itself, and potential users may be able to enunciate some requirements but not all. Assuming information requirements can be fully known in advance, whether the participants in the design can agree on them is another debatable question. The methodological approach to systems development further assumes that the system specification resulting from initial systems analysis is the right one. Not only do methodologies overly rely on the fixed-point theorem, but so does the resulting software engineering. At the extreme end of a continuum characterising these methodologies is SSADM. The fixed-point theorem of information systems lacks both theoretical and empirical evidence but has many counter-examples (Paul 1993).

A simplified scenario of using systems development methodologies in project-based system development might be typified as follows: methodologies assume systems analysts can provide a detailed specification of required functionality in a proposed system; analysts in turn depend on users to know what system functionality is required and to communicate that to them in detail to enable data modelling. Users will often want additional functionality or require changes to those already stated; such adjustments are difficult and costly to do in time and money after the design phase has begun and often meet developers' resistance. Analysts are frequently unable to communicate with users or understand their positions, making the whole requirements analysis reasoning unmanageable, resulting in systems developments that often disappoint their users' changing needs.

This line of dependency on users, with its emphasis on formal approval of specifications (Powers and Dickson 1973), rests uneasily on the false premise that users are capable of knowing what is required from a proposed system development and, more significantly, that they are able to articulate unequivocally that knowledge to analysts. An equally false premise is that analysts are capable of understanding users' requirements which are invariably stated in business nomenclature unfamiliar to them. Empirical evidence to support these premises is not available. However, plenty of examples reveal that such attempts remain unfulfilled and lead to incomplete systems specifications (therefore systems), and to disappointed users and analysts (Mouakket *et al.* 1994).

13.1.2 Rationale for Building Tailorable Systems

The user population of a given system will be quite diverse in its abilities to use a provided system and in its requirements from it. The requirements of the business are also in a constant state of flux. Such variety cannot be satisfied by a system developed on the basis of information gleaned from a sample of users' involvement, as occurs in the methodological approach. A system can only accommodate variety if it itself is adaptable, and the trait of adaptability is a central feature of tailorable information systems. The need for tailorable information systems also arises because of developments in end-user computing. Micro-computers, workstations, software packages and networks are replacing the familiar mainframe scene. These technologies have enabled computer systems downsizing to become a major phenomenon in businesses (Trimmer 1993). All these developments have been placed in the hands of numerous business users who have varied requirements. This variety can only be meaningfully accommodated by computer systems that users can tailor to their particular needs. Researchers have also identified tailorability as a major future development in computer systems by the year 2000 (Nielson 1993).

More importantly, there are real benefits to be gained from researching tailorable systems. The real benefits in terms of actual improvements are:

1. *Savings in maintenance costs*: it follows that if a system is tailorable by the user, he or she will tailor it to suit changes in requirements, thus saving on maintenance programming costs.
2. *Increasing the longevity of a system*: by enabling tailoring activity the system's life will be increased because the user will continually adapt the system to new environments.
3. *Increased computer systems usage*: a system that is tailorable will be more likely to be used because the user would be able to adapt it to his or her requirements.

All of the above should result in improved organisational group and personal productivity in terms of increased effectiveness and efficiency.

Business organisations in a market economy adapt as a matter of survival. It therefore follows that their manual procedures, processes and methods of operation must adapt too. If they did not then the business will not survive. That is a compelling justification for designing and building tailorable information systems which support those adapting aspects of a business. The ultimate purpose of designing and developing tailorable information systems is to improve both the performance of the computer system and its human user. This means increasing the use of available software and hardware systems, and improving the efficiency and effectiveness of users' decision making.

13.2 Customising and Tailoring

The concept of tailorability should not be confused with that of customising. Packaged software, mainly for non-mainframe computer systems, is often customisable, especially if it operates in the Windows environment. Standard dictionary definitions of customisation and tailoring do not provide any distinguishing features between the two. A technical distinction is therefore necessary. A distinguishing feature of a tailoring systems environment is that *design decisions are deferred* to the user. These decisions concern the functionality of a system. Apart from trivial screen layout and icon representation, control customisation does not allow design decisions to be deferred to a user. Although the provision of recording macros in spreadsheets extends the application's functionality it is limited because of its reliance on users having to learn a programming language for more sophisticated developments, and especially for editing a macro (Microsoft 1993).

A design decision is normally taken by a system designer before a system is delivered to its users and is an integral part of the delivered system. These decisions are about the functionality of a system, as well as its inputs and outputs. In systems development methodologies, these decisions are made by the systems designer. A prerequisite of tailorable information systems is that such design decisions be deferred to users to make whilst using a system in a particular organisational setting. So a central feature of systems' tailorability is deferring design decisions to users.

13.2.1   The Concept of Tailorability

Deferring design decisions to a user requires user controllable mechanisms. A tentative theoretical framework of tailorability is now offered which should enable building deferred design decisions into a computer system. A framework is a useful research device for gaining understanding of the research problem. It provides a shorthand language for describing relations and highlighting important and non-important dimensions (Booth 1992). Moreover, it provides a language for describing important elements of the research (Treacy 1986). Further research is required to operationalise the concepts presented here, research which will aid in designing and developing tailorable information systems.

The concept of tailorable information systems can be analysed into its constituent parts of user control, usability, interface, functionality and variability. The relative importance of the constituent parts of the framework has, on the whole, yet to be determined and so is the question of how to operationalise the concepts. Some empirical work was conducted to research the need for tailorable information system, specifically the hypothesis that information systems need to be responsive to changes in organisational tasks was investigated. Amongst other things, the evidence from the two commercial companies and two higher education institutions shows that users perceive their interfaces to be weakly adaptable to changes in their organisational tasks.

These constituents or attributes of tailorability require closer empirical scrutiny to gain a better understanding of the pragmatics and theory of tailorable information systems. It is also necessary to theoretically and empirically understand their inter-relationships. Such empirical study may reveal other attributes of tailorability which are currently not accounted for in the framework.

Figure 13.1 shows the major components of a tailorable system: its interface and functionality. By providing control to the user over these, the computer system aspects, such as dialogue for the interface and input for the functionality, can be adapted by the user to suit particular needs. The hierarchy is a valuable conceptual form of analysing the concept of tailorability. At its top is the concept itself; an idea seeking a realisation. The subsequent levels are attempts to move towards that realisation, until the bottom level is reached, where the concept acquires a practical application in the form of tailoring technology and tools.

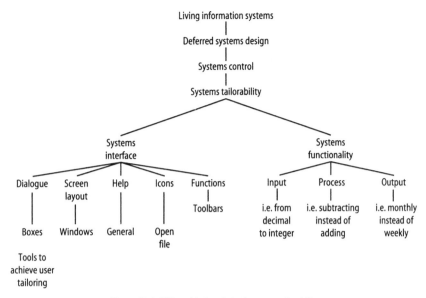

Figure 13.1. A hierarchical analysis of systems tailorability.

13.2.2   User Control

A computer system is tailorable if it provides a user with control over its operation. This means a user should be able to regulate or operate the system, thus providing ultimate power to direct or manipulate a system's behaviour. Humans are rational beings who will attempt to control their environments to achieve specific objectives. Present computer systems are not designed for rational humans and provide very little control to a user. Tailorable information systems are suitable for rational human behaviour. Fully automatic adaptive systems, because they remove control from the user, are not suitable and often result in dysfunctional behaviours (Robertson *et al.* 1991).

Tailorability can be defined with reference to the degree of user control available and the nature of that control over a computer system. A tailorable system would be built on the assumption of providing controllability to a user. A control is understood to be a device or interface widget that enables a user to regulate or operate a system, and provides the user with the power to direct or determine its state. The degree of control provided in a system determines its tailorability. Systems built using the fixed-point theorem do not provide controllability to a user and in this sense they are predetermined, automatic systems lacking the attribute of user control over operation. Such systems are unresponsive to their environments of which, it could be argued, a user is one facet, and unresponsive systems are destined to succumb to entropy.

It is postulated that there exists a direct correlation between the control that a user is provided with via an interface for a given system and the tailorability of that system's functionality. Control being the independent variable, and functionality the dependent variable. This is graphically depicted in Figure 13.2.

In living information systems thinking (LIST), human rationality is central to thinking of information systems as living entities. The fact that humans are potentially rational beings is thus fundamental to the notion of tailorable information systems, which

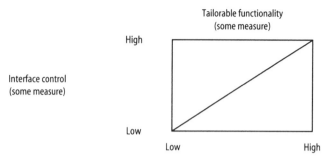

Figure 13.2. The relationship between an interface and systems functionality.

is founded on LIST. A necessary condition of human rationality is the need to be able to exercise control over things. It is thus necessary to provide users with interface widgets that enable them to control the systems they use, these are referred to as tailoring tools, or Ttools, and are the basis of tailoring technology. Thus, computer systems built to support organisational tasks also need to be controllable.

13.2.3 Classifying Computer Systems Along the Control Dimension

Computer-based information systems can be classified using control as a dimension. Where a user has little or no control, such systems are fully automatic, they may even be adaptable, but they are automatically adapting with no control by the user. Where users have greater control, such systems are tailorable, precisely because a user has direct control over the system. (As discussed earlier, user control over trivial aspects of interface aesthetics does not equal tailorability). This is graphically illustrated in Figure 13.3.

It is a necessary feature, but not sufficient, to provide the required control over a system to a user in order to deliver tailorable information systems which move beyond the fixed-point theorem. However the features of a system that should be provided for users to control will vary from application to application. For instance, the controls provided in an inventory system would be different from those provided for a financial system (Essinger 1991). How should the controllable features be determined is also a pertinent question which is discussed later.

13.3 Functionality

A second critical dimension of tailorability is system's functionality. Functionality too can be used to define whether a system is tailorable. Permitting a user to cus-

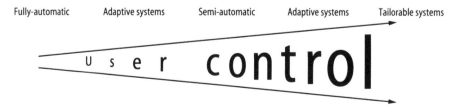

Figure 13.3. The span of user control over information systems.

tomise a system alone does not mean a tailorable system has been delivered. A truly tailorable system is one that can have its functionality altered by a user. When information systems built on the basis of the fixed-point theorem are delivered, often users subsequently require alterations to the provided functionality. Such alterations are dealt with by maintenance programmers, and although this work is referred to as maintenance, it is in fact a powerful indication of users' tailoring requirements.

A system's functionality is its ability to take inputs and process them to provide required outputs. Information systems delivered within the fixed-point theorem paradigm do not permit changes to this functionality by the user. The inputs, processing and outputs in such systems are rigid, and, as indicated above, are only alterable via maintenance programmers.

The functionality of a tailorable information system should be alterable by its user or it can be argued that functionality should be controllable by users. This can be termed 'internal tailorability'. The constituents of functionality are: input, processing and outputs. The ability to change a given input format of a delivered system is an example of a tailoring activity, as is changing the format of its outputs (see Figure 13.1). Tailoring inputs and outputs may be relatively simple to provide, but providing tailorable processing may be difficult to achieve. Although logically, tailorable inputs and outputs imply that processing is tailored too.

The question of determining what aspects of a system's functionality should be tailorable can be addressed by identifying junctures of required tailorability in a given information system. Junctures of tailorability can be defined with reference to data flow diagrams (DFD). A system's DFD shows the movement of data amongst its various processes. Each process receives data, processes them and, if required, sends them to the next process. It is often at these points that a delivered system has to be reprogrammed by maintenance programmers.

Another facet of a system's functionality is data communications. As shown above, a system is internally tailorable when its inputs, outputs and processing can be altered by a user. Such a system is inter-systems tailorable when its outputs can be communicated to other users or systems, and when these users can in turn tailor the received inputs in their various applications. Rank Xerox's Buttons technology is a case in point (Maclean *et al.* 1990). Inter-systems tailorability can be across various hardware and software platforms; from mainframes to micro-computers or workstations, or between micro-computers and workstations, or even on a network.

13.3.1 Variability

How much tailorability should be provided in an information system? To assess this issue it is necessary to somehow determine what a system's variability level is. It may be hypothesised that the degree of tailorability required in a system is directly dependent on the degree of variability in that system and its environment.

The variability of a system is the level of change that occurs in that system's operations. This reflects the various dimensions of variability. First, users' information needs vary over time and across organisational tasks. Second, the frequency of use of the system varies. Thirdly, there is also variation in the quantity of information required by users.

Decision making is an example of a variant in a system. A user's decision needs may change as the business processes change, and the outputs from an existing information system may not be relevant. An example of a system's environmental variability is changes in economic or governmental regulations. Tailorability is required at both these points of variability.

13.4   Usability

The usability of a system is a measure of the user's ability to achieve specific goals relating to the system. It measures a business system's effectiveness, efficiency, learnability, flexibility and user attitude (Davies 1992). To design tailorable information systems issues regarding usability need to be addressed. These issues concern both the design process and evaluating the designed system.

Just as the ability to exert control over a system is an important assumption and a prerequisite of tailorable information systems, the ability to use that control is equally important. Tailorable information systems should be usable. Issues regarding usability are now an accepted part of computer systems development (Nielson 1993). Such issues become more pertinent when designing tailorable information systems for business users whose time is a scarce resource.

13.4.1   Interface

The importance of a user interface in a tailorable system cannot be overstated. An interface is the medium through which a user can operate a given computer system. It therefore needs to be clear, informative and usable. An interface also provides a user with a model of the computer system's functionality. Major systems delivered within the fixed-point paradigm have failed because of poorly designed user interfaces. Such interfaces are developed as non-distinct features of the developed system's functionality. A better design option is to use user interface management systems (UIMS) which provide the flexibility of appraising an interface design and testing it empirically with users of the system before making it a feature of the delivered system (Easterby 1987). Trillium is a developers' tool for designing interfaces which can be appraised before becoming a permanent feature of a system. Trillium itself has tailorability built into it which makes it a powerful UIMS (Henderson 1986).

Computer systems have progressed from command interfaces through menu interfaces to graphical user interfaces (GUIs). This progression has seen a commensurate increase in the operability of delivered systems. Interfaces for tailorable information systems need to be GUI based.

The interface of a system manipulates the dialogue between the user and the system being operated. It also provides a help facility and is a critical determinant of a system's overall tailorability. It is postulated that there exists a direct correlation between the tailorability of an interface for a given system and the tailorability of that system's functionality. There is a direct hypothesised correlation between the tailorability of a system's functionality and the tailorability of its interface. The latter being the independent variable, and the former the dependent variable.

Table 13.1 shows types of interfaces that have been used to allow users to interact with a computer system. The amount of control the interfaces allow has increased over time. Command-based interfaces are very weak because they do not provide much real control in a user's hands and also require much memorisation by the user. The most commonly used interfaces now are direct manipulation types. These interfaces make use of metaphors and objects which can be manipulated by a user to decrease the burden on a user's memory. Tailorable computer systems would have to use direct manipulation interfaces because of their intrinsic operability and usability.

Table 13.1. The evolution of computer systems' interfaces

Type of interface	Hardware environment	Tailorability	Reason for use	Extra attributes	Adaptable
Command	Micro-computer; mainframe	Yes, through DOS, but complex	Historical precedent	–	No
Yes/no	Micro-computer	No	User	–	No
Form filling	Micro-computer; mainframe	No	Prevent user errors	–	No
Menu	Micro-computer		User-friendly	–	No
Direct manipulation	Micro-computer, workstations	Yes	Decreases memory load on user	1. Graphical reasoning 2. Graphical	No
Demonstrational	Micro-computer; workstations	–	–	Affordance	Yes

13.5   Further Research and Conclusions

It is necessary to operationalise the identified conceptual attributes or framework of a system's tailorability to enable empirical investigation. The current research into tailorable information systems will be progressed by:

1. Further efforts to deeply understand the concept of tailorability and its business validity.
2. Investigation of the tailorability needs of users.

This will be achieved by investigating means of operationalising the identified attributes of tailorability for the purpose of empirical research.

The intention of the present research effort is to provide empirical evidence for tailorable information systems and to use the data collected to inform the specification, design and development of tailorable information systems.

Present research is concentrated on specifying tailorable systems architectures for tailorable information systems. This work is being done in conjunction with the Department of Informatics at the University of Athens. Early research shows that there are existing technologies, particularly objected-oriented systems design and object-based graphical users interfaces, which can be used to objectify the notion of tailorable information systems.

Research into suitable systems analysis techniques for tailorable information systems is also underway at the Centre for living information systems thinking (LIST) at Brunel University's Department of Information Systems and Computing. A prototypical tool called 'Living Information Systems Analysis (LISA)' is being developed using hypermedia technology, which has been used previously for flexible systems development (Gardner and Paul 1994).

It has been argued in this paper that information systems research and development needs to make a paradigmatic shift away from the fixed-point theorem of information towards the design of tailorable information systems. The concept and attributes of tailorability identified thus far have been expounded in the form of a theoretical framework which can be utilised for further research.

References

Booth, P (1992) *An Introduction to Human–Computer Interaction.* London: LEA.

Davies, WS (1992) *Operating Systems, A Systematic View.* New York: Benjamin Cummings.

Dewan, P and Choudhary, R (1991) Flexible user interface coupling in a collaborative system. In *Reaching Through Technology.* Robertson, SP et al. (Eds). *Proceedings of CHI '91,* New Orleans, LA.

Easterby, R (1987) Trillium: an interface design prototyping tool. *Information and Software Technology,* **29**(4): 207–213.

Essinger, J and Rosen, J (1991) *Using Technology for Risk Management.* London: Woodhead Faulkner.

Gardner, LA and Paul, RJ (1994) A fully integrated environment for layered development in information systems. *International Journal of Information Management,* **14**: 437–482.

Henderson, DA (1986) The Trillium user interface design environment. In Mantei, M and Orbeton, P (Eds). *Proceedings of CHI '86.* Amsterdam: North Holland. April: 221–227.

Hesketh, RL (1992) *User Interface Development and Tailoring Tools.* Unpublished PhD thesis, Computing Science Department, University of Kent at Canterbury.

Maclean, A, Carter, K, Lovstrand, L and Moran, T. (1990) User-tailorable systems: pressing the issue with Buttons, ACM. *SIGCHI Bulletin,* Special Issue: 175–182.

Microsoft (1993) *Visual Basic User's Guide, Microsoft Excel Version 5.0.* Microsoft Corporation.

Mouakket, S, Sillince, AA and Fretwell-Downing, FA (1994) Information requirements determination in the software industry: a case study. *European Journal of Information Systems,* 3(2): 101–111.

Nielson, J (1993) *Usability Engineering.* London: Academic Press.

Paul, RJ (1993) Dead paradigms for living systems. In *Proceedings of the First European Conference on Information Systems.* Whitley, E (Ed.). Henley: Operational Research Society: 250–255.

Paul, RJ (1994) *Computer Science: A Model Perspective.* Professorial Inaugural Lecture, Department of Information Systems and Computing, Brunel University.

Powers, RF and Dickson, GW (1973) MIS project management: myths, opinions, and reality. *California Management Review,* 15(3): 147–156.

Robertson, SP, Olson, GM and Olson, JS (Eds) (1991) *Reaching Through Technology.* CHI 1991, Conference Proceedings, New Orleans, LA.

Treacy, ME (1986) *Toward a Cumulative Tradition of Research as a Strategic Business Factor.* Centre for Information Systems Research MIT, Sloan WP No. 1772-86, CIRS WP No.134 (WP).

Trimmer, D (1993) *Downsizing.* London: Addison-Wesley.

Watts, S (1992) Of mammon and the machines he employs. *The Independent on Sunday,* 8 November, London.

14 The Retail Industry and Information Technology

David Shaw and Anne Leeming

Abstract

As markets enlarge and become more complex, the once simple process of retailing is employing ever more sophisticated and intelligent retail information systems to cope with all the transactions involved. With the increasing globalisation of retailing, more efficient control of data, information and market knowledge is key to retaining competitive advantage. How effectively retailers strategically invest in and exploit retail information management is reviewed through case studies in the United States and the UK. We review existing models of retail information management which are rapidly being overtaken by continual technological innovation. The concept of the holistic retail information management system, in which all the essential information systems work in unison, appears to be several years away. The existence of the retail supply chain is under threat as information technology (IT), in the form of the Internet, challenges the basic premise of the physical existence of shops and sales staff. Findings are that IT is revolutionising, as well as adding value to, modern retailing. Retail information management is a top investment area for IT. Its benefits for the customer, currently poor in time although rich in cash, include the provision of time.

14.1 Purpose of this Chapter

The aim of this chapter is to critically examine the current use of retail information technology (RIT) by the UK's retail industry, to review how effectively fashion retailers, in particular, are utilising information technologies (IT) and information systems (IS) available to them. The speed of change within fashion retailing makes the way this area uses IT to support its operations of special interest.

This chapter also aims to review the increasing uses of IT in retailing. As the number of applications of IT expand exponentially, it is becoming clear that many retail organisations are suffering from 'data deluge'. The large volumes of data and information are becoming too complex for decision-making purposes.

New ways of coping with the data deluge using the newly named "detect and alert" systems are being developed. These help the increasingly complex work of the retail planner to spot trends and relationships within increasingly complex and volatile fashion offers. However, despite these advances, it would appear that retail organisational structures and practices are not keeping up with the speed of technological innovation. This chapter examines current organisational models and suggests alternatives to help use data more effectively. IT is increasingly having to traverse and underpin the supply chain to improve the interface between the supplier and the consumer. The retailer is rapidly becoming an information broker between the two key players: the supplier and the customer.

Retailers are now trying to use innovative IT applications as a source of competitive advantage, with variable success. These innovations are discussed and the chapter concludes by reviewing the future for technologically assisted vs conventional shopping.

14.2 Background

Since early times, shopkeepers have eventually adopted technologies which make their job easier. Originally scales, then cash registers, helped to control retailing transactions; to increase profitability for the retailer. By the early 1970s large retailers were using mainframe technology to control their businesses better; but, more importantly, to gain a competitive advantage.

The aim of IT in retail is to draw together data quickly enough to enable the decision-making process to be carried out effectively. The first applications of IT in retail were used to control stock and money more effectively. This phase is now completed. The development of technologies, such as Electronic Data Interchange (EDI), Electronic Point of Sale (EPOS) and Electronic Fund Transfer at Point of Sale (EFT-POS), has increased the process of data and information distribution. As markets become more competitive and fragmented, retailers are having to revisit the way in which they are using IT.

The supply chain is having to respond to change much more rapidly, and new developments and usage of EDI are well reported. There are many new areas that require integration and acceptance into Retail Information Systems (RIS). Undoubtedly, many subsidiary support systems, many based on PC technology, now fall under the generic name of the RIS. Space planning, store modelling and staff scheduling are good examples. The problem presented to retailers is how to integrate all this information into the decision-making process.

Recognition of this need is now understood, but due to data deluge the task of integrating systems and management structures has a new urgency. Actionable and understandable information is the one necessity to deal with the complexities facing the modern retailer. This speed of change, combined with the desire to obtain and maintain a strategic competitive edge, has long interested academics. Cash *et al.* (1992) examined the strategic impact of IT across different types of business. However, such simple models and matrices make little reference to the business strategies used, and the time scales and disruptions caused. The issues facing senior executives undergoing strategic IT change may have similarities, but retailing is overtaking banks and airlines in IT usage.

The reason for this has resulted from a combination of three factors.

1. The increasingly more complex retail IT applications and the vast amount of information that they generate.
2. The increasingly competitive retail environment, which has resulted in retailers turning once again towards the need to improve their processing of data and information more effectively.
3. The increasingly more complex and small-scale markets that have evolved within the fashion industry and the need to satisfy consumer demands more effectively. These we have called "micro-markets".

While there are many academic models concerning IT and business strategy related to retailing, in practice it is unclear that such a logical and strategic approach to the management of retail information systems is being utilised (Beaumont & Walters 1991). The lack of strategic use of IT in retailing was revealed in a study commissioned by Hewlett-Packard UK in 1992 and carried out by the British Market Research Bureau among 50 key clients, see Table 14.1.

The results in Table 14.1 indicate that only 10% of retail companies questioned had any formal IT strategy. Comparing this with the rise in concern among the senior IT executives, who participated in the Price Waterhouse survey, about the alignment of their IT strategies with corporate plans; we see how retailing lags behind other industries. (Grindley 1994). The investment into IT in retail and IS has been intensive over the past 20 years and rather unstructured. In Table 14.2 we see that the investment in retail IT is higher than IT investment in other commercial sectors.

In fashion retailing during the 1970s and 1980s, many large retailers such as the Burton Group and Sears, and particularly the British Shoe Corporation, invested heavily in IT, to gain better stock control and to rationalise ranges. This led to market domination in their respective sectors. Such successful applications of retail IT often go unrecorded in retailing, reducing the chance for performance assessment.

Increase in company size, turnover, profitability and market penetration were, and still are, the critical measures indicating the benefits of IT application. With the continually decreasing costs of technology, and increase in processing power, any competitive advantage derived from these in-house systems no longer became sustainable due to the development of many small packaged stock management systems developed during the late 1980s and early 1990s. IT was no longer the sole prerogative of large-scale retailers; small retailers were now able to use IT as a competitive strategy. UK fashion retailing is a mature industry and highly competitive; future success is likely to be derived by encroaching upon competitors' market share and by the more creative application of innovative information technologies. The vast historical investment in retail IT has left many retailers with large monolithic systems; many of which are now unsuitable for open systems applications.

Table 14.1. Companies with a long term IT strategy (Hewlett-Packard 1992)

	Manufacturing	Retail	Government/Public	Finance/Banking	Telecommunications
	%	%	%	%	%
Yes	30	10	30	30	30
No	30	60	50	30	50
Don't know	40	30	20	40	20

Table 14.2. Estimated annual IT spending of top 50 UK companies in 1994 (Corporate IT Strategy Magazine 1995)

	Annual turnover (£ million)	IT spending (£ million)	(%)
Retail sector (12 companies)	53 178	1098	2.06
Others (38 companies)	266 994	4392	1.64
Grand total	320 172	5490	1.71

14.3 Wal-Mart: A Brief Case Study in IT Strategy and Impact

Of all retail information strategists, probably the best known is Sam Walton of Wal-Mart, whose company has become the fastest growing retailer in the United States. As the classic retail IT case study, Wal-Mart has been well documented. As far back as 1966, Sam Walton enrolled himself in an IBM school for retailers. Walton believed that technology could help his business in three key areas:

1. distribution of stock;
2. supplier relationships;
3. management information systems/internal communications.

With currently 400 000 employees, 40 million customers each week and a 1995 turnover likely to be in excess of $50 billion, Wal-Mart stands as a shining example of the early strategic use of retail IT. In 1987 when Sam Walton forged supplier relationships, such thinking was revolutionary. Today his control of the supply chain and his mastery of quick response supply has pushed him to world number one in terms of growth and size. Wal-Mart has the largest privately owned satellite system and civilian database in the world. Using dedicated high-speed communication systems, together with 19 proprietary retail software packages, has made Wal-Mart the largest user of retail software packages in the world. Sam Walton's IS strategy has always been to use packages in preference to bespoke software. Never in retail history has so much IT investment been made to such a successful end (Discount Store News 1994).

Academic models in information management and IT investment abound, but the validity of some of these models needs to be reappraised, as new market situations and new technologies have altered the original premise upon which the models were based. We will also review some of the leading edge developments and issues that are likely to affect fashion retailers and their IT/IS requirements by the turn of the century.

14.4 The role of IT/IS in Helping the Retail Industry Meet its Objectives

Retailing is now a major contributor to the economic well being of Great Britain, with 40% of consumer expenditure, £282.6 billion in 1994, being spent in retail outlets. It is estimated that this year alone will see £20 billion spent on men's, women's and children's clothing in the UK (Mintel 1994) With such large sums involved, the effective use of retail IT becomes very significant to the economy.

Despite the current unclear economic conditions; parts of UK fashion retailing continue to perform reasonably well; with companies such as Marks & Spencer, NEXT and River Island increasing their market share annually (Textile Market Surveys 1995). There are successful new entrants such as Oasis and New Look, where the effective use of IT has been crucial to their growth. The fragmented nature of the UK fashion industry, the top five players having only 40% of the market, indicates the opportunity for new comers to gain market share. It is now possible for small retailers as new entrants to use affordable and innovative IT applications to their advantage; especially when there are no legacy systems to act as a barrier to

IT innovation. Britain as a nation, has an excellent track record in retailing, with no less than 12 companies in the top 30 European retailers turnover league (OXIRM 1995). Comparing return on assets in 1993–1994 (OXIRM 1995), Britain had 14 out of the top 30 (Management Horizons 1992). British retailers excel in terms of most financial performance indicators. British retailing must be uniquely placed to consider global expansion.

There have been several comparative analyses concerning the use of IT within retailing; many of which have tried to organise and analyse the functional aspects of retail information. Regrettably, these have quickly dated in view of the speed of development within retail IT (Murra 1991). The greatest spur to the majority of retail system investment has been the goal of cost and productivity benefit. Each differing technology seems to have a subsidiary objective, e.g. EDI was seen as a good way to "reconfigure the supply chain" (Bamfield 1994). New management objectives and vogues can also act a spur to IT developments throughout retailing, e.g. customer loyalty cards from Tesco in 1994.

Despite the lacklustre level of retail performance since its height at the end of the 1980s and the ensuing 1990s recession; the UK has seen the emergence of many small niche retailers, Sock Shop, Tie Rack, Knicker Box and so on. British consumers no longer accept universal products and brands, they have acquired affluence and more discerning tastes. Today's consumers are more precise and demanding, creating the problem for retailers of supplying a growing number of micro-markets. These can be defined as small, highly targeted, life-style specific and possibly geographically specific market segments; all requiring carefully targeted new products and/or services. There are fashion shops, brands and products to meet virtually any fashion taste. The mass fashion and retail following of the 1950s and 1960s no longer exists. Retailers and manufactures alike are selling less of individual lines now in comparison to 20 years ago. Despite the growth of the fashion market, consumers are buying less per line, from fewer better-run chains of shops. Fashion customers are becoming increasingly more volatile in their shopping habits, tastes and loyalties. The highly competitive nature of fashion retailing combined with the relatively low start-up costs has seen many chains and individual shops go out of business. In today's competitive retail environment, retailers have effectively three alternatives if they are to compete and survive:

1. to diversify into new products;
2. to develop internationally into new markets;
3. to acquire market share from competitors.

The intelligent use of IT/ISs can be used to underpin these options. We now propose to examine current IT usage within UK retailing.

14.5   Maximising Retail Resources by the Use of IT

Stock, staff and space are the three most important resources that a retailer has to optimise. In the market place, complete and accurate control of these is vital to maintaining a competitive stance. The gathering of information in these three key areas is at the heart of any modern RIS; in the past many of the applications and systems utilised have enjoyed varying levels of strategic importance. Many independent and free standing, functionally specific systems such as Geographic Information Systems (GIS) have been developed in isolation without integration to the stock control and financial management systems. Stock control and financial management were originally the key areas of IT/IS development in the early days of retail IT development.

In Figure 14.1 a conceptual view of the information domains requiring monitoring in the retail industry is seen. In Figure 14.1A the theoretically perfect level of integration, balance and synergy is shown; whilst Figure 14.1B shows the probable reality of most large companies' RIS at this time.

Currently, varying levels of control have been achieved in some functions by the development of free-standing IT solutions, which cannot be integrated with older systems. If retailers are to gain more effective control of their businesses, ultimately complete integration and control of all retail IT activity is desirable.

There are several well-known conceptual models of Retail Information Systems, two of which we propose to review briefly, those of Lewinson and Alter. These are based on assumptions which are not clearly stated and which are not relevant to all retail organisations/situations.

Lewison's theoretical model (see Figure 14.2) is still acceptable, but generalises greatly. It talks euphemistically of the "retail decision maker". This title fails to clearly explain the role, title or status of the person at the end of the chain. With mounting levels of data and information flowing around retail systems, it

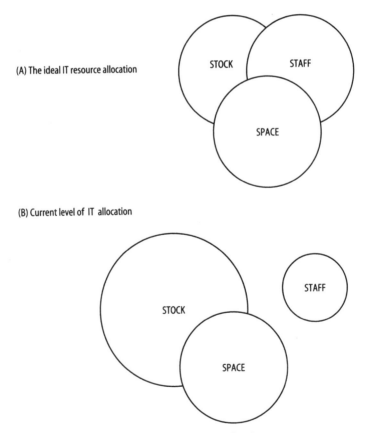

Figure 14.1. Retail IT resource allocation.

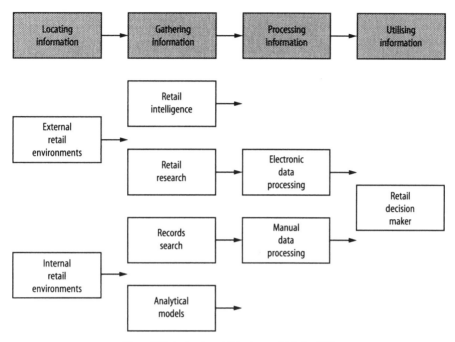

Figure 14.2. Lewison's model (Lewison and Delozier 1989).

would be interesting to speculate in which department of the organisation this super human being would sit, let alone the discipline in which they would have been trained!

More detailed RIS models, such as that of Alter (see Figure 14.3), show a more realistic flow of data and information, but his model focuses strongly upon EPOS and stock control as the most important areas. This 1989 view of a Retail Information System relies upon the enabling technologies and management vogues of the time, i.e. EFTPOS and EPOS, to improve important fashion business processes such as JIT, rather than separating the method of achievement from the goal required.

To overcome some of the deficiencies of Alter's and Lewinson's models we propose a new model which we call a Holistic Retail Information System. Figure 14.4 indicates three clear domains of activity, i.e. supply, operation and marketing. Each domain employs different types of IT activity. Again, we have deliberately shown the central part of the model to be focused on stock and financial management systems, whilst on the left-hand side there are systems connected with suppliers and external financial institutions. On the right-hand side there are the newer areas of customer and micro-marketing-related systems in the marketing domain. The central area of stock and financial management systems has, over the past 5 years, extended backwards along the supply chain and financial domains. This has come about as a direct result of the increasing use and standardisation of EPOS, EFTPOS and EDI; enabling technologies which whilst once revolutionary, are now taken for granted. However, under the marketing systems domain there are many new stand-alone systems, for example customer-centred applications such as loyalty, tracking and interactive shopping systems. It is in this domain of data gathering and information distillation where it is likely that there will be the greatest number of future initiatives.

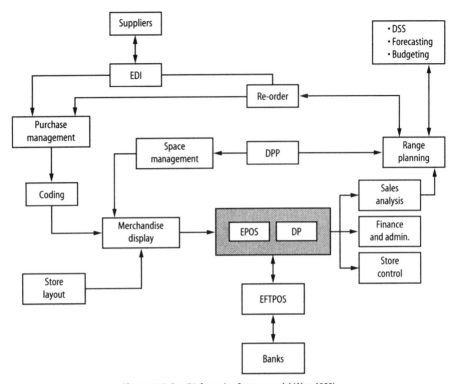

Figure 14.3. Retail Information Systems model (Alter 1989).

14.6   The Continuing Focus on Stock Control and Financial Management Systems in Retailing

It is evident that a great deal of current IT expenditure and investment is still being directed towards the effective control and management of stock levels, and the nature of their content. The highly complex multitransactional nature of high street retailing, combined with its spatial disaggregation, makes effective stock control high on the agenda of most retailers.

As stock management is the focus of most retailers' IT strategy, many are trying to use their stock transaction systems in more creative and intelligent-ways to maximise customer purchasing and loyalty. The old maxim of having the right stock in the right place at the right time is still an elusive objective for many large retailers. For the fashion retailers as opposed to food retailers; there are few staple and continuous products, e.g. sugar, tea, etc. The rapidly changing inventory of the fashion retailer combined with the much wider and multifarious purchasing decisions faced by the consumer is shown in Figure 14.5. There are 16 variables shown related to the fashion purchasing decision – this means that there are at least 65 536 decision options facing the consumer! Undoubtedly the decision numbers are greater, when considering that fashion decisions often defy simple yes/no logic. Many fashion decisions are scaled!

Fashion retailers, with complex offerings, often find it difficult to maintain high levels of stock availability at all times. Some may argue against this, in view of the

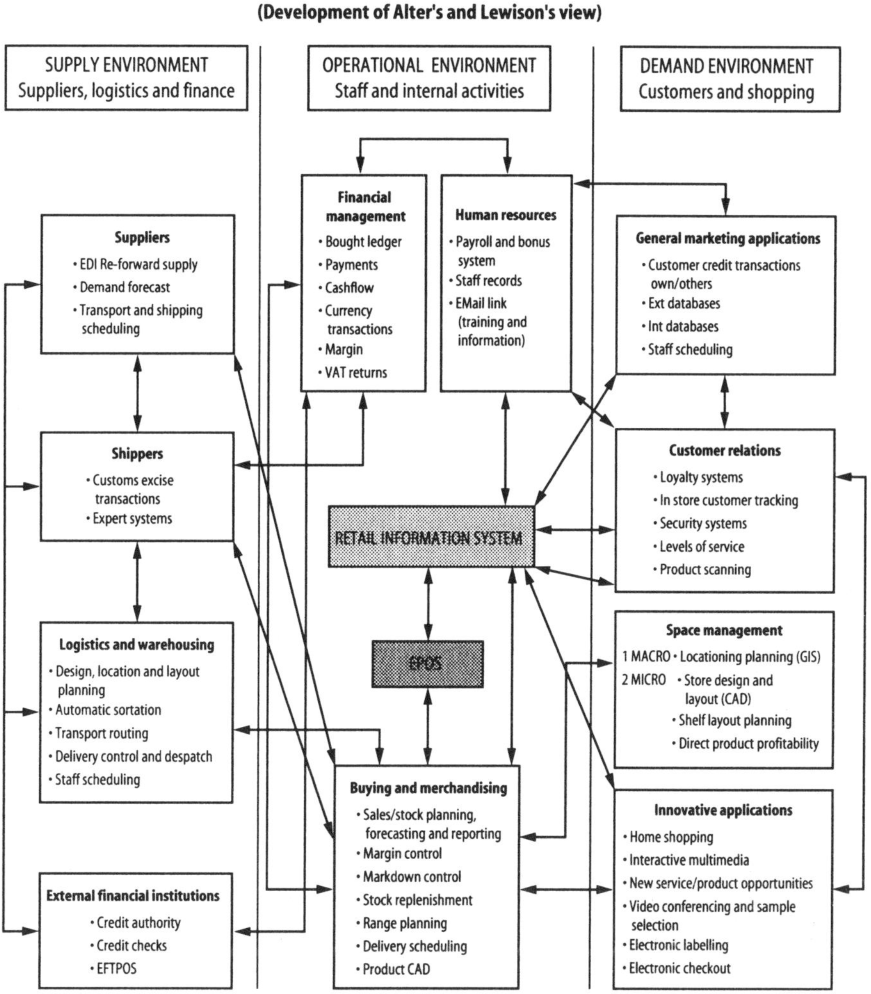

(Development of Alter's and Lewison's view)

SUPPLY ENVIRONMENT Suppliers, logistics and finance	OPERATIONAL ENVIRONMENT Staff and internal activities	DEMAND ENVIRONMENT Customers and shopping

Suppliers
- EDI Re-forward supply
- Demand forecast
- Transport and shipping scheduling

Shippers
- Customs excise transactions
- Expert systems

Logistics and warehousing
- Design, location and layout planning
- Automatic sortation
- Transport routing
- Delivery control and despatch
- Staff scheduling

External financial institutions
- Credit authority
- Credit checks
- EFTPOS

Financial management
- Bought ledger
- Payments
- Cashflow
- Currency transactions
- Margin
- VAT returns

Human resources
- Payroll and bonus system
- Staff records
- EMail link (training and information)

RETAIL INFORMATION SYSTEM

EPOS

Buying and merchandising
- Sales/stock planning, forecasting and reporting
- Margin control
- Markdown control
- Stock replenishment
- Range planning
- Delivery scheduling
- Product CAD

General marketing applications
- Customer credit transactions own/others
- Ext databases
- Int databases
- Staff scheduling

Customer relations
- Loyalty systems
- In store customer tracking
- Security systems
- Levels of service
- Product scanning

Space management
1 MACRO · Locationing planning (GIS)
2 MICRO · Store design and layout (CAD)
· Shelf layout planning
· Direct product profitability

Innovative applications
- Home shopping
- Interactive multimedia
- New service/product opportunities
- Video conferencing and sample selection
- Electronic labelling
- Electronic checkout

Figure 14.4. The Holistic Retail Information System.

oft quoted Pareto analysis that gives 80% of the sales from 20% of the stock. The Pareto analysis may hold a clue as to how poorly retailers are managing to maintain stock profiles to meet customers' demands. In-stock availability levels are a critical retail success factor, yet interestingly in-stock levels are rarely monitored and recorded. Retailers have always been more interested in what sales they have taken, rather than in the sales that they have missed (Hill 1992).

It is now clear that the use of basic automated stock control management systems is inadequate for today's fast changing and competitive retail environment. Sound forecasting is based upon clearly perceived trends. Some practitioners believe that forecasting may no longer be a worthwhile pastime; favouring a quick replenishment approach instead. Retailers and systems designers are now seeking outputs from stock control systems that are far more useful. Retailers still put the highest emphasis on IT investment into stock control and financial management systems, in

= 65,536 alternatives

Figure 14.5. The complexity of fashion purchasing decision making.

preference to staff and space control systems. They do not seem to have assessed whether systems to bring about more effective staff and space deployment would create greater competitive advantage.

14.7   New Tools to Help Manage Retail Information

Currently, simple stock control and management systems are moving towards more 'intelligent' Executive Information Systems, with a much higher emphasis on sophisticated forward planning. Such software innovation includes the proprietary names of Commander/Arthur Planning by Comshare and PlanIT by Multime/IBM. These systems act as a multiple tool kit for merchandise planning, range planning, and the allocation and replenishment of stock. Using an SQL database (e.g. Informix and Oracle), these powerful tools help to improve the accuracy of planning, control and support of decision making for the complex stock flows related to fashion retailing. These large-scale planning systems work well for large retailers, but there is also a range of smaller less powerful planning and control tools for the independent and smaller retail chains, e.g. Fashion Support, Radius and Prism by Pennine. The great majority of these contain their own financial planning and management systems, or integrate easily with other such systems. Primarily their function being to provide a platform with which to view easily the Retail Cube of product, location and time. This cube demonstrates the key merchandise planning parameters and their complexities (Figure 14.6).

Powerful planning tools such as Arthur and PlanIT, rebranded as MAKORO in 1997, have a 'slice and dice' facility to allow the drawing together or gap analysis of plans in different dimensions. Both are based upon an open client server architecture, enabling the high volume of, and intensive calculations related to, detailed panning (or sometimes called 'micro-planning') at both product and branch level.

A particular problem arising from the development of planning and modelling tools for stock planning and management is that their powerful 'what if' capabilities produce vast quantities of data, often leading to information overload. The prob-

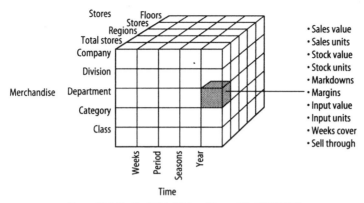

Figure 14.6. The PlanIT Retail Cube – 'Slice and Dice' (IBM 1995).

lem of 'data deluge', as it is popularly becoming known, is fast becoming the key issue facing retail IT departments. Combine this factor with downsizing and particularly the loss of 'grey management' (who had greater numeracy skills than their younger replacements), retailers are finding themselves facing an information Armageddon. So much information is now available that it is becoming almost impossible to decide on a clear course of action.

Decision Support Systems (DSSs) are being seen as the immediate answer, but unfortunately the constantly fluctuating patterns of the fashion trade make it almost impossible to create sets of intelligent business rules that can be used for any reasonable length of time. Data in business reputedly doubles every 2 years, but yet only 5% of it is acted upon. "If you can't or haven't got time to decide – don't capture it" must be the message.

To aid the current data overload, the development of data warehousing and data mining are at the forefront of retail systems designers. Data warehousing is the development of one or more consolidated databases from a multitude of stand-alone or partially integrated applications . Such stand-alone applications are clearly seen on the holistic RIS shown above. Data warehousing makes far greater analysis of customer and product purchasing patterns possible. For efficient consumer response, it is vital to have an efficient information response (Derr 1995).

The ability to slice and dice information from almost any perspective is the retail planners' dream, and to help this process we have seen the development of 'data mining'. It provides tools that help the planner identify where to seek information and trading patterns that were not immediately obvious.

Data mining has been successfully used by the Hertz Corporation to control over 250 000 daily prices. Such a competitive business needed to look deeply into its very competitive pricing structures in detailed way to ensure that it spots crucial trends, patterns and exceptions. Only data mining with detect and alert capabilities could undertake the task (Comshare 95).

To help retailers comprehend and act upon the information contained in data warehouses, 'detect and alert' systems have been created as a result of data mining and data warehousing. The detect and alert capabilities contained within a proprietary system, such as "Arthur" by Comshare, allow the use of software agent's aptly named robots, armed with business rule sets, to change information gathering patterns and allow interpretation paradigms appropriate for the retailer/ merchandise type concerned. These rule sets are built to suit each retailer and merchandise type. These types of agent-based systems will form the next wave of strategic information weapons that enable actionable information to be sorted from the unactionable.

14.8   Is Retail IT Aligned with Business Strategy?

The alignment of retail IT and business strategy has been well documented by Holland and Lockett (1992), and is shown in Figure 14.7. Their research revealed that retail IT strategies pass through three stages – isolation, integration and innovation, more importantly, they saw the need for the existence of a link between technological and organisational structure. In the final innovative stage of their model, they suggested that there is now evidence of the huge potential of information systems in service industries.

ISOLATION	**IT strategy**	**Business strategy**	Time
	Large, complex systems High maintenance costs Many upgrades to hardware and software Heavy reliance on technical staff Continuous change and improvement of existing practices Eventual collapse of system	Traditional data processing Structure Importance of information Technology increases	
	IT change ← →	**Organisational change**	
INTEGRATION	Use of new technologies e.g. fourth generation languages Use of development tools Common data shared between different applications and stored on advanced database IT infrastructure connecting different parts of the organisation together Integration of business functions	Strategy group needed to have major influence on design of new system New systems designed which need project management skills to make them work IT and organisation of work become intertwined Matrix structure for IT management	
	IT change ← →	**Organisational change**	
ISOLATION	Information systems extend outside the organisation Information as a product Novel applications: DSS, EDI, EIS, EFTPOS, database marketing, electronic mail New products and markets Novel delivery mechanisms	Experimentation and creativity to create new products and organisations New skills to support innovative business and technical activities Disintegration of organisational boundaries Common European market Globalisation	

Figure 14.7. Holland and Lockett's (1992) Retail IT Strategy Model.

Retailing organisations should re-assess their business strategies and consider the many opportunities now made possible by IT. They need to have a vision of the future. We propose that their model needs a fourth stage beyond innovation, to where the system is up and running and the retailer has a clear management structure. This fourth stage might be called the "involvement phase", in which both the information systems and the organisational structure are integrated.

As retail information systems are growing in importance so fast, it is vital for retail management to develop effective management structures to manage this new complexity. Retail organisational structures have remained unchanged, whilst IT/ISs have and still are changing dramatically. There is little evidence to suggest that retailers are grasping the need to rethink and restructure the historic roles and disciplines that are currently in existence.

A further useful model is that of Venkatraman and Henderson (1989) shown in Figure 14.8. This shows that to reap the full benefits of IT, business reconfiguration is ultimately necessary.

Venkatraman and Henderson's evolutionary stages accord with the Holland and Lockett model. However, it is clear that the latter's innovation stage is rather broad and ill defined. There is a need to encourage retailers to use IT in more revolutionary ways. The move from business process redesign to the business network redesign is the critical hurdle which is not happening quickly enough amongst UK retailers, as in most sectors. The need to identify the restraining factors and to produce clearer organisational methodology to achieve these fundamental shifts is a particular area of interest for my research. The need to clearly understand the restricting factors on management and structural re-alignment to match the increasing complexity of retail systems is vital. There needs to be a clearer understanding of the restraining forces at work.

So often, new retail systems fail to deliver after their initial introduction, usually as a result of a poor implementation process and a failure of management to break down the organisational barriers and preconceptions that have evolved. The historically based approach to retail decision-making processes may be the root cause of the problem. Retailers such as BHS are addressing the organisational issues, although they do appear to be starting to tackle the real problems. BHS have

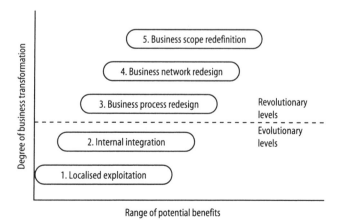

Figure 14.8. IT-induced reconfiguration (Venkatraman and Henderson 1989).

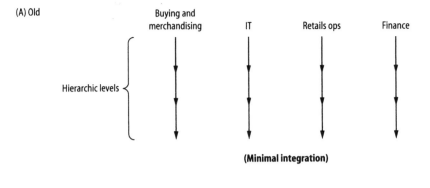

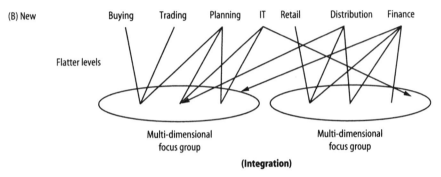

Figure 14.9. New organisational structures at BHS in 1995.

re-aligned their management planning teams into more multifunctional groupings of different disciplines. The hierarchical discipline-based approach to retail information management has started to evolve into a more integrated and multi-disciplined approach (see Figure 14.9).

From Figure 14.9 the development of new Multidimensional Focus Teams, drawn from four different disciplines, can be seen. Originally each team member would have worked under the old hierarchical structure based on the old disciplines. BHS called this their "Breakthrough" initiative and it was aimed at re-aligning business structures with both business and IT strategies. This example appears to be unique; most retailers preferring to retain hierarchical structures based on existing business disciplines. However, this BHS initiative, whilst addressing the structural/IT issues for the buying and merchandising office, has not yet addressed the other areas within the business also employing increasingly sophisticated IT applications. It is our proposition that more wide-ranging changes are needed to keep pace with IT innovation within all retail businesses. It is vital to produce effective models to help retailers break down the isolated functional approach.

As retail information expands and the demands for more integrated systems develop, it is likely that the multidisciplinary nature of the planning and control process within retailing will have to be widened. The old functional barriers of finance, buying and merchandising, and retail operations will need to crumble. The complexity of retail IT and systems is having a major impact on traditional management boundaries.

14.9   The Way Forward

With the emphasis moving towards the front end of the supply chain, hardly a day goes by without the announcement of some new technology to help us shop more efficiently. Soon the local supermarket will be devoid of human form as we place our groceries into a self-scanning trolley, attached to which will be a Mondex smart card swipe device. The doors will be triggered by radio signals and once the transaction has been verified the shopper will be released from retail Limbo and escape from its featureless domain. Customers will ask themselves whether they really need to come to the supermarket.

As traffic congestion builds and the population ages and becomes less mobile; shopping technology is beginning to provide interactive home ordering which is gradually attracting customers. The press reports surrounding initiatives such as QVC semi-interactive TV shopping and other Internet retail trading formats, was, in 1995, 'much ado about nothing'. 'Normal shopping', as understood by marketers, would be impossible due to the attributes of the current user base. For example, in 1995 85% of all Internet users were male and likely to be in management positions This contradicts the once popular imagery of the nerd, complete with anorak, locked away in his bedsit night after night trying to hack into a Pentagon modem. Interactive TV has had a slow start in the UK, and although established in America, where TV viewing is embedded in their way of life more than in the UK, it has not yet rocked traditional methods of retailing. For example, only in 1995 there were one million cable and three million satellite TV subscribers in the UK.

Examples of what is currently available for fashion freaks on the Internet is easier to find today than just a year ago. Many of the well-known high street retailers now have a presence on the Web giving a useful window on their style and their latest offerings geared to the shopping season. At the time of writing it is possible to visit Santa's grotto and shop as well as leave a message. The ability to shop for staple goods, such as food, and technically specified or known items is, at the time of writing, already feasible. Many cannot think of anything better than having the weekly groceries delivered, having sent the order ahead by e-mail or telephone. American initiatives in this field are proving very successful and the British have started. Despite scepticism of widespread interactive home shopping using current technology, it would be foolish to rule it out as technologies such as multimedia and 3D television/video on demand develop. Such improvements and innovations may make all products desirable. Evidence that large numbers of purchases are made from the pages of mail order catalogues suggests that it is quite possible to sell from the cathode-ray tube or its successor.

However, at the conventional front end of retailing, RISs are starting to improve customer service dramatically. Supermarket checkout queues could be a thing of the past due to store traffic monitoring systems. Stores can be adequately staffed at key times by using staff scheduling information systems. Even transaction speeds are getting faster. General levels of stock availability are improving, and targeting of marketing communications to customers is becoming more precise. More and more technology, helped by massive parallel processing, data mining and the extensive use of data warehousing, will enable the retailer to know more about individual shopping habits. This can help reduce shopping time for routine essentials, leaving the individual more time to shop for the more exciting things in life. Despite fear of unemployment, those in work are working harder than ever before and we are all becoming time paupers. Time is the new commodity that retailers can provide as a direct effect of good exploitation of IT.

Retailers must get better at managing information. In the words of Oliver Cromwell – "He who stops getting better, stops being good".

References

Alter, M (1989) *The UK Technology Market.* Business International Economist Intelligence Unit Ltd. 15 Regent Street, London SW1Y 4LR (http://www.eiu.com).

Bamfield, J (1994) The adoption of Electronic Data Interchange (EDI) by retailers. *International Journal of Retail and Distribution Management,* 22(2): 3–11.

Beaumont, JR and Walters, D (1991) Information management in service industries: towards a strategic framework. *Journal of Information Systems,* 1: 155–172.

Cash, J, McFarlan, F and McKenny, J (1992) *Corporate Information Systems Management – The Issues Facing Senior Executives* (3rd edition). Irwin: 17–26.

Comshare (1995) Communiqué 1.

Corporate IT Strategy Magazine (1995) Top 100 companies – review. *Corporate IT Strategy Magazine,* May.

Derr, R (1995) Efficient Consumer response requires efficient information response. *European Retail Digest,* Spring: 4–5

Discount Store News (1994) Logistical supremacy secures the base for Wal-Mart. *Discount Store News,* 5 December: 107–108

Grindley, K (1994) *Major Issues IT Review.* Price Waterhouse: 8.

Hewlett-Packard (1992) *Managers Concerns over IT and Open Systems Report.* The British Market Research Bureau: 1–17.

Hill, RM (1990) Measuring stock service levels. *International Journal of Retail and Distribution Management,* 18: 3.

Holland, CP and Lockett, G (1992) IT strategy in retailing: organisational change and future direction. *Journal of Strategic Information Systems,* 1(3): 134–142.

IBM (1995) *Plant IT Promotional Literature.* IBM.

Lewison, DM and Delozier, MW (1989) *Retailing* (3rd edition). Columbus, OH: Merril Publishing.

Management Horizons (1992) *International Retail Survey.*

Mintel (1994) *UK Clothing and Footwear Market Review.*

Murra, EF (1991) *Comparative Analysis of the Retailing Sector: Information Use and Systems.* M.Sc. thesis, London School of Economics.

OXIRM (1994) *Review of European Retailing.* Oxford: Oxford Institute of Retail Management.

Textile Market Surveys (1995) Market shares in retail clothing sector. *The Times,* 20 April.

Venkatraman, N and Henderson, JC (1989) *Strategic Alignment: A Framework for Strategic Information Technology Management.* MIT Management in the '90s Working Paper 89-076.

15 Information Systems at the Superstore Interface

Brian J. O'Connor

Abstract

This paper is written from the users' point of view. It describes how a company is pulling ahead of its competitors by using information systems focused on processes at the customer interface.

The company's objective is to support the retail customer better than any competitor.

The manufacturer has built his business by offering a 7-day delivery response to superstores through heavy investment in design and manufacturing.

He is increasingly looking to information technology to bolster market share in three specific ways:

1. point of sales information;
2. sales representatives who use *lap-top computers*;
3. a computer system *which can simulate* the appearance of the customer's home or office with the new product in place whilst still in the superstore.

In addition, the manufacturer is looking for improved ways to support the customer after they leave the superstore with their new product.

15.1   Introduction

This chapter is written from the users' point of view (retail customer, supplier, manufacturer and superstore). It describes how a company is pulling even further ahead of its competitors by using information systems focused on processes at the customer interface.

The company's objective is to support the retail customer better than any competitor from the moment they enter the superstore until the product is installed in their home or office.

The manufacturer has built his business by offering a 7-day delivery response to superstores through heavy investment in design and manufacturing. He is increasingly looking to information technology to bolster market share in three specific ways:

1. point of sales information which is relayed through *EDI* (Electronic Data Interchange) to manufacturing;
2. sales representatives who use *lap-top computers* to ensure that they are well briefed about each superstore at each visit;

3. prior to purchase of the product retail customers *can simulate* the appearance of their home or office with the new product in place using an in-store computer system.

In addition, the manufacturer is looking for improved ways to support the customer after they leaves the superstore with their new product.

For reasons of commercial confidentiality the identity of the companies involved is concealed.

15.2 EDI – The Data Highway Between Retail Customer and Machine Operator

This company is expanding rapidly in terms of annual sales, market share and variety of products offered to this market.

Sales forecasts on a monthly cycle are provided both by the superstores and the manufacturer's own salesmen.

The manufacturing facility is laid out for flexible flow production and is capable of producing large quantities of product at short notice. Prototypes for superstores are produced in days.

However, despite physical flexibility and short lead times in the manufacturing facility, production plans based on monthly sales forecasts have resulted in product staying far too long in the finished goods warehouse. In particular, optimistic sales forecasts for new products have resulted in the build up of excessive stocks.

As superstores qualify their own sales forecasts, with severe warnings about their accuracy, the tendency has been for production to produce their own sales forecasts based on extrapolation from previous periods. The superstores are demanding ever more customer service from suppliers as the number of stores increases and are moving towards *supplier managed inventories* where the manufacturer has full responsibility for ensuring that the product is available and on display when the customer enters the store.

This means that it is more important to improve the accuracy and timeliness of information from the market on which production plans are based.

EDI offers a step forward to improving information flow throughout the supply chain from retail customer to raw material supplier. EDI enables daily information from many hundreds of stores, by superstore, by product type, by price, etc., to be available to manufacturing.

This information by reason of its timeliness has enabled the manufacturer to bring his production plans closer to what retail customers are purchasing.

Using EDI in this way is a recent development in retailing, although it has been used in the automotive industry for many years. When the EDI information first became available in this company comparisons were made with the sales forecasts that had been used to drive production and the actual daily sales. The differences between forecast and actual sales were substantial and the manufacturing team looked to EDI to solve the challenge of inaccurate sales forecasts.

It was recognised that the daily information would provide benefits beyond improved communication in:

- cash flow;
- customer satisfaction;
- process efficiency.

Daily sales figures allow the manufacturer to plan his production lines to be closer to actual sales, thereby reducing costs in terms of inventory, labour (a small percentage of total costs) and transport costs.

In practice, although the EDI information is invaluable, production plans still take into account past experience of orders. In particular, forecasts are still required for intensive sales promotions through direct mail, weekly magazines and local TV, which result in heavy sales during specified weekends.

15.3   Sales Representatives and Lap-top Computers

The hundreds of superstore locations are serviced by representatives of the manufacturer who may be full- or part-time employees.

The objective of lap-top support is that the representative has real-time information available at his or her fingertips about each store. He or she can access data concerning:

- sales year to date to plan;
- shelf location of products;
- shelf layout;
- sales per product in timing, quantity and value;
- sales per promotion;
- comparative data for similar stores in other parts of the country;
- shipments;
- rejects by store and/or customer;

and plan his or her visit accordingly. This enhances the professional approach of the representative and helps them to focus on current opportunities for superstore and manufacturer.

Designed in the form of a checklist this enables every representative, irrespective of his or her personal qualities, to systematically service the stores across the country.

It is intended to take this further by making available an analysis of retail customers by age, sex, marital and social status, etc., when they purchase certain products.

15.4   Simulation of the Product in the Customers' Home

This computer system is located prominently in the superstore product display area and enables retail customers with the assistance of store staff to select combinations of products in the superstore within their budgets and then to simulate their appearance on a computer screen.

Just as product design is an ongoing activity, so the software is under review to 'seduce' the customer. It is customised to emphasise the unique features of the product design including its user-friendly aspects. Software suppliers are in continuous competition to develop improved simulation.

In a competitive situation where a number of manufacturers' products are displayed alongside each other in the store, the supplier with an easy to use simulation is favoured both by store staff and customers.

The resulting design to the customers' specification may be printed out on hard copy, although this is not always advisable as it allows the customer to approach other suppliers for competitive quotations.

Because customers are used to having restaurant bills handled on touch screens (the keyboard is no longer required) it is intended to improve the simulation in the store by means of touch screen. This will make the selection and design of the finished product even more user friendly and eye catching.

15.5   Taking the Systems into the Customers' Home

The above three processes improve customer service prior to purchase. But what can be done once the customer has placed the newly purchased product in his car?

Through customer research it has been determined that customer service can be improved by converting customers' criticisms to positive features of the product. This is under review at this time and will result in further computer support to retail customers.

15.6   Conclusion

High-quality, low-cost manufacturing has brought this company to its current position in a very competitive market, but this is no longer enough. In order to increase market share the manufacturer has to cocoon the customer in quality support.

As shown in Section 15.2, EDI helps production to ensure that the product is available to the customer at low cost, yet even more is required. As discussed in Section 15.3, the representative with his lap-top computer is able to service the store better than ever before to tailor his or her approach to the needs of the store manager and the store's retail customers.

In this TV age simulation of the product as in the customers' home is very impressive and gives the customer further impetus to go ahead with his purchase.

Yet, this is still not enough.

So how can the customer be helped once he or she has taken the new product out to their car in the superstore car park? What are the customers concerns? How can those concerns be converted into product features?

This involves rethinking the value of the product to the customer and involves a radical change in the supply chain from design to manufacture to display.

In a competitive market today's advance in customer support becomes tomorrow's standard. The winner with increasing market share to stay ahead will have to come up with enhanced customer support, and to do that he or she will look increasingly towards technological advances both in manufacturing and computer support.

Theme III

Modelling for Decision Support

16 Modelling for Decision Support in Simulation

Ray J. Paul and Robert D. Macredie

Abstract

This paper will look at two areas which are of importance to the field of decision support: 'artificial intelligence' and 'simulation modelling'. These areas are often brought together through aspects of expert systems which are used to model aspects of expert decision making. The chapter will introduce simulation modelling, acting as a background to several of the chapters in this theme, and will look at areas of expert systems which are used in simulation.

16.1   Introduction

This chapter looks at research into artificial intelligence (AI) and expert systems that support aspects of discrete event simulation modelling. This is an area of much research interest (see, for example, Futo and Gergely 1990; Henson 1988; Paul 1989a, 1989b; Uttamsingh 1988; Widman *et al.* 1989). One focus of the research has been on introducing intelligent reasoning into simulation through AI and expert systems techniques. Despite much research, there are few examples, arguably because of the challenges simulation itself holds as a statistical modelling approach with many inherent challenges.

This chapter introduces the field of discrete event simulation modelling as background to some of the chapters in this theme, and to inform discussion later in this chapter about the place of expert system and AI in supporting decision making in simulation. We will then go on to concentrate on three dimensions of expert systems in discrete event simulation: simulation program design; model formulation; and simulation program debugging. We will conclude with a short review of other relevant application areas.

16.2   Discrete Event Simulation

Simulation involves the setting up of a model of the system under study, in which all the relevant components are defined, and the way in which they change through time and effect each other are exactly specified. Typically the simulation model is stochastic because it will contain several random variables (for example, the inter-arrival times of ships at a port, or patients visiting a hospital accident and emergency department may be random). The model is 'run' and its behaviour is observed, with relevant data recorded for subsequent analysis. The output data for a stochastic process simulation model are themselves random and are therefore only estimates of the true characteristics of the model. If the model is of a real-world system, the outputs and behaviour of the model gathered over a set running time of the model can be compared to the values taken by the corresponding variables in the real system. If the correspondence is close, then the model may be considered to be a good representation of the real-world system. With close correspondence, the model provides a potentially powerful tool for conducting controlled experiments. Specific parameters can be systematically varied, with the model being re-run for each of the different set-ups of the model.

Simulation models of hypothetical systems can similarly be experimented with, although more caution has to be taken. Holder and Gittins (1989) provide an example of this type of model. They report on the effect of warship and replenishment ship attrition on war arsenal requirements. A group of such ships is simulated over extended periods in order to determine ship weapon usage. The model is used to study the impact of attrition, including the effects of preferential targeting, and the correlation between the usage of different weapon systems on war arsenal requirements.

The use of simulation has grown alongside developments in the power of computer systems. Simulation modellers were also quick to recognise the benefits of developing specialised simulation structures to promote the efficient construction and testing of large models. This, in turn, has led to developments in program generators which have further speeded up the process of model coding. There have also been changes in simulation, enabled by developments in computing, which has changed, and improved, the accessibility of simulation. These include the development of powerful portable machines, which has meant that simulation models can be taken to the user and experimented with through interactions between customer and analyst. This can lead to a better understanding of the situation being modelled and to greater commitment to the process and its recommendations on the part of the customer. The development of graphical techniques have also led to simpler and more intuitive simulation representations, such as iconic modelling and model presentation. Despite these developments, simulation is still a relatively expensive technique, although the relative expense of simulation now largely represents the function of the analyst rather than computer time.

16.3 Automating Parts of the Simulation Process: Opening the Way for Expert Systems

There has been a significant amount of research into ways of automating parts of the process of simulation modelling. One area of interest is developing computer aids for simulation modelling. Some possibilities are discussed here to illustrate potential areas of application for AI in simulation modelling.

The analyst, after consulting the decision maker(s) or client(s), formulates the problem in some structured way. The defined model logic is fed into an Interactive Simulation Program Generator (ISPG). These ISPGs interactively determine the characteristics of the problem, including quantitative information concerning sampling, arithmetic and initial conditions. The ISPG then automatically writes the simulation model using relevant software sub-systems. These would include a system concerned with model structure (such as the three-phase method – see Pidd 1988 for a description of this method) and various routines for data sampling, queue manipulation and recording, amongst others. Under control of the analyst, the model is run and output is produced. The output can be used to determine the 'correctness' of the model logic and of the automatically generated computer program (representing the model).

Assuming that the above process works satisfactorily, the labour intensive activities remaining are problem formulation and output analysis. These activities are 'intelligent' contributions of an analyst which tend to improve with experience. We feel that problem formulation is one area where the aid of an AI system could help the analyst formulate the problem with the customer. The expertise of the analyst might similarly be further captured in an output analyser to help decide what if anything is wrong and how to run the model to obtain satisfactory answers.

This type of modelling environment more closely represents practical as well as desirable model development, with the simulation environment not depicted as a single-pass system but as a continuous loop of activity. This enables gradual model development in small, easily checked stages, model correction in the light of program output, and determination of the running conditions and run lengths of the simulation model. The latter could be determined dynamically as a function of output and, hence, the feedback loop from the output analyser to the simulation model. The analyst is in control of, and participates in, this process. A major benefit of this type of rapid model development is that the client can participate in the modelling process as well. In these ways, integration of the system is advanced considerably.

It is clear that two potential areas of application for expert systems are in model formulation and output analysis, and that such systems could support rapid decision making in the initial formulation of the model. Before examining relevant areas, we will briefly look at how 'intelligence' could be incorporated into modelling approaches, from which it will be seen that simulation might profitably incorporate artificial intelligence ideas concerning software development.

16.4 'Intelligent' Modelling Approaches

In this section we will look at the possible ways in which AI could be used in different modelling approaches. We will concentrate on the three-phase modelling approach, as it is the one which we most commonly use in our research, but will then move on to consider briefly AI's application possibilities in other approaches to modelling.

In the three-phase simulation system which we use, described by Crookes et al. (1986), a library of Pascal routines support the writing of a problem-specific simulation program. The latter program is tightly structured into an executive controlling the three phases of the model; blocks of code for each event (the B and C events described below); and initialisation and report routines. Any three-phase structure would be similar to this.

16.4.1 A Production Rule Three-phase System

Such a structure can be redesigned as a production rule expert system in the following way. The knowledge base contains the set of rules that describes general knowledge about the problem domain. In this example, the rules have two compositions. The first, the B events, are the outcomes of the end of an activity, which occur when the simulation time reaches the activity ends. These events or rules can be considered as 'demons' in AI terminology as they do not have a non-temporal conditional part, only an action or series of actions. The rule waits to be fired when a certain event occurs, i.e. when the B event is at the front of the simulation timing mechanism. The C events are typical if–then production rules. Whenever a certain situation is encountered in the IF part of the rule, the actions in the THEN part are executed. In simulation terminology, when the necessary conditions for an activity to start are met, the necessary actions are taken. Examples of actions are queue manipulations, setting up the appropriate B events in the timing mechanism and sampling activity duration.

The working memory component of such a production system stores the current knowledge about the system. Its structures are assembled and manipulated from the inference engine by calls to the library of simulation units. The latter creates the requisite data structures and allows their updating or deletion. The main part of the working memory is made up of goals and facts as in any production system. The facts, the status of the simulation model at any point in time, are the states of the entities and queues which are used by the rules to make inferences. Goals are the elements of the timing mechanism which represent the scheduled bound or B events. As in any production system model, the goals provide a direction to the processing of the system by giving the status that must be achieved. In a three-phase simulation, the properties of the simulation goals that are used are time (when something will happen) and priorities (the relative priorities of activities). An auxiliary part of the working memory holds information about sampling and recording.

The inference engine controls the timing, model termination, B event demon calls and testing of all the C event production rules. The simulation system is not typical of production systems in its inferencing. In a simulation, a simple set of four 'meta-rules' could be executed in turn. The A phase meta-rule advances time to when something is bound to happen. The interrupt meta-rule, common to all production systems, checks for termination of the model run. The B event meta-rule executes all B events identified by the A phase meta-rule. Lastly, the C event meta-rule tests each C event production rule in turn and executes those which match the requisite data memory elements in the working memory. These four meta-rules are repeatedly applied until the interrupt meta-rule is positively invoked.

The inference engine follows a forward chaining method in matching and executing C event production rules. This is an obvious inferencing mechanism for a situation where there are many equally acceptable goal states and a single initial state. Also, there is no predetermined final state upon which backward chaining could be applied as the final state is what the model is attempting to uncover. The simplicity of the inference engine and knowledge base could lead to computer run-time inefficiency for complex problems. This could be alleviated using cellular simulation, as described by Spinelli de Carvalho and Crookes (1976), requiring a modification to the inferencing engine and the structure of the knowledge base.

16.4.2 Other Approaches

This discussion suggests potential for simulation models to be constructed with the logic of the model held in a knowledge base, as opposed to current methods where the logic is held in program code. An outcome of this approach should be faster model development. Some researchers have looked at this area. For example, Flitman and Hurrion (1987) have conducted experiments to test the feasibility of linking discrete event simulation models written in a procedural language (Fortran) with expert systems written in a declarative language (Prolog). The two systems have been written on separate, linked micro-computers. The combination can be used to develop and test expert systems, and to use an expert system as the control mechanism for a simulation.

Wahl (1986) reports on the use of declarative simulation programs that allow the inclusion of a rule-based system to augment numeric logic with human judgement. The application area is in aircraft fault isolation and diagnosis, where fault trees have been automated and supplemented by technician judgement.

Vaucher (1985) puts the main differences between the AI and simulation approaches as the stress on logical inference by the former as against the concern with the dynamic behaviour of systems by the latter. As seen above, there is some agreement on the power of the if–then or condition–action rules to describe state transitions. A further area of agreement is in the use of hierarchies of types to describe objects.

16.5   Expert System Application Areas

In this section we will look in more detail at the possibilities for the use of expert systems in the two areas of simulation: simulation problem formulation; and simulation program debugging.

16.5.1   Simulation Problem Formulation

The formulation phase of a simulation model is traditionally a costly and lengthy process, requiring extensive consultation and reworking of the specification, in common with any software system. A first attempt at using an expert system in this area is described by Doukidis and Paul (1985). The basic idea behind the expert system is to follow the life-cycle of an object to be modelled, ensuring that the cycle is only acceptable if it is complete (but not necessarily correct). A textual version of the problem can therefore be constructed.

Input is gather through a questionnaire approach. The system is initiated with an obvious action in the real-world problem, such as an arrival event. This determines the main object or entity whose life-cycle is to be evaluated. The system questions the user on what this entity does next, and under what conditions. Words which are new to the system are established as being new entities, entity attributes or activities. When the system recognises a closed cycle for the main entity, the user is then prompted to add sub-cycles, or a new main entity is selected from those mentioned in previous answers.

Whilst the expert system works, it has a number of drawbacks. Expert systems do not seem to be appropriate for handling what was essentially a Natural Language Understanding Problem (NLUS) (see instead Paul and Doukidis 1986).

16.5.2   Simulation Program Debugging

As noted in Section 16.4, at the heart of the simulation system which we use is a suite of Pascal routines that provide the support for writing discrete event simulation programs using the three-phase simulation structure (Crookes *et al.* 1986). This system is supported by an Interactive Simulation Program Generator (ISPG) that produces a Pascal simulation program using the suite of supporting routines (Paul and Chew 1987). Powerful though this type of ISPG is, some complex problem decision rules cannot always be handled directly, requiring an amendment to the generated code. Also, re-evaluation of the problem being modelled allows the analyst the choice of using the ISPG again or amending the code manually.

To support debugging of simulation models which is generally necessary for any but the most trivial modelling exercise, an expert system debugger called SIPDES (SImulation Program Debugger using an Expert System) has been developed (described in detail in Doukidis and Paul 1991).

SIPDES is designed to help an analyst discover where his or her simulation program written with the simulation systems that we use has gone wrong. The error may be a run-time error (for example, attempting to move an entity from an empty queue) or it may be an obvious mistake in the output (for example, nothing happened, or an entity disappears completely over time). The SIPDES system provides messages to facilitate the nature of the hypothesis being tested as well as the normal help facilities. SIPDES can be defined as an 'Expert Simulation System' as its goal is to remove the need for significant simulation training, supporting engineers, scientists and managers in conducting simulation studies correctly and easily (Shannon *et al.* 1985). SIPDES can also be considered as an 'advice-giving simulation expert system' (O'Keefe 1986), which supports decision making in simulation modelling. SIPDES's knowledge base concerns simulation in general, the systems of Crookes *et al.* (1986) in particular, and relevant aspects of Pascal (in which the heart of the system is written) as well.

SIPDES can explain its line of reasoning at any point on demand. It uses both the general explanation facility provided by the skeletal expert system ASPES (Doukidis and Paul 1987) and one specially designed for this domain. Knowledge acquisition in developing SIPDES was found to be one of the most difficult tasks. Top-down division of the problem into a knowledge tree was used. The construction of the knowledge-tree proved invaluable. It gave at a glance the number of errors acquired, their causes and any patterns that existed. A major proportion of the system development time was spent on the acquisition and development of the knowledge base to an acceptable level.

Hill and Roberts (1987) have similarly developed a prototype knowledge-based support system, written in PROLOG, which mimics the diagnostic process that teachers using the simulation package INSIGHT give students. Unlike SIPDES, the knowledge base contains knowledge concerning the assignments given to students. This should enable it to give more exact advice, whilst being restricted in its application.

Others also see decision support systems, where artificial intelligence aids the decision maker in interpreting simulation output, as an area of potential (see, for example, Moser 1986). Moser (1986) has developed a simple system to demonstrate the idea. The problem simulated is that of financial investment decisions, with the expert system interpreting the output from the simulation run for the decision maker. The system allows the decision maker to interrogate the results for a variety of possible outcomes. Spiegel and LaVallee (1988) also report on the use of an expert system to drive a simulation. The expert system is provided with a number of rules which describe, qualitatively, how various simulation parameters effect specific simulation results. The expert system is used to monitor simulation statistics and control simulation parameters.

16.6   Other Relevant Research

Taylor (1988), and Taylor and Hurrion (1988), report on an expert advisor for simulation experimental design and analysis. The work clearly demonstrates the feasibility of such systems. Users define the objectives of their study (with default values as alternatives). The system gathers information about the problem under consideration. An initial experiment is devised using production rules according to the objectives of the study. The analysis of the results of the first experiment may prompt the advisory system to refine the experiment or request further experiments before it can yield a sensible conclusion. The system demonstrates that such a framework for an advisor is robust.

Campbell (1986) and Elmaghraby and Jagannathan (1985) report on the separate development of expert systems which help a simulation analyst to select a simulation language to match the proposed model and the available computer resources. de Swaan Arons *et al.* (1986) describe an empty shell for building and consulting expert systems which has been used to find an appropriate model of a system to be simulated. It has also been used to recursively validate a simulation model using a knowledge base containing the expert's knowledge on validation.

Kornell (1985) has reported on the inclusion of expert systems within military simulation models to model the decision processes of individual commanders in combined arms scenarios. A further development is in a wargaming model where a human player on one side can be replaced by an automated decision module (or even both human players can be replaced). A later paper (Kornell 1987) discusses experiences by the author in using knowledge-based systems for military simulation. He emphasises the different nature of the task concerning the addition of knowledge-based sub-systems to existing simulations, to that of including such systems in the initial specification.

Elmaghraby *et al.* (1985b) describe the construction of an expert system designed to control a dynamic chemical process. The actual process considered is a distillation column. The distillation process consumes 30% of the energy consumption in the chemical industry. In order to aid the design and to test the expert system, a dynamic simulation of the process was interfaced with it. This provided the convenience of experimentation. Elmaghraby *et al.* (1985a) have developed an expert system for flexible manufacturing, with an interactive simulation system used to evaluate it. Both papers hint that the simulation can form the basis of a learning tool, to assist in redefining the expert system rules, and thereby optimise the process being modelled.

The increasing interest in flexible manufacturing systems has led a number of authors to consider an AI system that uses simulation. Ford and Schroer (1987) have developed an expert system with a commercial simulation language for simulating an electronics manufacturing plant. The goals of the system are to develop a simulation capability for the electronics facility, to provide a natural language interface so that the decision maker will not have to learn the simulation language and to embed in the system an expert system to assist the decision maker. The system incorporates a program generator which takes the natural language description as the basis for the specification. Mellichamp and Wahab (1987) have developed an expert system to take the output of a simulation of a flexible manufacturing system design as the basis of a redesign. In this way the expert system can iterate around the designs until some predetermined objectives are met. The limitations of the system are the ability to capture the richness and variety of modifications to designs that human designers display. The authors stress the potential for the system, in that, with time, the expert system will slowly improve towards the standard of a human expert.

One of the most important difficulties of developing expert systems in manufacturing scheduling or control, is to find the required knowledge. Pierreval and Ralambondrainy (1990) suggest simulation as a solution to the problem of finding knowledge about the manufacturing system behaviour. They propose learning algorithms that generate, from simulation experiments, a set of production rules. This set may be considered as a simulation meta-model, and may be used either directly by the shop manager, or inserted into a knowledge base. They illustrate their approach by the use of a learning program that generates rules related to the behaviour of a simplified flow shop when different dispatching rules are used.

Williams et al. (1989) have embedded a rule base advisor into a discrete event simulation model of the logistics of replenishing a naval warship group. This advisor provided an intelligent decision maker to automate the simulation model. The rule base was derived from interviews, observation and induction. The rule based was extrapolated by the commanders to handle the complex situations for which there was no previous experience. This enabled the simulation model to be run for extensive computer trials as an integrated system.

Rozenblit et al. (1990) describe the knowledge-based design and simulation environment called KBDSE. The environment supports the development of discrete event simulation models in hierarchical, modular fashion. The environment consists of two basic components: the front end for the model construction process; and an object-oriented simulator supporting evaluation of hierarchical, multi-component models. The multifaceted modelling methodology, that has been employed, has been implemented in LISP. Because the symbolic manipulation and object-oriented facilities of the environment make it relatively easy to code complex structures, KBDSE has been used successfully in many design examples.

Dewhurst and Gwinnet (1990) advocate an artificial decision analysis support (ADAS) system to unify the traditional scientific methodologies with AI approaches. Such a system would access the whole range of modelling techniques, including simulation. Intelligent simulation is seen to 'artificially' replicate some of the fundamental processes of human decision making, in particular the more experiential processes. Their proposal would require considerable development work, as well as there being significant problems associated with the elicitation of the required expertise from the decision analysts. The paper gives an insight into the possible future systems that may be built as the art of simulation and other techniques is enhanced with AI software applications.

16.7   Summary

This chapter has briefly looked at issues around artificial intelligence (AI) and expert systems that support aspects of discrete event simulation modelling. It has provided background that will be relevant to the chapters in this theme of the book and has also reported the issues on which our research in the area has concentrated.

References

Birtwhislte, G. (Ed) (1985). *AI, Graphics and Simulation* (San Diego, CA: The Society for Computer Simulation).

Campbell, RA (1986) Development of an expert system for simulation model selection. In *Intelligent Simulation Environments*. Simulation Series, Vol. 17(1). San Diego, CA: The Society for Computer Simulation.

Crookes, JG, Balmer, DW, Chew, ST and Paul, RJ (1986) A three phase simulation system written in Pascal. *Journal of the Operational Research Society*, 37: 603–618.

de Swaan Arons, H, Jansen, EP and Lucas, PJF (1986) Building and consulting expert systems in simulation with DELFI-2. In *AI Applied to Simulation*. Kerckhoffs, EJR, Vansteenkiste, GC and Zeigler, BP (Eds). Simulation Series, Vol. 18(1). San Diego, CA: The Society for Computer Simulation.

Dewhurst, FW and Gwinnet, EA (1990) Artificial intelligence and decision analysis. *Journal of the Operational Research Society*, 41(8): 693–701.

Doukidis, GI and Paul, RJ (1985) Research into expert systems to aid simulation model formulation. *Journal of the Operational Research Society*, 36: 319–326.

Doukidis, GI and Paul, RJ (1987) ASPES – a skeletal Pascal expert system. In *Expert Systems and Artificial Intelligence in Decision Support Systems* Sol, HG, Takkenber CATh and Vries Robbe, PF (Eds). Dordrecht, the Netherlands: D. Reidel: 227–246.

Doukidis, GI and Paul, RJ (1991) SIPDES: A SImulation Program Debugger using an Expert System. *Expert Systems With Applications*, 2: 153–165.

Elmaghraby, AS, Demeo, RS and Berry, J (1985a) Testing an expert system for manufacturing. In *Artificial Intelligence and Simulation*. Holmes, WM (Ed.). San Diego, CA: The Society for Computer Simulation.

Elmaghraby, AS and Jagannathan, V (1985) An expert system for simulationists. In *AI, Graphics and Simulation*. Birtwhistle, G (Ed.). San Diego, CA: The Society for Computer Simulation.

Elmaghraby, AS, Jagannathan, V and Ralston, P (1985) An expert system for chemical process control. In *Artificial Intelligence and Simulation*. Holmes, WM (Ed.). San Diego, CA: The Society for Computer Simulation.

Flitman, AM and Hurrion, RD (1987) Linking procedural discrete event simulation models with non-procedural expert systems. *Journal of the Operational Research Society*, 38: 723–733.

Ford, DR and Schroer, BJ (1987) An expert manufacturing simulation system. *Simulation*, 48: 193–200.

Futo, I and Gergely, T (1990) *Artificial Intelligence in Simulation*. New York: Ellis Horwood.

Henson, T (Ed.) (1988) *Artificial Intelligence and Simulation: The Diversity of Applications. Conference Proceedings*. San Diego, CA: The Society for Computer Simulation.

Hill, TR and Robert, SD (1987) A prototype knowledge-based simulation support system. *Simulation*, 48: 152–161.

Holder, RD and Gittins, RP (1989) The effects of warship and replenishment attrition on war arsenal requirements. *Journal of the Operational Research Society*, 40: 167–175.

Kornell, J (1985) Knowledge-based systems for military simulation: problems, experiences, lessons. In *AI, Graphics and Simulation*. Birtwhistle, G (Ed.). San Diego, CA: The Society for Computer Simulation.

Kornell, J (1987) Reflections on using knowledge based systems for military simulation. *Simulation*, 48: 144–148.

Mellichamp, JM and Wahab, AFA (1987) An expert system for FMS design. *Simulation*, 48: 201–208.

Moser, JG (1986) Integration of artificial intelligence and simulation in a comprehensive decision-support system. *Simulation*, 47: 223–229.

O'Keefe, RM (1986) Advisory systems in simulation. In *AI Applied to Simulation*. Kerckhoffs, EJR, Vansteenkiste, GC and Zeigler, BP (Eds). Simulation Series, Vol. 18(1). San Diego, CA: The Society for Computer Simulation.

Paul, RJ (1989a) Artificial intelligence and simulation modelling. In *Computer Modelling for Discrete Simulation*. Pidd, M (Ed.). Chichester: John Wiley.

Paul, RJ (1989b) Combining AI and simulation. In *Computer Modelling for Discrete Simulation*. Pidd, M (Ed.). Chichester: John Wiley.

Paul, RJ and Chew, ST (1987) Simulation modelling using an interactive simulation program generator. *Journal of the Operational Society*, 38: 735–752.

Paul, RJ and Doukidis, GI (1986) Further developments in the use of artificial intelligence to formulate simulation problems. *Journal of the Operational Research Society*, 37: 787–810.

Pidd, M (1988) *Computer Simulation in Management Science* (2nd edition). Chichester: John Wiley.

Pierreval, H and Ralambondrainy, H (1990) A simulation and learning technique for generating knowledge about manufacturing systems behaviour. *Journal of the Operational Society*, 41: 461–474.

Rozenblit, JW, Hu, J, Kim, TG and Zeigler, BP (1990) Knowledge-based Design and Simulation Environment (KBDSE): foundational concepts and implementation. *Journal of the Operational Society*, 41: 475–489.

Shannon, RE, Mayer, R and Adelsberger, HH (1985) Expert systems and simulation. *Simulation,* **44**(6): 275–284.

Spiegel, JR and LaVallee, DB (1988) Using an expert system to drive a simulation experiment. In *AI Papers.* Uttamsingh, RJ (Ed.). Simulation Series, Vol. 20(1). San Diego, CA: The Society for Computer Simulation.

Spinelli de Carvalho, R and Crookes, JG (1976) Cellular simulation. *Operational Research Quarterly,* **27**: 31–40.

Taylor, RP (1988) *An Artificial Intelligence Framework for Experimental Design and Analysis in Discrete Event Simulation.* Unpublished Ph.D. thesis, University of Warwick.

Taylor, RP and Hurrion, RD (1988) An expert advisor for simulation experimental design and analysis. In *Artificial Intelligence and Simulation: The Diversity of Applications.* Henson, T (Ed.). San Diego, CA: The Society for Computer Simulation.

Uttamsingh, RJ (1988) *AI Papers.* Simulation Series, Vol. 20(1). San Diego, CA: The Society for Computer Simulation.

Vaucher, JG (1985) Views of modelling: comparing the simulation and AI approaches. In *AI, Graphics and Simulation.* Birtwhistle, G (Ed.). San Diego, CA: The Society for Computer Simulation.

Wahl, D (1986) An application of declarative modelling to aircraft fault isolation and diagnosis. In *Intelligent Simulation Environments.* Luker, PA and Adelsberger, HH (Eds). Simulation Series, Vol. 17(1). San Diego, CA: The Society for Computer Simulation.

Widman, LE, Loparo, KA and Nielsen, NR (1989) *Artificial Intelligence, Simulation, and Modeling.* New York: John Wiley.

Williams, TM, Gittins, RP and Burke, DM (1989) Replenishment at sea. *Journal of the Operational Society,* **40**: 881–887.

17 The Strategic Role of Expert Systems in UK Organisations

Elayne W. Coakes and Kim Merchant

Abstract

A 1994 survey by Coakes and Merchant of the utilisation of computer information systems (CIS) by UK organisations found that those organisations that used expert systems had differing characteristics in the use of CIS from those organisations that did not use expert systems. This paper considers the effect expert systems have on organisational structure and change, and concludes that although they have a role to play in the strategic activities of organisations, they are not critical to organisations' changing role in business.

17.1 Introduction

Applegate *et al.* (1988) wrote "Expert and knowledge-based systems ... are rapidly appearing in commercial settings. Every large company we've polled expects to have at least one production system using this technology by late 1989".

In 1994 Coakes and Merchant conducted a wide-ranging survey of UK organisations and their utilisation of computer information systems (CIS). The results of the survey (detailed in Coakes and Merchant 1995) showed that 23% of respondents were using expert systems. The results also showed that those organisations that did use expert systems had differing characteristics in the use of CIS from those organisations that did not use expert systems. This chapter sets out to look at some of the differences in use of CIS, and proposes that development and use of an expert system (ES) may help define 'system maturity' and that lack of achievement of such a maturity level may help explain why Applegate's prediction has not yet come true.

In Millet and Powell (1993) the results of a survey into ES success are detailed. One of the more interesting findings was that organisational perception and culture had a correlation to the success or failure of an ES implementation. The more successful implementations were within organisations that had a higher score for being receptive to new technology (which would match with the idea of system maturity) and where there was rarely resistance to change, with the organisations having a highly decentralised decision-making process. Successful ESs have a relationship to how and where decisions are made, and this was borne out in this further study conducted by the authors of this paper, with the majority of respondents finding that their ES helped:

- enhance users' decision-making quality and consistency;
- decision makers to consider more factors before making decisions.

In some instances it also helped in saving experts' time and enabled them to make decisions more quickly, using company information more efficiently.

This chapter looks at how expert systems might contribute to overall organisational strategy both in information technology/information systems (IT/IS), and in structural changes that support business aims and strategies. A number of organisations from the original survey agreed to participate in a further study. Preliminary results of this latest research are included to support conclusions drawn.

17.2   Organisations and System Maturity

A number of authors (Hirschheim 1983; Nolan 1979; Porter 1988) have identified stages in organisational growth in relation to computer usage. These stages are intended to identify what level of maturity in CIS usage the organisation has achieved, and thus predict the type of applications that might be used and their purposes. They are also likely to predict the role of CIS strategy within organisational strategy.

17.3   System Maturity and Competitive Strategy

System maturity models are discussed in detail in Coakes and Merchant (1996), but the consensus viewpoint on the main criteria for maturity to have been achieved is an integration of CIS strategy into the strategic framework of the organisation, with the CIS being used as a competitive weapon. Cardinali (1992) states that information systems are increasingly being used to shape or support an organisation's competitive strategy. He divides the opportunities arising from information systems strategy into three areas: internal – to develop efficient and effective organisational structures and processes; business portfolio strategy – which concerns the choice of where to compete and how; and competitive strategy – which concerns itself with moves within the industry in which the organisation is competing.

17.4   Match of Organisations

In the Coakes and Merchant survey of 1995, 46% of respondents with an ES identified their system as being part of their strategic plan and 22% gave one of their reasons for using the ES as the fact that competitors used it. In the latest research of organisations with ES, the majority saw information technology (IT) and computerised information systems (CIS) as being a boost to their organisations against competitors, stating that the ES was of great benefit.

Schutzer (1990) states that to be competitive a system must be in a critical part of the business, be innovative, result in a large organisational change, result in an business performance improvement or be difficult to reproduce. For the system to be strategic he states it must be designed for maintaining competitive parity over the 'long haul', or must create the correct environment for innovation and competition. Finlay (1992) goes on to say: "It is only for novel or unique situations that IT can provide competitive advantage and this is rarely the province of ES". The current research shows that most organisations believe that ES would make them a lot more productive in the short term but that in the longer term (5–10 years) ES would provide few advantages.

17.5 Expert Systems and Organisational Change

17.5.1 Changing Structures

Keen (1991) gave five IT counter-measures against the organisational complexity caused by the current social and business environment. These measures were that it could recreate organisations; help support structure and location independent organisations; facilitate collaboration; make it easier to collaborate than not; and repersonalise management.

Miles and Snow (1986) say that "new organisational forms arise to cope with new environmental conditions" and describe their new organisational form as the "dynamic network". Applegate et al. (1988) describe this structure as a "cluster" where people will work together to solve problems and will then disband, technology will be used to support this process, in particular ES, executive information systems and cooperative work systems. Ferioli and Migliarese (1991) talk about the tools that IT can provide for possibilities and facilities for communication channels to support the exchange of information required by these emerging organisations.

17.5.2 Information Technology Push

Drucker (1988) wrote about the need for businesses to learn to use information more effectively and efficiently for diagnosis and decision-making. He felt that this would result in a flatter organisational structure with fewer layers of management (and supervisors). Wysocki and Young (1990) say that evidence shows that as this flattening occurs the "knowledge worker" emerges as critical to the performance of the organisation's work. Drucker foresaw a new looser organisation structure comprising a federation of task forces with requisite skills.

Main (1988) says that in the 1990s companies will need to develop products and make decisions faster:

> They will adopt fluid structures that can be altered as business conditions change. More than being helped by computers, companies will live by them, shaping strategy and structure to fit new information technology ... With the help of information technology, managers can increase by several magnitudes the number of people reporting to them.

Our recent survey asked whether organisational structure had changed over the last 5 years, the majority of respondents said 'yes', agreeing that there had been a flattening of the structure and that more team work was employed than previously. They stated that employees are more mobile in their roles (e.g. team leader to learner player), according to project, than they had been in the past.

In addition, they stated that there had been a loss of senior management or other management/supervisory roles during this period.

Most respondents felt that their new organisational structure was Networked (as opposed to Flat or Pyramid). When asked whether the ES employed had had any effect on the change in organisational structure, most stated that it had not, there had been other influences for change.

17.5.3   Enabling Technologies for Change

Cash *et al.* (1994) write about the effective organisation and the role that IT plays in enabling change. They say:

> When information technology substitutes for human effort it *automates* a task or process.
> When information technology augments human effort, it *informates* a task or process.
> When information technology restructures, it *transforms* a set of tasks or process.

They go on to say:

Today, the payback from IT investments comes, not from the one-shot ideas, but from outstanding execution of business processes ... use the technology to transform the business processes in three fundamental ways:

Shifting from *predicting events* to *managing uncertainty*;
Shifting from *discrete* to *continuous process*;
Increased emphasis on *horizontal information flows*;
IT and business transformation;
IT touches everything;
IT, per se, causes nothing;
IT innovation is not necessarily about being first – with a new technology, or with a new application.

In 1991, 1992 and, again, in 1993 the CSC survey of IS management issues asked the question: "What are the (three) emerging technologies of greatest interest to your company?".

Expert systems/artificial intelligence were considered amongst these three technologies by 35% of respondents in 1991, 18% in 1992 and only 5% in 1993.

When asked whether any organisational change was caused by IT/IS push or was enabled by changes in IT/IS, the majority of respondents to the current survey felt that it enabled. When asked about the specific technologies that supported this organisational change they cited client server computer architecture, networks, group work programs such as Lotus Notes, portable computers, e-mail and the Internet or other on-line external databases.

Venkatraman (1994) stated that IT has become the fundamental enabler in creating and maintaining a flexible business network. He distinguishes five levels of IT-induced business and organisational reconfiguration. By level 3 IT is being used as leverage for new organisation and business process redesign, by level 4 the nature of the exchange amongst the multiple participants in a business network is redesigned by IT, and by level 5 IT functionality has enabled and facilitated organisational change to the 'newer' organisational forms. As Venkatraman put it "from transaction processing to knowledge working".

17.5.4   The Role of Expert Systems in Change

The current survey found that few respondents felt that their ES had had an effect on organisational structure and change. This is likely to be because, as Finlay (1992) says:

> Little in ES is new. ES as presently implemented are suitable for well-structured situations. Thus their use, although likely to provide tangible payoffs is unlikely to result in sustainable strategic advantage.

Liebowitz (1990) goes on to say that:

In the coming years, businesses will continue to develop and integrate expert systems into their existing systems and daily operations. Expert systems will serve as vehicles to improve the productivity, effectiveness, and efficiency of selected business operations ... the company will be well on the way to better facing its competition in the near future.

In the current survey many respondents stated that IT/IS were planned at a strategic level using a 2–5 year horizon, in addition they said that this IT/IS strategy was part of the organisation's overall strategic plan. Some also replied that their organisation's use of IT was currently going through a period of upheaval and experimentation with how IT/CIS could improve or enhance business processes and techniques. Respondents also said that IT/CIS had made their organisation "a lot" more productive (on a scale of 1–5 with 5 being equal to "a lot"), and expected IT to continue to make their organisation more productive over the next 1–5 years but expected the benefits to tail off after that.

17.6   Conclusions

From the evidence supplied above, it would seem that although ES have a role to play in the strategic activities of organisations using them, they are not critical to the organisations' changing role in business. ES would seem to be supportive rather than instrumental of change.

Those organisations using ES feel that they are of competitive value, but that overall the productivity of their organisations was likely to be enhanced by any form of IT/IS only in the near future. Longer-term benefits were unlikely to accrue. With this attitude towards the use of IT/IS it is unlikely that the predicted large expansion (see the quote by Applegate *et al.* at the start of this chapter) in the use of ES will now occur. ESs are too expensive to develop on an individual basis and are difficult to use when bought in and customised. It seems likely that there will be only a slow incremental use in ES as part of the overall strategic role of IT/IS.

References

Applegate, LM, Cash, JI and Mills, DQ (1988) Information technology and tomorrowís manager. *Harvard Business Review*, November–December, 66(6): 128–136.

Cardinali, R (1992) A key ingredient to achieving organisational competitive strategy. *Computers in Industry*, 18: 241–245.

Cash, JI, Eccles, RG, Nohria, N and Nolan, RL (1994) *Building the Information-Age Organisation: Structure, Control and Information Technologies* (3rd edition), Harvard Business School.

Coakes, EW and Merchant, K (1995) Expert Systems – a survey of their use in UK business. *Information and Management*, 30: 223–230.

Coakes, EW and Merchant, K (1996) Expert systems in UK organisations: an empirical analysis. In *Third World Conference on Expert Systems*. Seoul, Korea. Elmsford, NY: Cognisant Communication Corporation: 1335–1342.

Drucker, P (1988) The coming of the new organisation. *Harvard Business Review*, 66: 1.

Ferioli, C and Migliarese, P (1995) Opportunities and drawbacks of information technology in the emerging forms of organisations. In *Proceedings of the Third European Conference on Information Systems*. Galliers, R, Jelass, T, Kremar, H and Land, F (Eds). 1–3 June, Athens: 559–576.

Finlay, P (1992) IT for competitive advantage: the place of expert systems. *Journal of Strategic Information Systems*, 1: 3.

Hirschheim, R (1983) Managing the growth of electronic office information systems in long range planning. *Harvard Business Review*, 16: 59–67.

Keen, P (1991) *Shaping the Future: Business Design through Information Technology*. Harvard Business School Press.

Liebowitz, J (Ed.) (1990) *Expert Systems for Business and Management.* Englewood Cliffs, NJ: Prentice-Hall.

Main, J (1988) The winning organisation. *Fortune,* 26 September: 50–60.

Miles, RE and Snow, CC (1986) Organisations: new concepts for new forms. *California Management Review,* **28**: 3.

Millet, D and Powell, P (1993) Measuring success in expert systems developments. *Journal of Information Systems Development,* **A24**: 41–59.

Nolan, A (1979) Managing the crisis in data processing. *Harvard Business Review,* **57**(2), March–April: 115–126.

Porter, M (1988) Reports. *Planning Review,* September–October: 26–27.

Schutzer, D (1990) Business expert systems: the competitive edge. *Expert Systems with Applications,* 1: 17–21.

Venkatraman, N (1994) IT-enabled business transformation: from automation to business scope redefinition. *Sloan Management Review,* Winter: 73–87.

Wysocki, RK and Young, J (1990) *Information Systems: Management Principles in Action.* Chichester: John Wiley.

18 Workflow Benchmarking for Improved Productivity in a Large Store Group

Anthony R. Ovenden

Abstract

This chapter reports on a successful study into the identification and introduction of improved management methods to a retail store group. The investigating team did not attempt to use traditional, scientifically rigorous, operational research techniques – instead, some basic operational analysis has resulted not only in large improvements but also in the continuation of training suggested by the consultants after their departure. Indeed, the technique has since been applied to other areas of the business.

18.1 Introduction

It is not every day that a relatively simple management technique is introduced into an organisation and provides benefits amounting to millions of pounds per year. Certainly very few, if any, of the mathematical or statistical solutions outlined in *Journal of the Operational Research Society* would be able to match this as an example of truly *operational* research.

This paper describes a productivity improvement study which was carried out for a well-known department store group. It was shown to be possible to achieve improvements in productivity of up to 30% in some of the back-room departments through the use of a benchmarking technique and by providing departmental managers with procedures which enabled them to control their workflows better. This approach was enthusiastically adopted by the management to such effect that the method is now used throughout the group. They estimate the financial benefits to be of the order of millions of pounds per year.

The research carried out in this study did not attempt the full scientific rigour which is so often associated with mathematical operational research (OR). Absence of such rigour does not mean, though, that the results are worthless or inapplicable. In terms of sheer value for money this study provided outstanding results; some basic operational analysis, together with the introduction of an improved management decision-making process, has resulted in enormous benefits for this leading store group. The decision-making process itself was straightforward and readily understandable by all concerned, and this probably contributed in no small way to the acceptability of the overall procedure.

18.2   The Reason For the Study

The retail marketplace has always been highly competitive. When electronic point of sales (EPOS) burst onto the scene and when desk-top computers were making their presence felt significant changes took place on the high street. The new technology provided a store with much better information for managing stocks, credit and so on, but it was not too difficult for its competitors to obtain precisely the same benefits; and, of course, they did just that.

The store group which commissioned this study recognised that real competitive advantage would be likely to accrue if better in-house managerial techniques could be applied, and they requested assistance in identifying and introducing improved management methods. Essentially they wanted to reduce costs and improve business effectiveness. This would provide the group with financial benefits and their staff with improved job security.

A team comprising two consultants and selected key executives was set up. This team would study how back-room clerical staff were managed, in a sample of six of the 50 stores selected to cover various sizes and types of store, and various patterns of demand.

18.3   The Preliminary Results

The review was carried out and indicated that, *using the performance levels already being achieved in each store,* there was 18–25% spare capacity in the clerical departments of five of the six stores sampled. Further analysis indicated that significant additional improvements could be obtained by bringing the performance of the not-so-good departments up to the level of the best.

18.4   Of Course Every Store is Different – But Not Greatly Different

During our review we came up against the usual statements and views. All investigators know them: "Ah, but we're different. We have special problems in our office/factory/type of business". And, of course, so they are. Perhaps they deal with larger quantities. Perhaps their time scales are tighter. Perhaps ..., etc. But it is rare to find that there are truly significant differences which make it impossible to apply the same or similar logic to a management investigation, and so it turned out. This was not one of those rare cases.

The statistics indicate that differences between stores concerning the workloads and the effort applied are not extreme. At any store:

- December accounts for between 15 and 19% of the annual sales value.
- Monthly sales are normally between 5 and 7.5% of the annual sales value.
- Saturday is the busiest day, with sales of about three times the average weekday sale.
- Full-time staff made up 70–80% of the total clerical man hours available (FTEs), with regular part-timers accounting for the remainder.

18.5   Nine General Areas of Clerical Work Were Studied

The Group had already introduced, some time previously, standard procedures for carrying out many of the back-room activities. No significant differences between stores were found in the manual procedures being adopted. One process was reviewed which at one store included the use of a PC, and it was found that the PC contributed little if anything to the productivity being achieved; in fact it was seen as being more a liability than an asset.

Pareto's 80:20 rule applies here. All the offices had a number of key tasks which accounted for the bulk of the total workload. This is not to say, of course, that the remaining tasks were not important, but merely that they did not take up as much time as the other tasks. The general picture is shown in Figure 18.1.

18.6   The Office Environment

The offices followed what many would recognise as the normal pattern of office life, with managers and supervisors looking after particular work sections. In this context, it was possible to make some general observations about management control and productivity.

18.6.1   Unless Controlled, Work Expands to Fill the Time Available

Parkinson's Law was almost certainly based on his own experience of people in their workplace, and anyone can confirm its accuracy by spending a little time as a fly on the wall in a general office. It is perfectly usual for experienced staff to carry out most of their work quite independently, and when new work arrives they share it out

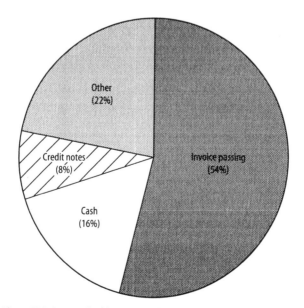

Figure 18.1. An example of departmental clerical workload, showing tasks involved.

amongst themselves without reference to their manager. Then, almost irrespective
of the amount of work to be done, the whole of the working day is taken up doing
it; if there is a large amount to get through they speed up so as to complete it – or
at least most of it – by 5 pm, and if there is only a little it gets spread more thinly
across the day.

18.6.2 Administrative Managers are Frequently Unaware of the Level of Workload

Administrative managers or supervisors typically concentrate on personnel matters
and on ensuring that the output is of a suitable quality. They become involved with
workloads only when problems arise. Although the manager may know that the
workload on his or her department fluctuates he or she is generally unaware of the
precise volume except when extremes of overload or underload occur.

Absence of such knowledge means that managers cannot have proper control over
the productivity of their staff.

18.6.3 Staff Tend to Specialise in 'Their' Tasks and Lack Task Flexibility

If a member of staff likes a particular task and is able to do it well then that task
tends to be taken over by that person. In many offices each routine activity generally has a single person who deals with it, either formally or informally. This specialisation is beneficial insofar as the work can be done without reference to the
manager unless unusual problems arise. Conversely, however, these specialists prefer to work on 'their' tasks and may be unwilling – and possibly unable – to work
on any of the other office activities.

Such specialisation is fine if there is always work for the specialist and the specialist is always available to do it. But when the work dries up or the specialist is
absent then problems arise. Staff absence would mean that the office was actually
unable to fulfil its purpose within the organisation.

18.7 Calculating Task Performance Rates

After an analysis of what was involved in the back-room clerical work a single feature, such as number of items or number of payments, was identified for each task
and was used as the measure of the volume of work. The number of man hours
applied was used as the measure of effort. The performance rates on these tasks over
a given period was then calculated as the volume of work divided by the effort
applied.

In setting an initial measure of task performance there was no stop-watch timing or detailed work study as these techniques would have been completely unacceptable in this environment. The consultant made an wrist-watch estimate of the
time taken to process a certain volume of work. Then the result was discussed with
the staff concerned and with the manager, and a consensus was arrived at which took
into account likely interruptions, breaks and so on.

The single measure is easy to calculate and it concentrates on the most significant feature of performance. This approach is simple, understandable and above all
powerful, because the managers and staff involved can readily see its relevance. It
does not attempt to be accurate to the n-th degree because the variability would be

quite large in any case, and the result is presented not as a precise measure of performance but rather as a rough measure; on a chart it would be represented not as a dot but as a circle covering a recognisable area.

Managers were requested to start to maintain records of the quantities of the key types of work passing through their department, together with the staff time which was used in processing it. The resulting performance figures were recorded and used for comparison purposes.

18.8   Task Performance Comparisons Showed Large Differences From Day to Day at a Store, and Also Between Stores

Large differences in store task performance were found, as exemplified in Figure 18.2.

The comparisons were reviewed with the managers of the departments concerned and possible reasons for differences were discussed. The two major reasons for differences in performance were identified as:

- lack of management procedures for scheduling and controlling clerical work;
- poor flexibility of staff in terms of the types of work they could carry out.

18.9   The Potential For Improvement

Figure 18.2 shows that a task at a single store will be carried out at different performance rates on different occasions. The differences may be because different people were performing the task, or because there were fewer interruptions, etc., but the question has to be asked: "If it is possible to work at a high performance rate at one time then why is it not possible to do so at other times?". On this basis an analysis showed that *using performance levels already being achieved in each store* there was between 18 and 25% spare capacity in five of the six stores studied. If this figure had been, say, 2–5% then it could be argued that this was probably within reasonable lim-

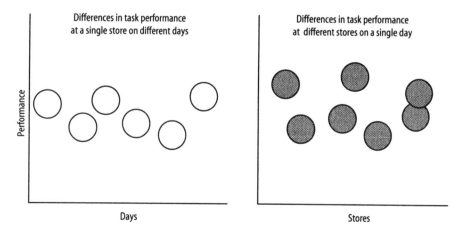

Figure 18.2. An example of task performance comparisons.

its of error in calculating the performance rates, or that it was only reasonable to expect a variation because people are not automata, but such a large value indicates that there is indeed scope for productivity improvement.

In addition, from the task performance comparison chart shown in Figure 18.2, it is clear that there is scope for improvement through bringing the performance of the worst-performing stores up to the level of the best ones.

Because productivity is calculated according to the time spent in carrying out a particular task, then if a person works twice as fast the time required will be halved and his or her productivity will have doubled. Although this is an obvious relationship it is not what the most effective productivity studies are about. The aim should be for staff to work at their normal rate but to use the very best methods and to be able to work more consistently. They do not work harder but they are more productive.

18.10   Converting Potential Benefit into Real Benefit

It is one thing to predict benefits but it is almost invariably more difficult to achieve them in reality. In order to achieve these benefits six separate types of management information and training were introduced.

1. *Skills inventory.* Documentation was prepared to identify the task skills of departmental staff, enabling comparisons to be made with departmental task requirements. Numerical measures of staff and departmental flexibility are now routinely available.
2. *Staff mobility.* Maintaining details of staff capable of providing assistance to other departments should the need arise and should the staff be underloaded in their home department.
3. *Forward planning.* A special spreadsheet was developed for departmental managers so that they could readily assign their expected staff capacity to expected volumes of tasks, and could also monitor the actual performance levels achieved. The managers could thus know how the time of their staff was spent, and ensure that it was used most effectively.

    This procedure ensures that whenever possible the expected future workload will be matched by the presence of staff to meet that load. It has highlighted the importance of ensuring that full-time staff are trained so that they can operate flexibly and be assigned to whatever work needs to be carried out at any particular time. It has also highlighted the importance of having part-time staff available to accommodate normal peak volumes and short-term overload situations.
4. *Managerial training.* A course was prepared and delivered to departmental managers to train them in the new techniques which they would be expected to apply.
5. *Management reporting.* A management reporting procedure was developed so that store results could be reviewed and compared weekly, and transmitted to higher management. This has promoted a benchmark ratcheting process, where competition between stores is encouraged.
6. *Dissemination of best practice.* The best performing stores get the kudos. At the same time they are expected to give procedural help to the not-so-good ones, by receiving staff from other stores and explaining/showing how they achieve their high productivity. This process is effective largely because store managers are encouraged to adopt an attitude of cooperation in association with friendly competition.

18.11   Extension Throughout the Store Group – and Beyond

After the departure of the consultants the in-house team continued the training process and extended the scope to the clerical departments at all the stores.

Improvements in performance of between 20 and 30% were achieved at all stores.

Subsequently the in-house team applied the technique to the store assistants serving customers. The same general level of benefit was achieved.

The Group was taken over by another retail organisation with massive representation throughout the UK. Workflow benchmarking has now been applied for monitoring and controlling staff utilisation throughout the whole of the newly formed larger organisation.

A representative recently stated that these techniques had saved them tens of millions of pounds since they were introduced.

19 Adding Value Through Simulation by Focusing on Process

Brian Lehaney

Abstract

This Simulation is a powerful modelling methodology, but it has no inherent means to address the 'messy' stages of modelling. Soft Systems Methodology (SSM) provides a recognised approach to problem structuring and conceptual model development, but it has no means to assess the feasibility of options. This chapter discusses how SSM may be combined with simulation to provide an iterative, framework which utilises the problem structuring capability of SSM and the feasibility-testing capability of simulation.

19.1 Introduction

This chapter outlines a methodology for combining the two modelling approaches of simulation and Soft Systems Methodology (SSM). Simulation provides a powerful tool to model complex problems, but has no inherent means to identify system activities or system boundaries. SSM was developed by Checkland (1981) and Wilson (1984) as a means to achieve consensus on system specification, and may therefore be useful in the early stages of modelling, even when simulation has already been chosen as the modelling tool.

A study on the use of simulation has shown that "awareness of the technology in industry is very low and some £300m pa of benefits is being missed" (Hollocks 1992). The apparent under-utilisation of simulation may be linked to the difficulties associated with a major modelling element. That is, the process by which real-world problems are developed as logical models. It is in this area which SSM has a particularly strong claim. The approach discussed in this chapter has been developed through modelling out-patient facilities at a general hospital, but it may be used for other 'messy' problem situations.

19.2 Simulation Modelling

Law and Kelton (1991) note that "As a technique, simulation is one of the most widely used in operational research and management science". Surveys by Beasley and Whitchurch (1984), Christy and Watson (1983) and Hollocks (1992) consistently demonstrate that simulation is one of the most popular techniques used by practitioners. This view is also expressed by authors such as Blightman (1987), Jasany (1989) and Kochhar (1989).

There are a number of reasons why simulation might be used:

- "[N]o advanced mathematics is required, and realistic models become possible" (Kleijnen and Van Groenendaal (1992).
- "[T]o facilitate choice among several different and competing schemes" (Lewis and Orav 1989).
- "The system as yet does not exist ... Experimentation with the system is expensive ... Experimentation with the system is inappropriate" (Davies and O'Keefe 1989).
- "Most important of all, the very act of studying a real system may change it and render our observations about it invalid" (Carroll 1987).
- "Frequently, however, the analytical approach either does not permit an adequate model or is found unhelpful and not particularly compelling by a mathematically sophisticated management ... the working of the system as a whole may be beyond the capabilities of existing analytical techniques, without drastic and unjustifiable simplification" (Paul and Balmer 1993).

Simulation is not without its drawbacks. The time and expense involved in developing a simulation model being major concerns. However, if simulation is viewed as part of a problem-structuring and problem-resolution process, which includes finding out about the system and the problem area, achieving agreement on what is to be modelled and building client confidence in the model, then much of the cost attributed to simulation would arise regardless of the chosen modelling methodology. This process of simulation modelling is defined in different ways by different authors, but, often in essence, with the same result:

- "[T]hree broad steps in simulation. problem definition, model development and decision support" (Mathewson 1989).
- "[A] project can be viewed as having three phases:
  - modelling;
  - computing
  - experimentation" (Pidd 1984).
- "The phases of a typical management science simulation project are:
  1. formulation and model specification;
  2. model development;
  3. model verification;
  4. model validation;
  5. experimental design;
  6. implementation" (Hurrion 1989).
- "Simulation ... can be divided into three major, usually overlapping, areas:
  1. Setting up the simulation problem. This includes identification of the question being asked ... .
  2. Running the simulation on a digital computer ... .
  3. Analyzing the output" (Lewis and Orav 1989).

Despite the possibility of authors' good intentions, simulation textbooks tend to ignore, or only fleetingly mention, the important processes of problem formulation and logical model development. As Paul and Balmer (1993) note "Experience of this process of model formulation is not easy to provide in the context of the

essentially artificial 'practical' exercises in either a textbook or academic course".
In fact, simulation texts give no real guidance as to how this process should be
undertaken.

19.3   Problem Structuring

Operational research could lay claim to providing management with the tools needed to forecast, manage, monitor and plan, yet managers often ignore the methodologies provided by this discipline (Lehaney et al. 1993). The reasons for this are
manifold, and within OR there has been a great deal of argument as to why, in practice, greater use is not made of modelling methodologies. The following background
discussion provides a brief outline of the debates which have risen in the operational
research and systems arenas from World War II until the present day. Much fuller
treatments are given by Checkland (1981), Jackson (1992), Lewis (1994), Rosenhead
(1989), and Wilson (1984).

Operational research came to the fore during World War II, when military problems typically required optimisation, subject to constraints. The nature of the armed
forces, and the high level of secrecy required during war time, meant that decisions
were imposed from above, and that personnel had as little involvement as possible
in decision making and operations. The successes of operational research during the
war were hoped to be mirrored in both private- and public-sector post-war organisations:

> In its heyday of the 1960s and early 1970s this approach was widely seen as the ratio-
> nal way to take decisions.
>
> *Rosenhead 1989*

> It is, then, proposed that the development of man–machine digital systems be conducted
> as an applied scientific enterprise, regulated in accordance with an evolving set of
> hypotheses that relate systems design to systems performance, and are experimentally
> tested in anticipation of, and in response to, changing conditions.
>
> *Sackman 1967*

The hopes for operational research were dented as a result of the more flexible
and open social structures which existed in Western countries after World War II.
Whilst technically-based problems suited a technique-oriented approach, many post-
war organisational difficulties had much more to do with social science than physics:

> Unfortunately 'management science' has not been able to resolve these problems. Hence
> there is an incentive to examine alternative paradigms to those of natural science,
> while continuing to build on the scientific bedrock: rationality applied to the findings
> of experience.
>
> *Checkland 1981*

> [T]he basic philosophy and methodology of the 'hard' systems approaches makes them
> unsuitable to applications in social situations, for there exists much corroborating
> evidence of failure in such situations.
>
> *Lewis 1994*

A much-quoted example of such failure is the RAND Corporation's experiences with
the New York public health sector, using methods which had proved successful
with the New York fire service (Greenberger et al. 1976). Critics of OR in practice
argue that failures have arisen because of OR's concentration on problems which
have clearly defined, agreed, objectives. (e.g. Ackoff 1979; Churchman 1967).
Reportage of many cases tends to concentrate (often exclusively) on the 'hard' aspects

of modelling, with little or no information given on the modelling process. What information is provided is often sketchy, and indicates a variety of ad hoc methods for model development.

It is not easy to distinguish whether the criticisms of 'hard' methods are of the methods themselves, or of the application of those methods in practice. In some ways, however, this distinction does not matter if the perception is one of failure. As a response to this 'failure', a range of so-called 'soft' methods has been developed over the last 30 years or so. These 'soft' methods address the problem-structuring side of modelling:

> The growing interest in understanding the practice of OR has, not unnaturally, tended to concentrate on experience with those 'soft' methodologies which address both process and content management issues.
>
> *Bryant 1988*

The use of problem structuring methodologies has a number of benefits:

- a reference framework for the less experienced analyst, which may be particularly useful in tricky situations;
- improved communication through the use of a common modelling methodology;
- an important reminder of the process to authors who are writing up case material.

Soft Systems Methodology (SSM) is one such approach to modelling developed by Checkland (1981) and Wilson (1984), and is intended for use in human activity systems, which are likely to have problem areas that are not clearly identified and which are unstructured.

SSM enables the people involved in running a system ('actors'), those responsible for controlling it ('owners') and those who receive its benefits ('customers') to participate in the process of developing a system model, which is likely to encourage acceptability of the model. SSM may be used to aid the identification of system boundaries and system activities, particularly in complex systems. This is particularly useful in a case where a 'hard' technique may eventually be applied, such as in the simulation of an out-patients system. Activity areas within the National Health Service (NHS) are typically 'messy', and are particularly suited to an SSM approach. The seven general stages of Soft Systems Methodology, as developed by Checkland (1981) and by Wilson (1984), are shown in Figure 19.1. The methodology is iterative in approach, and is not prescriptive as to a starting point.

A primary task root definition is a description of a system which is based on neutral or obvious real-world activities, such as "file papers", "enter data", etc. As such, a primary task root definition may result in a conceptual model which is fairly similar to an existing organisation chart.

The aim is to get to a position of consensus on the following:

- *owners*, the roles of monitoring and taking appropriate control actions;
- *actors*, the roles of running the system;
- *customers*, the beneficiaries of the system;
- *transformation*, the system inputs converted to outputs;
- *weltanschauung*, the world view, the perspective taken in defining the system;
- *environment*, the constraints on the system.

The above can be formed as the mnemonic CATWOE, and may be used to deter the modeller from omitting important system elements. Any omissions should be deliberate and rational.

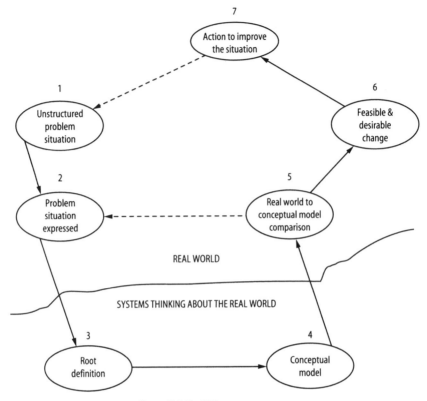

Figure 19.1. The SSM seven-stage process.

19.4   Simulation and SSM Combined

The idea for combination was developed during the modelling of a 'messy' problem situation, in which there were differing views of the system of out-patient facilities at a general hospital. However, it was recognised that many simulations have failed to provide client confidence, and that resolving the varying perceptions of a single system is a difficult and complex task (Lehaney and Hlupic 1995; Lehaney and Paul 1994a). SSM was used at an early stage to develop end-user confidence, and to produce a conceptual model. This gave rise to the problem of how the necessary conditions of a conceptual model could be developed as the sufficient conditions of an activity cycle diagram, and an approach to overcoming this modelling difficulty has been described by Lehaney and Paul (1994b).

The general approach proved to be successful, but was undertaken on a rather ad hoc basis, and a structure for combining the two powerful modelling approaches of Soft Systems Methodology and simulation would be more helpful. Simulation itself does not provide an approach to obtain consensus on a system specification, whereas SSM does. SSM itself has no structure for assessing the feasibility of actions, nor can it demonstrate easily and quickly a number of options from which those that are desirable can be chosen. By using simulation to model a range of options, their desirability and feasibility may be assessed, and informed choices can be made.

The combination of SSM and simulation may be viewed as a means to operationalise Phase 6 of the SSM process, in which feasible and desirable actions are identified. A seemingly different view of it is that the combination provides a means to operationalise the early stages of simulation methodology, in which the analyst finds out about the problem and structures it as a logical model. These views are, in fact, different perceptions of the same eight-phase process, and are only differentiated by the entry point to the same methodological cycle.

The approach is iterative, and regardless of starting point both the 'hard' and 'soft' aspects of modelling may be undertaken. A 'hard' approach modeller might (ostensibly), for instance, begin by producing an Activity Cycle Diagram. Once in the methodological cycle the 'soft' modelling activities would simply occur later in the process. (see Figure 19.2).

Phase 1 comprises the early stages of SSM, in which finding out about the problem situation is undertaken, the problem situation is expressed (rich picture), and the system is described (root definition). From the root definition, a conceptual model is formed which contains the minimum set of activities needed to support the root definition. The conceptual model is compared with the system (Phase 1a), and, where appropriate, the root definition is changed, and a new conceptual model is developed. If the activity level of the conceptual model is too broad, selected activities are expanded until the appropriate level of resolution is reached.

As primary task root definitions are used, it is likely that the systems identified within the conceptual model will match those of the organisation. Following temporary entities through the system may result in systems which do not match those of the organisation and which may not have owners. At this stage, if such systems are identified, it may be that control actions are taken. If the organisation appoints an owner of a newly identified system, for example, this may be sufficient to address any problem situations which have arisen.

If Phase 7 indicates that model output and system output do not match as well as is desired, the route of change must be through Phase 4. Adjusting the model ad hoc

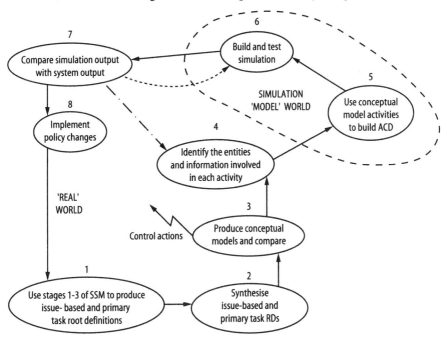

Figure 19.2. Simulation modelling process.

is likely to lead to self-fulfilling validation prophecies. (The modeller must make a judgement regarding minor changes.) The route through Phase 4 preserves the integrity of the model, and mimics the 'rich picture–root defintion–conceptual model–rich picture–root definition' circle of SSM, which should not be broken by direct input from the Rich Picture to the Conceptual Model. (The latter should be built solely from the root definition.) In turn, SSM mimics hypothetico-deductive methodology which does not permit data which have been used to formulate a hypothesis to test the same hypothesis.

If the conceptual model development has been undertaken rigorously and with sufficient participation, it should be unnecessary to revisit the early SSM stages. Any model–system mismatches should be addressed by the Phase 4–Phase 7–Phase 4 iteration.

Once policy changes have been explored and implemented, the system, being dynamic, should be re-examined using SSM. The cycle then continues.

19.5   Conclusions

This chapter discusses a process for formally linking the two approaches of simulation and SSM. It enables the modeller to utilise the problem-structuring capabilities of SSM to help define a system and its parameters with the associated increases in model confidence experienced by the use of participatory methods. The approach also enables the effectiveness of simulation to be utilised in assessing the feasibility of a range of options.

Combining simulation and SSM in a formal structure provides analysts with a methodology for addressing 'messy' problem situations in which there may be no consensus on the system to be modelled, but where a 'hard' simulation model is a requirement of the end user.

The approach suggested offers relatively inexperienced analysts a means to explore a problem situation in the difficult early stages of modelling. It affords experienced analysts with an approach that may be wholly or partly employed as circumstances require.

Using a soft approach increases the likelihood of end-user acceptance of simulation models, and thus reduces wasted cost. Hence, value is added by means of focusing on the process as a whole.

References

Ackoff, RL (1979) The future of operational research is past. *Journal of the Operational Research Society,* 30:189–199.
Beasley, J and Whitchurch, G (1984) O.R education – a survey of young O.R workers. *Journal of the Operational Research Society,* 35: 281–288.
Blightman, B (1987) Where now with simulation? *Journal of the Operational Research Society,* 38(2): 769–770.
Bryant, J. (1988) Frameworks of inquiry: OR practice across the hard–soft divide. *Journal of the Operational Research Society,* 39(5): 423–435.
Carroll, JM (1987) *Simulation using Personal Computers.* Englewood Cliffs, NJ: Prentice Hall.
Carter, L and Huzan, E (1973) *A Practical Approach to Computer Simulation in Business.* London: George Allen & Unwin.
Checkland, PB (1981) *Systems Thinking, Systems Practice.* Chichester: Wiley.
Christy, DP and Watson, HJ (1983) The application of simulation: a survey of industrial practice. *Interfaces,* 13(5): 47–52.
Churchman, CW (1967) Wicked problems. *Management Science,* 14: 141–142.

Davies, RM and O'Keefe, R (1989) *Simulation Modelling With Pascal*. Englewood Cliffs, NJ: Prentice Hall.

Greenberger, M, Crenson, MA and Crissey, BL (1976) *Models in the Policy Process*. New York: Russell Sage.

Hollocks, B (1992) A well kept secret. *OR Insight*, 5(4): 12–17.

Hurrion, RD (1989) Graphics and interaction. In *Computer Modelling for Discrete Simulation*. Pidd, M (Ed.). Chichester: John Wiley: 101–119.

Jackson, M (1992) *Systems Methodology for the Management Sciences*. London: Plenum.

Jasany, LC (1989) Simulation software update: kudos and caveats. *Automation (P.D.E)*, 36(2): 27–29.

Kleijnen, J and Van Groenendaal, W (1992) *Simulation A Statistical Perspective*. Chichester: John Wiley.

Kochhar, A (1989) Computer simulation of manufacturing systems – 3 decades of progress. In *Proceedings of the 3rd European Simulation Congress*. San Diego, CA. Computer Simulation Society. 3–9.

Law, AM and Kelton, WD (1991) *Simulation Modelling and Analysis*. New York: McGraw-Hill.

Lehaney, B and Hlupic, V (1995) Simulation modelling for resource allocation and planning in the health sector. *Journal of the Royal Society of Health,* 115(6): 382–385.

Lehaney, B and Paul, RJ (1994a) Using soft systems methodology to develop a simulation of out-patient services. *Journal of the Royal Society for Health,* 114(5): 248–251.

Lehaney, B and Paul, RJ (1994b) Developing sufficient conditions for an activity cycle diagram from the necessary conditions in a conceptual model. *Systemist* 16(3): 261–268.

Lehaney, B, Warwick, S and Wisniewski, M (1993) The use of quantitative modelling methods in the UK: some national and regional comparisons. *Journal of European Business Education,* 3(2): 57–71.

Lewis, P (1994) *Information-systems Development*. London: Pitman.

Lewis, PA and Orav, EJ (1989) *Simulation Methodology for Statisticians, Operations Analysts, and Engineers,* Vol 1. California: Wadsworth and Brooks/Cole.

Mathewson, SC (1989) The implementation of simulation languages. In *Computer Modelling for Discrete Simulation*. Pidd, M (Ed.). Chichester: John Wiley: 23–56.

Paul, RJ and Balmer, D (1993) *Simulation Modelling*. Bromley: Chartwell Bratt.

Pidd, M (1984) Computer simulation for operational research in 1984. In *Developments in Operational Research*. Eglese, RW and Rand, GK (Eds). Oxford: Pergamon Press.

Rosenhead, J (Ed.) (1989) *Rational Analysis for a Problematic World*. Chichester: John Wiley.

Sackman, H (1967) *Computers, Systems Science and Evolving Society: The Challenge of Man-Machine Digital Systems*. New York: John Wiley.

Wilson, B (1984) *Systems: Concepts, Methodologies, and Applications*. Chichester: John Wiley.

20 The Centre for Applied Simulation Modelling

Ray J. Paul

Abstract

The Centre for Applied Simulation Modelling (CASM) started in 1982. Since that time a number of software developments have taken place which have been reported on in the literature. These developments reflect the research group's views on one of the ways in which simulation modelling could be conducted in practice in order to add value to business, commerce and government policy. This chapter re-examines these views with respect to the underlying methodology of simulation modelling, discusses the latest version of the simulation software developed by members of the CASM team and mentions the method of organisation of the CASM research team. Some comments on the success or otherwise of these endeavours are made and on the future anticipated research endeavours of the group.

20.1 Introduction

The Centre for Applied Simulation Modelling (CASM) was initiated in 1982 and its fundamental approach to simulation enunciated by Balmer and Paul (1986). This research is continuing at Brunel University. Paul (1992b) and Paul and Hlupic (1994b) reported on the work of CASM up until 1994 and this chapter revises that work. The objectives of the research group were based on the teaching and consultancy experience of the project's directors. Research work is undertaken by a continuous stream of bright would-be Ph.D. students, who tackle specific parts of the research programme. Sixteen students have already succeeded in obtaining their Ph.D.s (Abdurahiman 1994; Angelides 1992; Au 1990; Barakat 1992; Chew 1986; Domingo 1991; Doukidis 1985; El Sheikh 1987; Fatin 1996; Hlupic 1993; Kienbaum 1995; Knox 1988; Mak 1993; Mashhour 1989; Mejia 1992; Mukhtar 1997) and four students are likely to complete in 1998. There are 10 research students currently working on the project. The research group also includes several academics from institutions in various countries such as the United States, Croatia, Slovenia, Brasil, Greece and Hong Kong. Many papers have been published in the research literature and these are given in the References, in a fairly complete listing of all the CASM papers and theses.

The CASM research group concentrates on problems related to discrete event computer-based simulation modelling. This area of modelling is particularly popular amongst the operational research and information systems fraternities. Whilst continuous modelling, differential equations, systems/industrial dynamics and other temporal modelling systems are undoubtedly of interest, being related to discrete event modelling, at the current time CASM is restricting its research interests in order to make progress in one of these dimensions.

In the next section, the process of simulation modelling is examined and the problems associated with simulation modelling, as seen by the author, are outlined. Following this, the objectives and underlying methodology of the CASM research group are described. Some of the modelling environments that have been developed are described in the following section. Application areas are covered next. This chapter concludes with the experiences and future anticipated research of members of the research group.

20.2   Simulation Modelling

In many textbooks on operational research and in some textbooks on simulation modelling, the simulation process is described as follows. There is a real-world problem. This problem is formulated as a logical model. Logical models can be activity cycle diagrams, flow charts, block diagrams, etc. There are a variety of ways to represent the logic of a formulated problem. The next step is to convert the logical model into a computer model; sometimes it is a computer program, sometimes it is a data driven generic simulation system. This computer model is verified and tested to see if it is doing what the analyst wants it to do. The model is used as an operational model to produce some results, or some conclusions, or for implementation after the operational model has been validated against the real world. An implicit assumption is that the product of the modelling process is a set of results, usually numerical, which lead decision makers and/or analysts to some conclusions, from which some decisions are implemented. Many textbook expositions point out that the process is not quite as linear as has just been described. There are many iterations or feedbacks in the process as understanding of the real-world problem changes.

In many real-world situations, however, the above description of the simulation process is inadequate. Real-world problems are owned by interest groups. The definition of the problem is influenced by the owners of the problem, especially for complex strategic decision making. Such problems are usually owned by many interest groups, some of whom may be in conflict. Because the problem is complex, formulation is a very difficult task. The construction of a logical model representing the formulation of the problem is, in many instances, the most difficult aspect of the problem. In fact, understanding what the problem is may be the object of the whole exercise. The analyst should be prepared to constantly undertake problem reformulation to obtain a common understanding of the problem, as part of the modelling process.

A dynamic (changing) logical model needs to be turned into a computer model with relative ease. Otherwise, if this part of the process takes a long time, contact with the real-world problem starts to diminish. If the analyst discusses the computer model with the decision makers infrequently, then the chance that the computer model represents the real-world problem is small. In many instances, the function that the computer model serves is to perform a medium of communication for the structuring of the problem for all participants in the decision-making process.

It is obviously necessary to verify that the computer model does what one thinks it should. But it is questionable as to how much emphasis should be placed on producing the operational model which is going to be used for experimentation purposes. In many cases, the production of a computer model which secures problem definition agreement amongst the decision makers may be sufficient to satisfy all participants. It may not be necessary to actually pursue the modelling process to the point of getting statistically valid results. In the event that the latter should be required, it is usually a minor part of the whole modelling process. It is curious that so many textbooks concentrate on the theoretical aspects of this part of the modelling process.

In summary then, the problems associated with using simulation modelling as a decision aiding technique are as follows. First of all, most problems to which one applies simulation are poorly defined. In fact, one might go further and claim that if the problem is not poorly defined, there are probably better and more reliable methods of solving the problem than the rather crude technique of simulation modelling. Secondly, any problem of any complexity which is important will probably involve conflicting interests and understanding. One must anticipate that if the modelling process is going to lead to change in the organisation, then it is unlikely that all decision makers will see these changes as favourable to them. The analyst must anticipate negative attitudes and spoiling tactics. As much as possible, the modelling process is used in a neutral way to help the participants in the decision-making process understand their problem and come to a resolution amongst themselves. The third problem associated with simulation modelling is that there never exists a static specification of the problem, it is always dynamic. Even if one succeeds in satisfying the conflicting views of the decision makers, it is probable that for complex problems the specification still undergoes change. The real world is dynamic and therefore the perceived problem will be dynamic as well. The fourth problem with simulation modelling is the question of 'model confidence', which is better terminology than the commonly used description of verification and validation. No computer program of any size can possibly be verified. No model of any size can possibly be validated against the real world, especially given that the real world is not static. The model cannot be proved to be correct. The aim should be to use methods that demonstrate confidence in what the model is doing and the way it is doing it.

Simulation modelling is involved in decision aiding. Discrete event simulation modelling is a quantitative technique. The outputs are numerical, and numerical values tend to indicate that one course of action might be better than another. However, such a numerical technique cannot represent all possible factors in the problem scenario. It can crudely represent most or some of them in a quantitative way, but it cannot represent subjective factors. It must be remembered that the simulation modelling process is not designed to find the answer or answers. It is there to help decision makers take decisions, or to help decision makers gain an understanding of their problem. The numerical output of the simulation model in itself may often be of no particular intrinsic value. Learning about the processes of the interactions that go on within a complex environment, the relationships between the variables, is probably the dominating characteristic of interest in simulation modelling.

20.3   CASM Objectives

CASM is researching into simulation modelling, with a view to producing computer systems that automate, as much as possible, the simulation modelling process. The aim is to make simulation efficient, as a modelling tool for helping decision makers understand their problems. It is impossible to produce an all-purpose simulation modelling system that can handle any problem that one might wish to model. The analyst is restricted to what a simulation system can handle or the simulation system must provide programming code that can be modified to do the task that has been set. In this latter context, CASM are dedicated to the production of transparent models (i.e. program code that can be read by somebody else). Gifted amateurs not only produce program code that cannot be read by other programmers, but after a short lapse of time, cannot even be read by themselves! It is therefore quite apparent that a highly stylised, highly structured method of writing computer simulation models is required, so that anyone familiar with this structuring and style is able to read and understand it.

CASM is a research group operating within a university environment, so the computer systems that are researched into must also help in the teaching of simulation modelling, as well as assisting in further research into simulation modelling. Other apparently relatively insignificant factors need to be taken into account. A variety of career paths for the research participants must be satisfied. If this were not so, then individuals would feel free to go in any direction that appeared to satisfy their goals. Lastly, but not least, in a research environment it is important that the individuals concerned enjoy what they are doing. If the researchers do not enjoy their work, a variety of reasons will be found for why things are not working, not being done, or not happening.

20.4   The CASM Approach to Environments

Figure 20.1 illustrates the sort of simulation environment that CASM envisages would help the analyst assist the decision maker. This environment is more extensively described by Balmer and Paul (1986). The analyst and customer, or decision maker, would use a system that assisted in problem formulation. This problem formulation system would essentially capture the model logic of the problem to which could be applied to an Interactive Simulation Program Generator (ISPG). The ISPG would produce a simulation model which called on a library of software subsystems to actually run the simulation itself. Simulation model output would be analysed by an output analyser which would, again under analyst control, help determine experimental design for running and controlling the simulation model. It is anticipated that the problem formulator and output analyser would close the loop, so that the analyst and decision maker could collectively use the complete system.

Attempts have been made by CASM to develop a problem formulator. These attempts are described by Doukidis (1985, 1987), Doukidis and Paul (1985, 1986, 1987b), Paul (1987) and Paul and Doukidis (1986). The final system, which works, is a natural language understanding system. Using an activity cycle diagram paradigm, the natural language understanding system asks questions of the analyst at a computer terminal. This system has been demonstrated to work, in that the model logic for a problem can be determined in this way. Curiously enough, however, the system is not used in practice. The reason is that the purpose of the system, to help the analyst formulate a problem in conjunction with the decision makers, is not practically feasible in this way. One cannot expect a decision maker, or decision makers, to sit in front of a screen, talking sideways to an analyst who is being controlled, in a textual sense, by the computer. This is a completely unnatural way for humans to

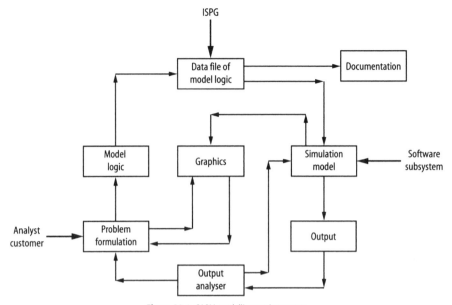

Figure 20.1. CASM modelling environments.

hold a discourse. The terminology that the natural language understanding system uses is also unnatural for the decision maker, albeit well understood by the analyst.

The latest attempts at applying intelligent systems to problem formulation are described by Abdurahimin and Paul (1994). A system is being developed using inductive learning, where the problem is hypothesized using positive and negative examples of aspects of the problem. The resultant formulation is logically correct, although there is no guarantee concerning its validity.

The ISPG part of the environment has been researched into throughout the duration of the CASM research project. First attempts emulated the work of Clementson's (1982) CAPS/ECSL package. The second version, called AUTOSIM, made some minor improvements (Paul and Chew 1987). A later version, VS6, is described by Knox (1988). All these interactive simulation program generators generate program code in a high-level programming language, in this case Pascal. A high-level programming language was deliberately selected because of the availability of expertise and assistance on a broad level. Many simulation systems develop simulation code in their own purpose-built language. These languages have undoubtedly been developed to a high degree of sophistication suitable for simulation modelling purposes. However, they require participants in the modelling process to learn the language in order to use it. CASM has concentrated on using a high-level programming language to avoid the problem of scarcity of experts.

In order to handle the problem of simulation-specific code, CASM have produced well-written modifiable libraries of simulation routines. These routines enable the commonplace parts of any simulation model to be easily accessed. The generated program code for any particular problem is written in a three-phase structure, as described by Crooks *et al.* (1986) and Paul and Balmer (1993). This structure has the virtue of describing the control of flow in any model accurately and is easy to modify. Bearing in mind the earlier points made about the need for dynamic model development, it is clear that this ease of modification is an essential characteristic of any generated simulation program. Apart from the virtue of writing simulation models in a highly stylised structured way, an interactive simulation program generator also has the advantage that it produces models in which one may have a high degree of confidence. As the ISPG is applied to more and more problems, the errors in the system itself are slowly removed, so that the generated code is more likely to be correct. Another virtue of using an ISPG is the ability to undertake rapid prototyping. This means that if the specification of the problem changes, as it almost invariably does, then the ISPG can be reapplied to write a new program each time.

In theory, if the description of the model logic is adequate enough for an ISPG to produce the simulation code, then it must be adequate enough for documentation of the simulation model to also be automatically produced. Whilst this is almost self-evident, it seems that the task of producing a system that automatically documents programs is not quite as exciting for prospective researchers as many of the other tasks available within the research project!

The last part of Figure 20.1, the output analyser, presupposes that the large body of published statistical knowledge describing how to analyse output from simulation models can be encoded into some sort of intelligent system. Regrettably, however, it turns out that the statistical knowledge available, largely tested on simple simulation models, does not appear to work so readily on the complex sort of models that one generally applies simulation to. Therefore, research in this area is into simple ways of analysing the output from simulation models. Some early results that reinforce this approach are emerging in work undertaken by Mejia (1992).

20.5   Modelling Environments

20.5.1   Specification Methods

Surprisingly, given the relative length of time that simulation modelling has been undertaken on computers, there is no fixed method for specifying simulation problems. There are a large number of diagrammatic techniques, such as activity cycle diagrams and Petri nets, and semi-formal methods as exemplified by Zeigler's (1984) work. The basic problem in specification appears to be as follows. If specification is going to be used as a vehicle for communication, it must have a simple structure. However, many simulation models inherently model complex situations and the combination of objects or entities in an activity requires some complex conditions to be stated. If these conditions are described explicitly in the specification method, then the specification becomes very difficult to follow.

At one extreme are the diagramming methods, which give a very simple representation of the basic simulation model structure. At the other extreme are the formal methods or mathematical approaches, which make everything explicit, but suffer from a heavy use of mathematics, and therefore, not understandable by very many people. Ceric and Paul (1989) describe a brief survey of available diagrammatic methods that are commonly used in simulation modelling. In a later paper, the principle of Comprehensive Harmony is expounded for the requirements of a specification method. This principle quite simply requires that the specification method must be reasonably comprehensive. However, this comprehensiveness must be balanced by a harmony in the method of specification that makes it intelligible to the active participants in the simulation modelling process. It is anticipated that such comprehensive harmony might be provided by a mixture of diagrammatic methods with a hierarchy of descriptions leading to formal methods at the lowest level.

Domingo (1991) describes a range of simulation specification methods leading up to possible ways of using formal methods as the specification approach. Some research is going on into visual formulation methods, which include diagrammatic methods such as activity cycle diagrams and Petri nets, and simulation graphs. More particularly, specification languages and the systems theoretical approach by Zeigler are being examined. Some of this research encompasses an examination of formal languages such as Z and VDM. Whilst these languages have not been designed for simulation specification, and in particular are not very adept at handling temporal issues, it is felt that an attempt to use such methods for simulation specification will assist in the derivation of a language in its own right. The main advantage of using formal methods is that the specification is provable in some sense. In other words, the model logic is at least consistent, albeit it can never be known if it is exactly what is required.

Mak (1993) has shown that the activity cycle diagram specification of a discrete event simulation model can be translated into a Systems Dynamics diagram. There are certain extra pieces of information required and the translation can require intelligent transformation. Curiously, the reverse translation proved to be very difficult as the Systems Dynamics model needs much less structure than the discrete event simulation.

20.5.2   Graphics Driven Environments

Since the inception of CASM, the creation of a simulation environment has been one of the main objectives of the research group. Chew (1986) produced the first of CASM's Interactive Simulation Program Generators (ISPGs) which form the basis for a three-phase simulation system written in Pascal. Later work on graphics, adding a picture to the simulation modelling process, is described by Knox (1988).

The latest development in these environments is described by Au (1990) and Au and Paul (1993, 1994, 1996, 1997). This graphics driven environment allows the users, the analyst and the customer, to specify the problem using iconic representations for the objects in the system. The icons are laid out on the screen in a logical fashion, intelligible to the user as well as to the analyst. No particular formalism is used for this, in terms of diagrams or methods, although underpinning the method is the activity cycle diagram concept. This system was developed on the Macintosh microcomputer, which is an ideal environment for mixing graphics display with text. The system provides the user with assistance in the construction of the logic of the problem and in the addition of quantitative and conditional information to the model logic.

A feature of this system, called MacGRaSE, is that different levels of detail concerning the problem are constructed in parallel, by a mixture of diagramming methods and tabular information. So, for example, if the users specify an object such as a person in the system, then this person can be represented by an easily identifiable icon. At the same time, a description of what type of object or entity a person is can be input to a table. The MacGRaSE system allows the user to draw the equivalent activity cycle diagram for the problem. The problem can be run in interpretative mode, so that the dynamics of the system can be visually seen on the screen, checked and verified as much as any such visual representation can verify anything. Some complex simulations might be difficult if not impossible to completely describe using such a graphics driven specification environment. MacGRaSE allows a more basic model to be input and generated as a Pascal program, so that the particular idiosyncratic difficulties can be edited into the program code. Such complexities usually revolve around the conditions for an activity to start and often involve several levels of conditional statement, which is difficult to encompass entirely within a graphics driven environment.

Future work in this area is intended to remedy some of the possible deficiencies in the complexity of the problem that can be handled by this system. This might be achieved using a mixture of graphics and artificial intelligence techniques. Further enhancements might, in any case, be provided, by producing a richer mixture of interrelated screens for the analyst to specify the problem with, plus some better help facilities for reminding the user of what is required for a complete specification. Hopefully, in the not too distant future, one might build such an environment and incorporate the benefits of the research in formal methods described above.

Another research direction, which incorporates many aspects of artificial intelligence, is a simulation system which is very different to the ones described above. This simulation system is based on a spreadsheet approach to simulation software. This approach was adopted as it was felt that many potential users of simulation modelling are already familiar with spreadsheet packages such as Lotus 1-2-3. So, the interface to this package is basically similar to Lotus 1-2-3 itself. A description of the simulation problem can be written in natural language form, and then the simulation system will interpret this natural language using some artificial intelligence approaches such as semantic networks. So, one spreadsheet level in the simulation package, as described by Barakat (1992), is a semantic network connecting the objects in the system to their definition, such as entities, activities and so on. A second equivalent level to this, in spreadsheet terms, provides an activity cycle diagram for the problem. A third equivalent level in the spreadsheet system provides the numerical data required to actually run the simulation model. It is also possible to add to the system an iconic visual representation which can be run dynamically.

20.6   Application Areas

The CASM research group is constantly aware that its research endeavour into simulation modelling needs to be related to the real world if the research is not to become esoteric. There are a number of application areas that we are looking at.

Kuljis *et al.* (1990), Kuljis and Paul (1994, 1995), Paul (1995a) and Paul and Kuljis (1995) have built an out-patients clinic model using commercial application packages. This out-patients clinic has been built so that OR analysts in the health service can go to the administrators and doctors who operate, or who are responsible for such clinics, to demonstrate the feasibility of different clinic practices. A common problem with clinics is the waiting time of the patients at various stages throughout the process and it is hoped, by showing a visual simulation representation of these clinics for different clinic operating practices, that the people concerned might be persuaded to operate practices that are more beneficial to the patients and at no loss to them. The system is currently undergoing trials.

Lehaney and Paul (1994a, 1994b, 1996a, 1996b) and Paul and Lehaney (1995) describe work that is being conducted on an out-patients clinic in the UK. Here, the purpose of the exercise is to use Soft Systems Methodology to understand the problem sufficiently to build a simulation model. The soft modelling approach added to the hard simulation language is proving both effective and acceptable to the 'customer'.

El Sheikh et al. (1987) have described the application of early CASM simulation systems to a port problem. This particular application demonstrated that simulation was a powerful tool for handling a potentially difficult political situation. The results of the simulation were reasonably well known in any case. The simulation model's benefits derived from the discussion that took place around the results. Participants suggested that things would be different if parameters changes were made. The simulation model enabled such parameter changes to be rapidly tested, showing that some if not all of the suggestions made were, in fact, erroneous.

Paul (1989c) describes how simulation modelling has potential applications in the area of stock control. It is quite clear that in the world of increasingly complex and flexible methods of manufacturing, simulation modelling is an inexpensive method of testing such new approaches, without actually building a factory or a stock control system and then finding out too late that it does not do as required. Hlupic and Paul (1992, 1994b) describe work being carried out in the area of Flexible Manufacturing Systems, which includes an extensive case study with a manufacturing company (Hlupic and Paul 1993c, 1994a, 1994b, 1994c, 1994d).

Our early CASM systems, described by Crookes et al. (1986), have been used in a number of military applications. These are described by Holder and Gittins (1989), Stapley and Holder (1992) and Williams et al. (1989). The interesting characteristic of the use of the simulation systems by these groups is that they partially replaced previous systems quite successfully and very effectively. The models described by Holder and Gittins (1989) and by Williams et al. (1989) were eventually joined together in a reasonably short space of time. It is pleasing that the claimed flexibility and effectiveness of these systems has actually been demonstrated in a real application and the systems are continuing to be of use (Ceric and Hlupic, 1993; Stapley and Holder, 1992).

20.7   Other CASM Research Areas

There are several other research areas covered by the members of the CASM research group. For example, Hlupic (1993) researches into simulation modelling software approaches to manufacturing problems. The major part of this work relates to simulation software evaluation criteria and software selection methodology (Hlupic and Paul 1993a, b, 1995a, b, 1996).

Angelides and Paul (1993a, b, 1995) research into combining simulation games and intelligent tutoring systems. Mukhtar (1997) has demonstrated how to build such a system. Hirata and Paul (1996) examine an object-oriented programming architecture for simulation modelling. Mladenic et al. (1993, 1994) research into using machine learning techniques to interpret results from discrete event simulation. Paul and Chanev (1998) have investigated the potential of genetic algorithms in simulation model optimisation.

Some members of CASM are researching into object-oriented program generators for simulation modelling. As a part of this research, a Model Description Language is proposed for the specification of models based on the process interaction approach, and is used inside a program generator currently under development (Kienbaum 1995; Kienbaum and Paul 1994b).

Future CASM research will explore the areas of graphical problem formulation to drive the software systems that automate the simulation process. Research into expert system development for simulation software evaluation has been initiated. Some work has started on determining the relationships between discrete event simulation modelling and more general forms of modelling of systems over time, such as systems dynamics (Mak 1993), control theory, differential equations and queueing theory.

20.8   Experiences and Conclusions

The CASM simulation systems have been tested on many groups of students over the last 12 years. It is good experience for students who are going to work in operational research to use systems that are not fully tested. It teaches them to be more than a little wary of software! One of the features of the systems developed is the concentration on activity cycle diagrams. However, activity cycle diagrams are not all-embracing. It is very easy to construct examples of problems where the logic of the problem is not captured in the activity cycle diagram. For example, in the port problem described by El Sheikh *et al.* (1987), the activity cycle diagram is very simple. It has two small cycles and only two activities, but the logic in the model is very complex. The rules for engagement of ships and berths require a matching between the ship cargo, the handling facilities of the berth, the priorities that various ships have on different berths and so on. These priority rules cannot be visually displayed on an activity cycle diagram, but they are an essential component of this particular simulation problem.

In conclusion, CASM believe that their research approach will lead to a concentration on the more difficult tasks of simulation modelling. These are: problem definition and understanding, improving model confidence, experimental design and 'implementation'. These are the intellectual tasks facing analysts in helping the decision maker. They are often not given the effort they require because of the time taken in the more mundane programming elements of the simulation model. If the analyst can concentrate, with the assistance of efficient low-cost software support, on these more difficult intellectual tasks, then the analyst will be able to work more closely with the decision maker. There is no doubt that collaboration between analyst and decision makers in decision aiding is synonymous with success, however one defines success.

References and associated reading

Abdurahimin, V (1994) *Towards Inducing a Simulation Model Description.* Unpublished Ph.D. thesis, Brunel University.

Abdurahiman, V and Paul, RJ (1994) Machine learning and simulation model specification. *Journal of Simulation Practice and Theory,* 2(1): 1–15.

Aharonson-Daniel, L (1996) *Application of Operations Research in Studies of Ambulatory Care Services.* Unpublished Ph.D. thesis, Hong Kong University.

Aharonson-Daniel, L, Hedley, AJ and Paul, RJ (1995) Computer simulation of a general outpatients department. In *Proceedings of the Third Hong Kong (Asia Pacific) Medical Informatics Conference.* MGhee, SM, Hedley, AJ, Wong, CP and Ho, LM (Eds). Hong Kong Society of Medical Informatics Ltd and Hong Kong Computer Society: 134–139.

Angelides, M (1992) *Developing the Didactic Operations for Intelligent Tutoring Systems: A Synthesis of Artificial Intelligence and Hypertext.* Unpublished Ph.D. thesis. University of London.

Angelides, MC and Paul, RJ (1993a) Developing an intelligent tutoring system for a business simulation game. *Journal of Simulation Practice and Theory*, 1(3): 109–135.

Angelides, MC and Paul, RJ (1993b) Towards a framework for integrating intelligent tutoring systems and gaming-simulation. In *Proceedings of the 1993 Winter Simulation Conference*. Evans, GW, Mollagha-semi, M, Russell, EC and Biles, WE (Eds). New York: Association for Computing Machinery: 1281–1289.

Angelides, MC and Paul, RJ (1995) Providing intelligent tutoring within a gaming-simulation environment for learning. *Journal of Intelligent Systems*, 5(2–4): 319–350.

Au, G (1990) *A Graphics Driven Approach To Discrete Event Simulation*. Unpublished Ph.D. thesis, University of London.

Au, G and Paul, RJ (1993) Computer simulation modelling using hypercard. *Journal of Computing and Information Technology*, 1(1): 1–13.

Au, G and Paul, RJ (1994) Graphical simulation model specification based on activity cycle diagrams. *Computers and Industrial Engineering*, 26(2): 295–306.

Au, G and Paul, RJ (1996) Visual simulation modelling: a pictorial approach. *European Journal of Operational Research*, 91(1): 14–26.

Au, G and Paul, RJ (1997) A graphical discrete event simulation environment. *Information Systems and Operational Research*, 35(2): 1–17.

Balmer, DW (1987) Polishing the analysis of the statistical output of comparative simulation experiments. *Simulation*, 49(3): 123–126.

Balmer, DW and Paul, RJ (1986) CASM – the right environment for simulation. *Journal of the Operational Research Society*, 37(5): 443–452.

Barakat, M (1992) *Semantic Modelling for Discrete Event Simulation*. Unpublished Ph.D. thesis, University of London.

Ceric, V and Hlupic, V (1993) Modelling a solid-waste processing system by discrete event simulation. *Journal of the Operational Research Society*, 44(2): 107–114.

Ceric, V and Paul, RJ (1989) Preliminary investigations into simulation model representation. In *Proceedings of the 11th International Symposium on "Computer at the University"*. Zagreb, Croatia: University of Zagreb Computer Centre.

Ceric, V and Paul, RJ (1992) Diagrammatic representations of the conceptual simulation model for discrete event systems. *Mathematics and Computers in Simulation*, 34(3/4): 317–324.

Chew, ST (1986) *Program Generators For Discrete Event Digital Simulation Modelling*. Unpublished Ph.D. thesis, University of London.

Clementson, AT (1982) *Extended Control and Simulation Language*. Birmingham: Cle.Com Ltd.

Crookes, JG, Balmer, DW, Chew, ST and Paul, RJ (1986) A three-phase simulation system written in Pascal. *Journal of the Operational Research Society*,. 37(6): 603–618.

Domingo, LT (1991) *Formal Methods in Specifying Discrete Event Simulation Models*. Unpublished Ph.D. thesis, University of London.

Doukidis, GI (1985) *Discrete Event Simulation Model Formulation Using Natural Language Understanding Systems*. Unpublished Ph.D. thesis, University of London.

Doukidis, GI (1987) An anthology on the homology of simulation with artificial intelligence. *Journal of the Operational Research Society*, 38(8): 701–712.

Doukidis, GI and Paul, RJ (1985) Research into expert systems to aid simulation model formulation. *Journal of the Operational Research Society*, 36(4): 319–325.

Doukidis, GI and Paul, RJ (1986) Experiences in automating the formulation of discrete event simulation models. In *AI Applied to Simulation*. Kerckhoffs, EJH, Vansteenkiste, GC and Zeigler, BP (Eds). Simulation Series, Vol. 18(1). San Diego, CA: The Society for Computer Simulation: 79–90.

Doukidis, GI and Paul, RJ (1987a) ASPES: A Skeletal Pascal Expert System. In *Expert Systems and Artificial Intelligence in Decision Support Systems*. Sol, HG, Takkenberg CATh and de Vries Robbe, PF (Eds). Dordrecht, the Netherlands: D. Reidel: 227–246.

Doukidis, GI and Paul, RJ (1987b) Artificial intelligence aids in discrete event digital simulation modelling. *IEE Proceedings*, 134(4): 278–286.

Doukidis, GI and Paul, RJ (1991) SIPDES: A SImulation Program Debugger using an Expert System. *Expert Systems With Applications*, 2(2/3): 153–165.

Doukidis, GI and Paul, RJ (Eds) (1992a) *Artificial Intelligence in Operational Research*. Basingstoke: Macmillan.

Doukidis, GI and Paul, RJ (1992b) Operational research participation in artificial intelligence: practical experiences. In *Artificial Intelligence in Operational Research*. Doukidis, GI and Paul, RJ (Eds). Basingstoke: Macmillan: 3–7.

Doukidis, GI and Paul, RJ (1992c) Combining operational research and artificial intelligence. In *Artificial Intelligence in Operational Research*. Doukidis, GI and Paul, RJ (Eds). Basingstoke: Macmillan: 63–69.

Doukidis, GI and Paul, RJ (1992d) Methodological issues in artificial intelligence and operational research. In *Artificial Intelligence in Operational Research*. Doukidis, GI and Paul, RJ (Eds). Basingstoke: Macmillan: 303–310.

El Sheikh, AAR (1987) *Simulation Modelling Using A Relational Database Package*. Unpublished Ph.D. thesis, University of London.

El Sheikh, AAR, Paul, RJ, Harding, AS and Balmer, DW (1987) A microcomputer based simulation study of a port. *Journal of the Operational Research Society*, 37(8): 673–681.

Fatin, F (1996) *A Programming Structure for Parallel Simulation*. Unpublished Ph.D. thesis, Brunel University.

Giaglis, GM, Paul, RJ and Doukidis, GI (1996) Simulation for intra- and inter-organisational business process modelling. In *Proceedings of the 1996 Winter Simulation Conference*. Charnes, JM, Morrice, DJ, Brunner, DT and Swain, JJ (Eds). Baltimore: Association for Computing Machinery: 1297–1304.

Hirata, CM and Paul, RJ (1996) Object-oriented programming architecture for simulation modelling. *International Journal in Computer Simulation*, 6(2): 269–287.

Hlupic, V (1993) *Simulation Modelling Software Approaches to Manufacturing Problems*. Unpublished Ph.D. thesis, University of London.

Hlupic, V and Paul, RJ (1992) FMS scheduling strategies using the simulation package SIMFACTORY II.5. In *Proceedings of the 8th International Conference on CAD/CAM, Robotics, and Factories of the Future*. Metz: 1672–1686.

Hlupic, V and Paul, RJ (1993a) Simulation software in manufacturing environments: a users' survey. *Journal of Computing and Information Technology*, 1(3): 205–212.

Hlupic, V and Paul, RJ (1993b) Selecting software for manufacturing simulation. In *Proceedings of the XV International Conference on Information Technology Interfaces*. Zagreb, Croatia: University of Zagreb Computer Centre: 387–394.

Hlupic, V and Paul, RJ (1993c) Simulation modelling of an automated system for electrostatic powder coating of metal components. In *Proceedings of the 1993 Winter Simulation Conference*. Evans, GW, Mollaghasemi, M, Russell, EC and Biles, WE (Eds). New York: Association for Computing Machinery: 1324–1329.

Hlupic, V and Paul, RJ (1994a) Simulating an automated paint shop in the electronics industry. *Journal of Simulation Practice and Theory*, 1(4): 195–205.

Hlupic, V and Paul, RJ (1994b) Simulation modelling of flexible manufacturing systems using activity cycle diagrams. *Journal of the Operational Research Society*, 45(9): 1011–1023.

Hlupic, V and Paul, RJ (1994c) A critical evaluation of modelling an automated manufacturing systems using the simulation package WITNESS. In *Advances in Manufacturing Systems: Design, Modeling and Analysis*. Sodhi, RS (Ed.). Amsterdam: Elsevier: 1–6. (*Proceedings of the 9th International Conference on CAD/CAM, Robotics, and Factories of the Future*, 18–20 August 1993, Newark, NJ.)

Hlupic, V and Paul, RJ (1994d) Evaluating the simulation package "WITNESS" on an automated manufacturing system. *Informatica*, 18(4): 337–345.

Hlupic, V and Paul, RJ (1994e) How to improve manufacturing simulators. In *First Joint Conference of International Simulation Societies Proceedings*. Halin, J, Karplus, W and Rimane, R (Eds). Zurich: ETH Zurich: 450–453.

Hlupic, V and Paul, RJ (1994f) Modelling an automated manufacturing system using activity cycle diagrams. *International Journal of Manufacturing System Design*, 1(2): 119–128.

Hlupic, V and Paul, RJ (1995a) Manufacturing simulators and possible ways to improve them. *International Journal of Manufacturing System Design*, 2(1): 1–10.

Hlupic, V and Paul, RJ (1995b) A critical evaluation of four manufacturing simulators. *International Journal of Production Research*, 33(10): 2757–2766.

Hlupic, V and Paul, RJ (1996) Methodological approach to manufacturing simulation software selection. *Computer Integrated Manufacturing*, 9(1): 49–55.

Holder, RD and Gittins, RP (1989) The effects of warship and replenishment ship attrition on war arsenal requirements. *Journal of the Operational Research Society*, 40: 167–175.

Kienbaum, G (1995) *A Framework for Automatic Generation of Object-oriented Simulation Models*. Unpublished Ph.D. thesis, Brunel University.

Kienbaum, G and Paul, RJ (1994a) H-ACD: Hierarchical Activity Cycle Diagrams for object-oriented simulation modelling. In *Proceedings of the 1994 Winter Simulation Conference*. Tew, JD, Manivannan, S, Sadowski, DA and Seila, AF (Eds). New York: Association for Computing Machinery: 600–610.

Kienbaum, G and Paul, RJ (1994b) H-ACDNET: an object-oriented graphical user interface for simulation modelling of manufacturing systems. *Journal of Simulation Practice and Theory*, 2(3): 141–157.

Knox, PM (1988) *Automated Graphically-based Discrete-event Simulation Systems*. Unpublished Ph.D. thesis, University of London. Zagreb, Croatia: University of Zagreb Computer Centre: 401–407.

Kuljis, J and Paul, RJ (1991) Human–computer interfaces for modelling systems. In *Proceedings of the XIII International Conference on Information Technology Interfaces*. Zagreb, Croatia: University of Zagreb Computer Centre: 401–407.

Kuljis, J and Paul, RJ (1994) Organising outpatient clinics using simulation modelling. *International Journal of Management and Systems*, 10(3): 299–306.

Kuljis, J and Paul, RJ (1995) Outpatient clinic waiting times: a visual simulation approach revisited. In *Proceedings of the Third Hong Kong (Asia Pacific) Medical Informatics Conference*. MGhee, SM, Hedley, AJ, Wong, CP and Ho, LM (Eds). Hong Kong Society of Medical Informatics Ltd and Hong Kong Computer Society: 140–143.

Kuljis, J, Paul, RJ, Malin, H and Thakar, S (1990) Designing an out-patient clinic modelling package. In *Proceedings of the 11th International Symposium on "Computer at the University"*. Zagreb, Croatia: University of Zagreb Computer Centre.

Lehaney, B and Paul, RJ (1994a) Using Soft Systems Methodology to develop a simulation of out-patient services. *Journal of the Royal Society for Health*, 114(5): 248–251.

Lehaney, B and Paul, RJ (1994b) Developing sufficient conditions for an activity cycle diagram from the necessary conditions in a conceptual model. *Systemist*, 16(4): 261–268.

Lehaney, B and Paul, RJ (1996a) Soft Systems Methodology and simulation modeling. In *Proceedings of the 1996 Winter Simulation Conference*. Charnes, JM, Morrice, DJ, Brunner, DT and Swain, JJ (Eds). Baltimore: Association for Computing Machinery: 695–700.

Lehaney, B and Paul, RJ (1996b) Simulating out-patient services at Watford General Hospital through a soft systems approach. *Journal of the Operational Research Society*, 47(7): 864–870.

Macredie, RD and Paul, RJ (1995) Simulation modelling in manufacturing system design: an overview. *International Journal of Manufacturing System Design*, 2(3): 233–247.

Mak, H-Y (1993) *Systems Dynamics and Discrete Event Simulation Modelling*. Unpublished Ph.D. thesis, University of London.

Mashhour, A (1989) *Automated Simulation Program Generation using a Relational Database Simulation System*. Unpublished Ph.D. thesis, University of London.

Mejia, A (1992) *Output Analysis in Discrete Event Modelling*. Unpublished Ph.D. thesis, University of London.

Mladenic, D, Bratko, I, Paul, RJ and Grobelnik, M (1993) Using machine learning techniques to interpret results from discrete event simulation. In *Proceedings of the XV International Conference on Information Technology Interfaces*. Zagreb, Croatia: University of Zagreb Computer Centre: 401–406.

Mladenic, D, Bratko, I, Paul, RJ and Grobelnik, M (1994) Using machine learning techniques to interpret results from discrete event simulation. In *Proceedings of the European Conference on Machine Learning*.

Mukhtar, MS (1997) *Application of Gaming Simulation to Intelligent Tutoring Systems*. Unpublished Ph.D. thesis, Brunel University.

Odhabi, HIA and Paul, RJ (1995) Accessible simulation modelling for manufacturing system design. *International Journal of Manufacturing System Design*, 2(2): 145–151.

Paul, RJ (1987) A.I. and stochastic process simulation. In *Interactions in Artificial Intelligence and Statistical Methods*. B. Phelps (Ed.). Aldershot: Gower Technical Press: 85–98.

Paul, RJ (1989a) Artificial intelligence and simulation modelling. In *Computer Modelling for Discrete Simulation*. Pidd, M (Ed.). London: Wiley.

Paul, RJ (1989b) Combining artificial intelligence and simulation. In *Computer Modelling for Discrete Simulation*. Pidd, M (Ed.) London: Wiley.

Paul, RJ (1989c) Use of simulation to investigate stock control policies. In *Proceedings of the Technical Overview Symposium on Management Control Systems and Information Technology Implementation Issues of Inventory and Stock Control Systems*. London, June: 42–53.

Paul, RJ (1989d) Visual simulation: seeing is believing. In *Impacts of Recent Computer Advances on Operations Research*. Sharda, R, Golden, BL, Wasil, E, Balci, O and Stewart, W (Eds). Publications in Operations Research Series, Vol. 9. New York: North Holland.

Paul, RJ (1991) Recent developments in simulation modelling. *Journal of the Operational Research Society*, 42(3):217–226.

Paul, RJ (1992a) Outpatient clinic waiting times: a visual simulation approach. In *Proceedings of the Second Hong Kong (Asia Pacific) Medical Informatics Conference*. Hong Kong Society of Medical Informatics Ltd and Hong Kong Computer Society: 136–140.

Paul, RJ (1992b) The computer aided simulation modeling environment : an overview. In *Proceedings of the 1992 Winter Simulation Conference*. Swain, JJ and Gainsman, D (Eds). New York: Association for Computing Machinery: 737–746.

Paul, RJ (1993a) AI and simulation. In *AI and Computer Power: The Impact on Statistics*. Hand, D (Ed.). London: Chapman Hall.

Paul, RJ (1993b) Activity cycle diagrams and the three phase method. In *Proceedings of the 1993 Winter Simulation Conference*. Evans, GW, Mollaghasemi, M, Russell, EC and Biles, WE (Eds). New York: Association for Computing Machinery: 123–131.

Paul, RJ (1995a) Outpatient clinics: the CLINSIM package. *OR Insight*, 8(2): 24–27.

Paul, RJ (1995b) Towards a gaming-simulation environment with intelligent tutoring support. *Journal of Computing and Information Technology*, 3(1): 45–58.

Paul, RJ and Balmer, DW (1993) *Simulation Modelling*. Lund, Sweden: Chartwell-Bratt Student-Text Series.

Paul, RJ and Ceric, V (1990) Conceptual modelling in discrete event simulation using diagrammatic representations. In *Proceedings of the IMACS European Simulation Meeting on Problem Solving by Simulation*. Esztergom: Hungary, August.

Paul, RJ and Chanev, TS (1998) Optimising simulation models using a genetic algorithm. *Journal of Simulation Practice and Theory*, in revision.

Paul, RJ and Chew, ST (1987) Simulation modelling using an interactive simulation program generator. *Journal of the Operational Research Society*, 38(8): 735–752.

Paul, RJ and Doukidis, GI (1986) Further developments in the use of artificial intelligence techniques which formulate simulation problems. *Journal of the Operational Research Society*, 37(8): 787–810.

Paul, RJ and Doukidis, GI (1992a) Operational research approaches to artificial intelligence in production planning and scheduling. In *Artificial Intelligence in Operational Research*. Doukidis, GI & Paul, RJ (Eds). Basingstoke: Macmillan: 135–138.

Paul, RJ and Doukidis, GI (1992b) Artificial intelligence and expert systems in simulation modelling. In *Artificial Intelligence in Operational Research*. Doukidis, GI & Paul, RJ (Eds). Basingstoke: Macmillan: 229–238.

Paul, R.J. and Hlupic, V (1994a) Designing and managing a Masters degree course in simulation modelling. In *Proceedings of the 1994 Winter Simulation Conference*. Tew, JD, Manivannan, S, Sadowski, DA and Seila, AF (Eds). New York: Association for Computing Machinery: 1394–1398.

Paul, RJ and Hlupic, V (1994b) The CASM environment revisited. In *Proceedings of the 1994 Winter Simulation Conference*. Tew, JD, Manivannan, S, Sadowski, DA and Seila, AF (Eds). New York: Association for Computing Machinery: 641–648.

Paul, RJ and Kuljis, J (1995) A generic simulation package for organising outpatient clinics. In *Proceedings of the 1995 Winter Simulation Conference*. Alexopoulos, C, Kang, K, Lilegdon, WR and Goldsman, D (Eds). Baltimore: Association for Computing Machinery: 1043–1047.

Paul, RJ and Lehaney, B (1995) Soft modelling as an approach to determining the basis for simulating out-patient services. In *Proceedings of the Third Hong Kong (Asia Pacific) Medical Informatics Conference*. MGhee, SM, Hedley, AJ, Wong, CP and Ho, LM (Eds). Hong Kong Society of Medical Informatics Ltd and Hong Kong Computer Society: 39–45.

Paul, RJ and Thomas, P (1994) Computer-based simulation models for problem-solving: communicating problem understandings. *Electronic Journal on Virtual Culture*, 2(2).

Saliby, E and Paul, RJ 91993) Implementing descriptive sampling in three phase discrete event simulation models. *Journal of the Operational Research Society*, 44(2):.147–160.

Stapley, NR and Holder, RD (1992) The development of an amphibious landing model. *J. N. S.*, 18(3): 193–202.

Thomas, P, Macredie, R and Paul, RJ (1995) Games, simulations and human–computer interfaces. *Journal of Intelligent Systems*, 5(2–4): 79–87.

Williams, TM; Gittins, RP and Burke, DM (1989) Replenishment at sea. *Journal of the Operational Research Society*, 40: 881–887.

Zeigler, BP (1984) *Multifaceted Modelling and Discrete Event Modelling*. London: Academic Press.

21 Combining Modelling Approaches in Library Systems Analysis

Jon Warwick and Shamim Warwick

Abstract

The analysis of systems within which actors make decisions based on their expectations of system behaviour (and the observed or predicted behaviour of other actors) can be a difficult proposition, and the construction of robust models with which the effects of system change can be predicted would be valuable. In this chapter one such system (an academic library) is described, and the conflicting interests of actors within the system are discussed, these conflicting interests making traditional modelling approaches seemingly inadequate. Examples of such models which try to capture the interaction between actor and system are given, and a more general framework is described within which both hard and soft modelling approaches might be used in conjunction to give models effective in both explanation and prediction.

21.1 Introduction

Effective modelling within the domain of business and management problem solving seems to require an ever-expanding appreciation of the tools and methodologies of both 'hard' and 'soft' systems approaches. In this context the 'hard' aspects might include quantitative and clearly measurable variables and parameters together with the mathematical and logical relationships that relate them. The 'soft' aspects might include non-quantitative (qualitative) factors, human aspects, judgements and actions not so easily transferable to standard model forms. At the current time, no truly unified methodology exists for application to these problems in general, and much of the modelling work reported seems to be rooted firmly in one or other of the two camps. In reality, of course, most reasonably complex management-type problems have aspects that encompass both, and there would seem to be advantages to be gained from addressing both the 'soft' and 'hard' issues of such problems, particularly in cases where there is significant human involvement, and the dynamic behaviour of a system is dependent on the actions of those involved. For example, the demand for goods in classic stock control models may be significantly affected by the occurrence of stockouts, or the arrival rate and behaviour of customers at a queue by the perceived waiting time or queue length. Of course, assumptions regarding this type of behaviour can be made to produce tractable models and to aid model transparency, but as representations of reality, such models can sometimes be questionable.

Here we consider the example of a complex system which is subject to dynamic behaviour caused by the behaviour of the people involved, and shows how the modelling of both 'soft' and 'hard' aspects could be combined to produce a more general realisation of the system involved.

21.2   Problem Context

Resource provision within universities has, in recent years, become of central importance as the combined pressures of increasing student numbers and decreasing financial support have focused attention on maximising benefit at the minimum cost. University libraries have not been immune from this, even though they provide to students what one could argue is one of the most crucial resources of all – textbooks and information. Cuts in the funding to academic libraries have had a profound effect on the services they provide. Most academics would tell the same stories as subscription to journals and periodicals are cut, new titles in their subject areas can not be afforded (or at best with only few copies), requests for new additions of standard texts are rejected, etc. Of course, library management allocate as much money as possible to the provision of learning resources but the constraints are heavily binding, and the effective allocation of limited financial resources is an acute problem. This situation would seem to be tailormade for the operational researcher, and indeed much modelling work has been undertaken in order to provide some (scientific) rationale for the allocation of resources. A quick glance at the literature (Warwick 1992) will, however, highlight the diversity of models proposed, the approaches suggested and the assumptions made. In all but a few cases, the modelling has seemingly had little impact on the problems concerned, with the vast majority of models being exclusively quantitative and hard-systems oriented. Indeed, the diversity of models available can be taken as evidence of the complexity of the problem situation and perhaps the need for a rather more holistic view of the system under study.

Within this context, some modelling ideas are presented that mix both hard and soft aspects of the problem to capture some of the dynamic aspects of the system, and to provide a framework within which other existing models might fit.

21.3   Problem Description

There are a variety of system parameters that are under the direct control of the academic library management team, and with which the management team exact partial control over the interaction of the library and its customers (users). We will consider the problem from the point of view of the provision of textbooks and, relating to this, the main control parameters are usually taken as:

- the loan period;
- the level of duplication (number of copies of each title available);
- the borrowing capacity of customers (how many books can be borrowed at one time).

To get a feel for the problem situation we should first perhaps consider the main parties involved in the library system and what their requirements of the system might be. Essentially there are four broad groups of people involved: students (including full-/part-time, undergraduate/post-graduate), library management staff, academic staff and the university senior management team. As to their requirements of the system, we might classify these as follows.

1. Students:
   - comprehensive choice of textbooks;
   - availability of books on demand (high duplication level);
   - long loan period;
   - adequate borrowing capacity.
2. Library staff:
   - student satisfaction across courses and faculties;
   - reasonable budgets;
   - investment in new technology;
   - staff development;
   - timely information regarding proposals for new acquisitions, new courses, etc.;
   - schedules for assessment, reading lists, etc.
3. Academic staff:
   - provision of new titles on demand;
   - provision of multiple copies dependent on class size;
   - library staff with technical/subject expertise;
   - support for 'student-centred learning'.
4. University management:
   - adequate resource base for all courses;
   - adequate resource base for research students and staff;
   - investment in new technology;
   - cost effectiveness.

These requirements are by no means an exhaustive list, but illustrate the diversity of interests and requirements of the different groups. Common to all groups, however, is the general desire to see the library providing adequate resources for students in breadth and depth, i.e. both in terms of the variety of books to support academic courses/research and the number of copies of the main books to satisfy student needs, even for large classes. However, the resource allocation (book provision) problem is subject to a number of external influences (external to the library system although not necessarily to the university) and these influences can be grouped generally as follows.

- *Student numbers*: the number of students studying within the Higher Education sector has grown remarkably from around 50 000 in 1945 to 700 000 in 1990 (Department of Education and Science 1992), and has continued to expand, although the number is now stabilised to a certain extent. All the parties involved are keen to see at least an adequate resource provision, and effective planning under such growth is difficult.
- *Student-centred learning*: the popularity of this approach to teaching and learning has placed an emphasis on the library as an information source as students are encouraged to become active learners rather than passive recipients of notes and handouts from academic staff. Predicting the demand and demand fluctuations for library resources therefore becomes a central problem.
- *Rapid changes in courses*: coupled with the rapid changes in established subject areas (e.g. computing) is the rapid development of new 'hybrid' areas of study

(e.g. Business Information Technology) which require new learning support materials and will possibly make older books obsolete – the balance of books between subject areas within the core collection changes quite markedly over time and the subject specialities of the book collection must reflect the courses taught.

- *Conflicting requirements within parties*: within the groups identified as having an interest in the operation of the library system, there will be conflicting requirements. For example, senior management within a university will be required to limit the funds available to the academic library as there will be other competing resource demands within the university. On the other hand, committees concerned with the maintenance of academic standards will be keen to see the library system adequately resourced. As another example, within the student group, those students who are able to get copies of the books they want will be keen to hold on to them for as long as possible (suggesting long loan periods), whereas those who have made reservations for a book not available will want the book returned as soon as possible (suggesting short loan periods).

There are clearly a number of issues here that would need to be addressed if modelling is to be an effective tool in assisting in general resource allocation within academic libraries. The system is heavily constrained financially and in most subject areas the demand for books far outstrips the supply. It is unlikely that the supply side can be significantly enhanced so there is a continual search to find ways of getting greater use from the existing book stock. What 'greater use' actually means though is a difficult question. To some it has meant circulating the items at a faster rate so that in theory more people get the book but for shorter times, others prefer to see books in the library and on the shelf as often as possible so that they are available when required, still others have argued that books should be out of the library with students as much as possible, so that learning can take place. So, one question of central importance would be to decide what constitutes an effective library system. This would depend on the user concerned and that user's particular requirements of the system.

A second consequence of the excessive demand situation is that users will find alternative sources of supply for their information. In cases of sufficient supply, circulation statistics can be used to give a fairly accurate picture of general demand. In the current situation it is no longer the case that past use of library materials is a sufficient indicator of future use, and therefore the analysis of current circulation rates (as a surrogate for demand) is not sufficient as there is likely to be a large component of unsatisfied demand that will not register in circulation statistics. In other words, user behaviour is an important element in the assessment of demand, and, as a second question, we would need to consider how we can generally model the changing pattern of demands made of the system in response to external pressures such as changes in student numbers/ class sizes, new courses/areas of study, new technology alternatives to books and journals, etc.

The first question requires consideration of some of the generally held measures of library effectiveness. The second question has not been particularly well addressed in previous modelling studies and it may be looked at in two ways: can current models that try to reflect dynamic system behaviour benefit from the inclusion of softer, behavioural models? and how could static models of library system performance be included within a general modelling framework that includes the interaction of the library system with it's users?

21.4   Assessing Library Effectiveness

A number of measures have been suggested for assessing the effectiveness of a library system (Evans *et al.* 1972) and these have been included as elements in cost–benefit analysis.

- *Cost*: measured by staff size, skills and characteristics; unit costs; the ratio of book budget to user population.
- *User satisfaction*: this might include user satisfaction with services provided; the number of user activities in the library.
- *Response time*: here we would include the speed of services; the ratio of the time to secure a document to the time it is of value.
- *Use*: the statistical evidence in terms of book circulation rates, book stock usage, numbers of book reservations.

Many of these elements are directly measurable and give some indication of library performance. Unfortunately, this is really only part of the picture. User satisfaction could be seen as the crucial customer measure as it provides an external view of the system and has a direct effect on many of the others. Dissatisfied users may opt not to use the system at all preferring to borrow books from elsewhere, buy their own copy of important books or sub-borrow from other users. The loss of these users may well give a distorted picture of system performance as measured by other means. For example, fewer library users may well improve response times within the library, reduce the number of reservations for books (indicating an adequate book supply) and reduce the number of issues of important core textbooks. Consequently, predicting the demand, or potential demand, for new titles and assessing the need for duplicate copies of books becomes difficult, as unsatisfied demand is not measurable through the usual book circulation statistics, they only measure what *did* happen, and not what *might* have happened.

Much of the modelling work relating to book acquisition policies, determining optimal loan periods and the general management of book collections use current or forecast book demand and circulation rates. Both of these necessarily imply no change in user behaviour even though suggested changes in library policy or book collections will have changed the system, user satisfaction with the system and therefore the way users will interact with the system. In this sense such models are essentially static. A more complete picture of system effectiveness will be given if the modelling includes the interaction between user and system so that the effect of system change can be reflected in the predicted effect on user behaviour. This would then lead to a more detailed assessment of the demand for library services which other models could then draw on. In this way, existing models that have hitherto addressed the quantitative aspects of library effectiveness, based on inadequate input forecasts, can now give a more holistic view as the effects of proposed system change on user satisfaction are assessed via an intermediate modelling stage.

21.5   Modelling User Demands

Over the years, a number of authors have recognised the fact that the behaviour of library users is likely to be responsive to changes in the library system. One simple example is that of Hindle (1977), who noted that the attractiveness of a library is likely to increase if the availability of books increases. In particular, shortening the loan period or buying extra copies of books will increase the likelihood of books being on the shelf when required, and so an increase in demand for the books is likely. He proposed a simple model to demonstrate this, based on queuing theory. In his model, the availability of books (A) is assumed to be a function of the rate of demands (l) and the rate at which books are returned (m). Now, if users can keep the book off the shelf by placing reservations then $A = 1 - (l/m)$. Using an analogy with economic supply and demand theory he proposed that:

$$l_t = f(A_{t-1})$$
$$A_t = f(l_t, m_t)$$

Now in order to express the relationship between demand and availability, he used a simple linear form so that $l_t = a(A_{t-1})$, where a is the slope parameter. This gave the relationship between availability and the loan period, L, where $L = 1/m$ as

$$A^* = 1/(1 + aL)$$

demonstrating that the shorter the loan period, then the higher the equilibrium level of availability.

We might also consider here the quantitative model by Bookstein (1975) which, although not directly modelling dynamic system change, tries to factor perceived demand into three components. This model, based on those of Morse (1968), yields equations that link the loan period to the number of transactions at the circulation desk (a surrogate cost measure), although it can be extended to investigate the effects of book duplication. The objective was to use the loan period to minimise costs subject to a constant level of real demand. In the model, it is recognised that demands occur as a result of first-time visits, returns from unsatisfied initial demands and returns from satisfied initial demands who require more time with the book. Thus, modelling demands as a generally Poisson process, Bookstein represented the average actual demand rate for a book, l, as

$$l = l_0 + aU + bR$$

where l_0 is the underlying demand rate, U is the number of unsatisfied demands resulting from l_0 and R is the number of successful borrowers who require more time, and hence might try to re-borrow the book. The constants a and b represent the proportion of these users who actually do return.

Both of these examples acknowledge the fact that demands for library resources will reflect the perceived effectiveness of the system. In the first case book demands are responsive to the availability of books, and in the second a certain proportion of users return to generate further demands and these proportions would presumably reflect the likelihood of the demand being successful. Unfortunately, the modelling is at its weakest in the very areas where the models seek to say something useful. Hindle (1977) assumes a simple linear relationship between availability and demand, and Bookstein (1975) says little about the estimation of a and b. We would expect that both a and b together with l_0 would be functions of system effectiveness, so that they could be estimated using the results of the behaviour model. Furthermore, Bookstein's model becomes a more dynamic representation of the real system as the behavioural model invokes parameter changes in his model under alternative library policies.

21.6   A Modelling Framework

Academic libraries have objectives that are relatively easy to state and are required to operate within strict financial constraints. Difficulties arise when one tries to establish what constitutes success in achieving objectives and how objectives can be measured. In answering "What if ..." questions in the development of new management policies, the changes in system performance can be modelled more effectively if both 'hard' and 'soft' aspects are considered. Restricting this discussion to the problem of book duplication, i.e. how to allocate money between providing additional copies of existing texts, and buying one or more copies of new titles, the following combination of 'hard' and 'soft' elements would be appropriate:

- *soft elements*: modelling user responses to system change providing explanation and prediction of any changed user behaviour;
- *hard elements*: forecasts of student numbers, financial constraints, levels of existing book provision (if any) and the use of existing operational reseserch (OR) models *given* predictions of user behaviour within the system.

The book duplication problem is often considered in tandem with the problem of determining the correct loan period, since shortening the loan period is often considered as a substitute for buying more copies (core textbooks are often housed in short or restricted loan collections). Diagrammatically, the decision framework would be as in Figure 21.1

Modelling the behaviour of users in a library system is difficult as behaviour will reflect not only perceived changes in the system, but also the observed changes in the behaviour of other users and possibly the expected changes in behaviour of others. Previous work in this area (Warwick 1986) has resulted in a model based around

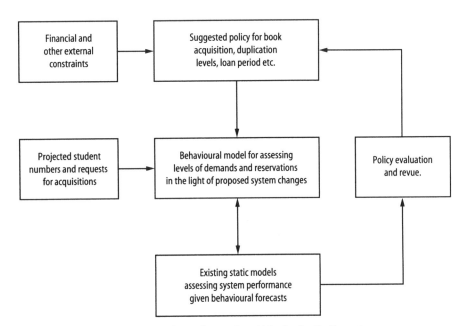

Figure 21.1. The decision framework combining 'hard' and 'soft' aspects.

the notion of rational expectations, under which a user's actions are a function of his or her expectations (predictions) of system performance under the expected actions of others. So from the model we can predict that if a user takes action a, then system performance will be $s(a)$, and if the user expects performance s then his or her behaviour will be $R[s]$. So the action must satisfy

$$a = R[s(a)]$$

In this way a set of implicit equations can be formed representing the possible actions.

Previous work has established three decisions to be made by users in following a recommendation to obtain a book:

- Whether to buy a copy or try to borrow it from the library.
- Whether to reserve it if it is not available on demand
- Whether to return at a later date if it is not available and no reservation is made.

Simple utility functions were developed that defined the utility gained by a user in possessing a copy of the book dependant on the time in possession of the book and any delay experienced before it was acquired. Under the assumption that users are attempting to maximise their own utility, the model was able to estimate the probability with which users would attempt any of the three following actions:

- Buy a copy and make no attempt to borrow it.
- Place a reservation if it is not available on initial demand.
- Return at a later time to look for it if it is not immediately available and no reservation is made.

Now any changes in the system can be seen to effect user behaviour. For example, if extra copies of a title are purchased, then a user would expect to derive increased utility from an attempt to borrow it (it would be available sooner) so the probability of purchase would decrease, and the probability of placing a reservation would increase. This utility-based, rational expectations approach was used originally to investigate user behaviour in response to book recommendations by academic staff. As such, the model considered demand as peaked around the time of the recommendation and not, as more general Poisson processes assumed, by many researchers. The point is, however, that this approach could be modified for inclusion into a variety of models as the changes in the actions of users can be investigated under any assumed demand pattern.

So, with this combined approach, the demand elements in Bookstein's model could each be represented using, inter alia, utility functions within a rational expectations framework so that changes to, say, the loan period would yield new predictions of the underlying demand, the proportion of unsatisfied users who return and so on.

21.7   Conclusion

There are a number of areas within the domain of human decision making where significant modelling problems arise directly resulting from the human activity within the system. The library system is a good example because important decisions have to be made regarding the allocation of resources but the allocation made will change the system, and hence the action of users within the system. A wide variety of modelling techniques have been employed to tackle some of the problems, but these have been mainly from the 'hard', quantitative viewpoint, and have ignored some of the important, but difficult to model, aspects of changing system behaviour. Academic libraries have an important function in serving the student community, and their effectiveness is measured partly by user satisfaction. Moreover, the performance of the library system is governed by the action of the users within the system so it would seem logical to include some reference to these actions, and how they might change, in modelling studies. This argues for a combination of approaches in which the modelling work encompasses both 'hard' and 'soft' aspects to give a more complete representation of the system.

These comments are not confined purely to the case discussed here. Many of the models found in the traditional home ground of operational research can be equally criticised. For example, inventory models do not usually model customer actions in response to lead time changes, stockouts or backorders. Queuing theory makes assumptions regarding the 'good' behaviour of customers queuing for service. One could argue that such models are at their most useful in situations where systems are perceived as under-performing in some way (long queues building up, lost customers through frequent stockouts) and need correction. Understanding customer–system interactions could then be very important in understanding how problems have arisen so they can be corrected.

Clearly, assumptions are made to simplify models and allow easier solution processes, but a willingness to tackle some of the less clearly defined system interactions can yield far greater understanding on the part of both the modeller and, ultimately, the model user.

References

Bookstein, A (1975) Optimal loan periods. *Information Processing and Management,* 11(8/12): 235–242.

Department of Education and Science (1992) *Statistical Bulletin. Student Numbers in Higher Education – Great Britain 1980–1990.* Government Statistical Service 8/92.

Evans, E, Borko, H and Ferguson, P (1972) Review of criteria used to measure library effectiveness. *Bulletin of the Medical Library Association.* **60** (1): 102–110.

Hindle, A (1977) A theoretical note concerning the adaptivity of demand for library documents. *Journal of Documentation,* 33(4): 305–308.

Morse, P (1968) *Library Effectiveness.* Cambridge, MA: MIT Press.

Warwick, JP (1986) A rational expectations approach to duplication policy. *OMEGA,* 14(4): 325–331.

Warwick, JP (1992) A review of some modelling approaches to the loan and duplication of academic texts. *Journal of Librarianship and Information Science,* 24(4): 187–194.

22 The Usability of User Interfaces to Simulation Systems*

Jasna Kuljis

Abstract

This chapter introduces the area of simulation modelling and will discuss the importance of considering users in the development of simulation systems that support the modelling process. The aim of this chapter is to examine the issues that influence 'usability' of simulation systems. We examined six representative simulation systems in terms of their usability by identifying first general usability principles and then examining which of these principles are applied. We identified both good practice and usability defects in these systems. Based on these observations we proposed improved integrated simulation environments that facilitate: design of problem domains; better support for data input/model specification; better support for visual simulation; better support for simulation statistics/results; and better user support and assistance. In conclusion, we suggest several future research directions which may lead to developments of better simulation environments.

22.1 Introduction

The aim of this chapter is to examine the issues that influence 'usability' of simulation systems. Particular attention is therefore placed on investigating issues related to interaction styles, interaction objects, screen layout design, navigation through interfaces, user support and assistance. To accomplish these objectives, we conducted an examination of several representative simulation systems. The usability evaluation was carried out using structured walk-through, i.e. we worked through a series of tasks the user might be expected to perform looking for sources of potential difficulties. We have based the examination on simulation software for personal computers partially because the issues of interaction are not dependent on the computer platform and partially because the PC platform predominates amongst commercial simulation software. Therefore, the results and findings can be generalised across the whole spectrum of simulation software regardless of the host system.

---

*This paper is a slightly modified version of the paper "Usability of manufacturing simulation software" published in 1995 in the *International Journal of the Manufacturing System Design*, 2(2): 105–120.

To achieve the above objective we have reviewed six discrete simulation systems: XCELL+; Taylor II; ProModel for Windows; Micro Saint for Windows; WITNESS for Windows; and Simscript II.5 for Windows. Two of the systems are general purpose (Micro Saint, Simscript II.5) whereas the other four are manufacturing or mainly manufacturing. We are interested in discovering to what extent these systems foster model development. We are also interested in finding out whether simulation software developed for modelling problems offers a better modelling environment than general purpose software. We examine the user interface to three key areas of each system which we can think of in terms of tasks that users may wish to undertake: data input/model specification; simulation experiments; and presentation of output results. We review the interfaces from two perspectives: (i) their general usability, allowing the user to achieve particular goals in their application domain; and (ii) more specific interaction elements, including adopted interaction styles, modes of interaction, screen design and layout, interaction flexibility, supported functionality, navigation styles, use of colour, and the possibility to import and export data to and from the system.

This chapter is organised as follows. We will first provide a brief overview of simulation and simulation models. We will then discuss user interface features that are common in the above systems. These include interaction styles, navigation styles, modes of interaction, screen layout and design, interaction flexibility, supported functionality, and the possibility to import and export data. We will then assess the usability of these six systems by identifying first, general usability principles, and then examining which of these principles are applied. We will also identify usability defects in these systems. We will then propose how a user interface can be improved to provide a better, more usable modelling environment. In conclusion, we suggest several future research directions which may lead to developments of better simulation environments.

22.2   Simulation Systems

Simulation is the process of designing a model of a real-world system; experiments can then be conducted with this model for the purpose of either understanding the behaviour of the system or for evaluating various strategies relating the real-world system's operation (Shannon 1975). Application areas for simulation are numerous and diverse. Law and Kelton (1991) provide a list of particular classes of problems for which simulation has been found to be a useful and powerful tool.

- Designing and analysing manufacturing systems.
- Evaluating hardware and software requirements for a computer system.
- Evaluating a new military weapons system or tactic.
- Determining ordering policies for an inventory system.
- Designing communications systems and message protocols for them.
- Designing and operating transportation facilities such as motorways, airports, subways, or ports.
- Evaluating designs for service organisations such as hospitals, post offices or fast-food restaurants.
- Analysing financial or economic systems.

A distinction can be drawn between models of continuous and discrete systems. In continuous systems the changes through time are predominantly smooth, and are conveniently described by sets of difference equations. A discrete system changes at specific points in time and a model of such a system is concerned only with these events (Paul and Balmer 1993). The simulations and models that we consider in this chapter are discrete event simulation models.

The simulation model can be used to compare alternative systems, or the effect of changing a decision variable; to predict what would happen to the state of the system at some future point in time; and to investigate how the system would behave and react to normal and abnormal stimuli (Pidd 1992a). The model is used as a vehicle for experimentation, where trial and error and learning methods of experimentation help support management decision making. The research nature of modelling means that there is an active need for the users of simulation systems (whom we can also refer to as the problem owners) to participate in the modelling process. Requirements and specification are particularly subject to change as an understanding of the problem being modelled evolves, for both the users and the developers. This can lead to severe difficulties in implementing models. One aim in these situations might be to determine general principles concerning the flexibility of applications to meet specifications and specification changes, and customisability.

Recent advances in micro-computer technology have had a major impact on simulation modelling and the use of graphics in particular. Visual representation in simulation modelling comes in a variety of forms. There are a number of ways of visually representing the logic of a simulation model whilst it is running. Graphical interfaces can be extremely useful in the development of sophisticated training and simulation environments. Users of such interfaces are able to obtain a much more immediate impression of what is happening to the object or system in question by looking at a graphical representation than by looking at a textual or symbolic representation of a mathematical model.

22.3   User Interface Features in Simulation Systems

Current simulation software comes in a variety of forms. Pidd (1992a) classifies simulation software into: languages and simulators. A simulation language is a computer package that is general in nature but may have special features for certain types of applications. A simulator is a computer package that allows one to simulate a system, contained with a specific class of systems, with little or no programming. Most of the special-purpose simulation languages that are commercially available are suited to only certain types of systems. Many recent simulation products can be classified as data driven systems in which a graphical user interface is a fundamental part of their operation. These systems handle a limited class of problems generally restricted to some aspects of manufacturing. Some of the systems use special diagrammatic methods to represent graphically the logic of the models on the computer screen with occasional textual inputs. Some of these systems also provide menu driven environments in which the graphical construction of the model logic can sometimes be one of the options.

Most simulation software has some kind of graphical user interface. Interrupting the running program, modifying the appropriate variables and restarting the simulation from its previous state are becoming more commonly available features in commercial simulation packages. When properly designed, a graphical display can give a very good idea of the logical behaviour of the simulation program. The client may quickly gain an idea of whether the model logic is correct or not. The graphics are an aid to effective experimentation on the model and may help to reduce the potential set of feasible experiments. Graphical facilities for the representation of simulation statistics are quite common. Besides the standard reports for commonly occurring performance statistics (e.g. utilisation, queue sizes and delays, and throughput) most of the newer software allows the development of tailored reports. The user can choose the form of representation (e.g. textual output, table, representational graph, bar diagram, pie chart, histogram, time series, etc.), colours, labels, etc. In most of the visual interactive simulation software (VIS), partial statistical results can be viewed during the simulation run.

We have reviewed six discrete simulation systems: XCELL+; Taylor II; ProModel for Windows; Micro Saint for Windows; WITNESS for Windows; and Simscript II.5 for Windows. Table 22.1 provides a summary of the main characteristics of each system examined and general user interface features for each of the reviewed systems. Five of these simulation systems are data driven simulators (XCELL+, Taylor II, ProModel for Windows, Micro Saint and WITNESS for Windows) that use some sort of diagrammatic tools for representation of model logic, and one is a simulation language (Simscript II.5 for Windows). All six systems provide modelling environments. Two systems are general purpose (Micro Saint and Simscript II.5), whereas the other four are manufacturing or mainly manufacturing.

We examine the following interaction characteristics of these systems: input–output devices employed, interaction styles and use of graphics. For each simulation system we examine the user interface for the three identified modules: data input/model specification, simulation experiments and presentation of output results. We are interested in adopted interaction styles, modes of interaction, screen design and layout, interaction flexibility, supported functionality, navigation styles, use of colour, and the possibility to import and export data. We also examine what kind of user support and assistance is provided and analyse how this provision is facilitated. We try to identify which of the general usability principles are applied, and also establish where the usability defects are in each examined system. When examining the user interface we are particularly interested in three aspects:

- How the user interface for a particular system aids the user in a model development process.
- Can the user modify the existing interface to either accommodate the user's own preferences or to adjust the modelling environment to the needs of a particular model.
- Does the system facilitate user interface development.

Table 22.2 summarises user interfaces for data input/model specifications for the systems examined. Most of the systems keep data in text files that can be accessed and modified from other environments. None of the examined systems provides database facilities. Simulation languages, like SIMSCRIPT II.5 for example, can provide most of the data input features (menu driven system, data-input forms, on-line help, data validation, etc.) but at the expense of an extensive time-consuming programming effort. Some of the systems provide limited input error checking and model verification facilities. Graphic elements for the representation of the model logic are predefined for all simulators, and cannot be changed for two of them (XCELL+ and Micro Saint). Names of model elements (i.e. machines, parts) are predefined and cannot be changed for any of the simulators, although the user can provide labels for individual instances of elements to describe better the domain-related elements. Similarly, all examined simulators use fixed, predefined, and

Table 22.1. Main system characteristics

	XCELL+	Taylor II	ProModel	Micro Saint	WITNESS	Simscript II.5
Application area	Manufacturing	Mainly manufacturing	Mainly manufacturing	General purpose	Mainly manufacturing	General purpose
Software type	Data driven simulator	Data driven simulator	Data driven simulator	Data driven simulator	Data driven simulator	Language
Interaction style	Menus and fill-in forms	Menus and fill-in forms	Windows GUI	Windows GUI	Windows GUI	Windows GUI
Interaction devices	Keyboard	Keyboard and mouse	Keyboard and mouse	Keyboard and mouse	Keyboard and mouse	Keyboard and mouse
Navigation facilitated using	Function keys	Mouse, arrow keys and function keys	Mouse, arrow keys and F1	Mouse, arrow keys and function keys	Mouse, arrow keys and F1	Mouse, arrow keys and F1
Terminology	Manufacturing	Manufacturing	Manufacturing	No specific domain	Manufacturing	No specific domain
Screen layout	Overcrowded	Good	Good	Good	Poor	Good
No. of colours	12	16	64	16	16	64
Use of colours	Hideous	Good	Good	Good	Too extensive	Good

unmodifiable attribute names (fields). Data entry is usually facilitated through pre-defined, unmodifiable fill-in forms which use the system's own element names and attribute names (fields), which usually have default values provided. Data validation is not a common facility (available only in Taylor II and ProModel for Windows).

Most of the current simulation systems have some form of visual animation of a simulation run. Table 22.3 provides a summary of some of the user interface features that are relevant for the design of simulation experiments. Background drawing tools are rarely facilitated (Taylor II, ProModel for Windows and Simscript II.5 for Windows), as is importing graphics from other applications (ProModel for Windows, Micro Saint and Simscript II.5 for Windows). Icon editors are more common (not provided in XCELL+ and Micro Saint), even though the majority of them only provide elementary drawing capabilities. Visual interactive simulation systems, in particular, support many diverse graphical tools. Visual programming tools are standard features in all VIS systems, and drawing tools are very common. Dynamic icons and animation are supported by most visual simulation systems. The interactive change of the simulation parameters and of the speed of animation, whilst the simulation is being executed, are also often provided. Panning and zooming is another quite common facility.

Table 22.4 gives a summary of presentation capabilities of the reviewed software. Most simulation software offers graphical facilities for the representation of simulation statistics. Besides the standard reports for commonly occurring performance statistics (e.g. utilisation, queue sizes and delays, and throughput) some of the newer software allows the development of tailored reports. The user can choose the form of representation (e.g. textual output, table, representational graph, bar diagram, pie chart, histogram, time series), colours, labels, etc. In most of the VIS software, partial statistical results can be viewed during the simulation run. Graphs are updated dynamically during the simulation run. Some of the software has facilities to save the statistics into files that can then be printed. Only rarely is there a facility to print the whole screen at any point of a simulation run or when the statistics are displayed/presented on the screen.

22.4   Usability of Simulation Systems

There is no agreed definition of usability. A definition of usability proposed by the ISO and listed in Booth (1989) states: "The usability of a product is the degree to which specific users can achieve specific goals within a particular environment; effectively, efficiently, comfortably, and in acceptable manner". A more operational definition of usability is given by Shackel (1991) who suggests that any system should have to pass the usability criteria of effectiveness, learnability, flexibility and user attitude. Effectiveness refers to levels of user performance, measured in terms of speed and/or accuracy, in terms of proportion of task(s), proportion of users, or probability of completion of a given task. Flexibility refers to variations in task completion strategies supported by a system. Learnability refers to the ease with which new or occasional users may accomplish certain tasks. Attitude refers to user acceptability of the system in question. The primary objective of an interactive system is to allow the user to achieve particular goals in some application domain. This means that the interactive system must be usable. First, we investigated issues that influence usability of simulation systems in general and to what extent the usability is supported in six examined systems. Secondly, we investigated whether there are factors that support usability.

Table 22.2. Data input/model specification

	XCELL+	Taylor II	ProModel	Micro Saint	WITNESS	Simscript II.5
Model logic representation	Diagrammatic tools	Diagrammatic tools	Diagrammatic tools	Diagrammatic tools	Diagrammatic tools	Program
Graphic elements	Predefined cannot be changed	Predefined can be changed	Default or user selected	Predefined cannot be changed	Predefined can be changed	Not provided
Model elements	Predefined	Predefined	Predefined	Predefined	Predefined	User defined
Element names	Up to 10 characters	Up to 8 characters	Up to 80 characters	Up to 20 characters	Up to 8 characters	User defined
Attribute names	Predefined cannot be changed	Predefined cannot be changed	Predefined cannot be changed	Predefined cannot be changed	Predefined cannot be changed	User defined
Default values provided	Yes	Yes	Yes	No	Yes	Can be programmed
Fill-in forms design	Not applicable	Good	Good	Well balanced	Poor and often confusing	Not applicable
Importing files supported	No	Yes	Yes	No	Yes	Yes
Data validation supported	No	Yes	Yes	No	No	Can be programmed
Model validation supported	Partially	No	No	No	No	Can be programmed

Table 22.3. Simulation experiment

	XCELL+	Taylor II	ProModel	Micro Saint	WITNESS	Simscript II.5
Background drawing tool	No	Yes	Yes	No	No	Yes
Icon editor	No	Yes	Yes	No	Yes (limited capabilities)	Yes
Importing graphics supported	No	No	Yes	Yes	No	Yes
Zooming supported	No	No	Yes	No	Using virtual windows	No
Panning supported	No	Limited (with arrow keys)	Yes	No	Limited	No
Interactive speed change	Yes	Yes	Yes	Yes	Limited to 3 speeds	Yes if programmed
Interactive time change	Yes	Yes	Yes	No	No	Yes if programmed
Interactive change of other simulation parameters	Yes	Yes	Yes	No	No	Yes if programmed

Table 22.4. Simulation results

	XCELL+	Taylor II	ProModel	Micro Saint	WITNESS	Simscript II.5
Control of statistics collection	System	System User partially	System User can only reduce the set	User	System	Modeller
Default statistics provided	Yes	Yes	Yes	Yes	Yes	NA
Graphics supported	No	Yes	Yes	Yes	Yes	Yes
Graph types	NA	Histogram, Pie chart, Bar, Line, Scatter, Gantt, Area graph	Pie chart, Plot, Histogram, Bar, Line, Vertical line, Step graph	Bar, Line, Scatter, Step graph	Histogram Time series	Histogram, Pie chart, Line graphs, Dynamic bar graphs, Trace and X–Y plots Dials, Meters
User defined presentation	No	Partially	No	Partially	Partially	Yes
Flexibility of presentation	None	Small	Small	Small	Small	Great
Tabular form statistics	Yes	Yes	Yes	Yes	Yes	Yes
Exporting files supported	Yes	Yes	Yes	Yes	Yes	Yes
Printing statistics tables	Yes	No	Yes	Yes	Yes	Yes
Printing graphs	NA	No	Yes	Yes	No	No

Standards of user documentation are improving but there are still many problems that have to be encountered. Table 22.5 gives a summary of provision in examined simulation systems. On-line help, if available, usually does not extend to anything more than an overview of basic system concepts. Context-sensitive help is scarce and good context-sensitive help is almost non-existent (the exception is ProModel for Windows). On-line help for error messages is not available on the examined systems. On-line help facilities, when available, provide a limited help to the model builders as can be seen in Table 22.6.

The customisation of the modelling environment is a virtually unknown commodity. A limited customisation is offered only in ProModel for Windows. The user is rarely allowed to control statistics collection (only in Micro Saint and Simscript II.5) and the way the statistics are displayed (only Simscript II.5 gives complete freedom). Report customisation is rarely allowed. If this facility is provided, only a limited set of options can be exercised. The development of separable user interfaces for particular simulation problems is possible only in Simscript II.5 for Windows, which facilitates user interface development by providing templates for menus, fill-in forms and several types of graphs that can be then tailored to suit the problem.

We identified general usability principles which are essential for supporting the usability of graphical user interfaces: simple and natural dialogue, the terminology that is familiar to the user, consistency, minimised the user's memory load, provision of feedback, provision of clearly marked exits, provision of shortcuts, good error messages and prevention of errors. These usability principles support the four identified usability dimensions. Effectiveness is supported with the following usability principles: simple and natural dialogue, minimal memory load for the user, consistency, provision of feedback, provision of clearly marked exits, good error messages and prevention of errors. Effectiveness of the system can be hindered if there are: defects in navigation through the system, problems in screen layout and design, inappropriate terminology, inappropriate feedback or complete lack of feedback, problems with modality, inconsequential redundancies and problems in matching with user tasks.

Learnability is supported with the: simple and natural dialogue, using the user's language and consistency. Learnability can be impeded if there are: defects in navigation, problems in screen design and layout, inappropriate terminology, inappropriate feedback or complete lack of feedback and problems in matching the user tasks. Flexibility is supported by providing shortcuts. Flexibility is impeded if there is no user control over the system and if the system imposes the order in which the steps in a task are performed. Positive user attitude is supported with the following usability principles: simple and natural dialogue, minimal memory load for the user, using the user's language, provision of feedback, good error messages and prevention of errors. The user attitude towards the system can be seriously affected by any of the above usability defects.

We identified which of the usability principles that support the usability of graphical user interfaces are applied in six examined systems. Only Pro Model for Windows provides an adequate level of usability support by providing a consistent user interface that employs natural dialogue with an appropriate feedback that minimises the user's short-term memory load. ProModel for Windows is also the only product that facilitates shortcuts, appropriate feedback for error messages and clearly marked exits. Acceptable user manuals are provided by ProModel for Windows, and to some extent by XCELL+ and WITNESS for Windows.

The following usability defects were identified in examined simulation systems. When there are problems in understanding where the user currently is in the

Table 22.5. Printed manuals

	XCELL+	Taylor II	ProModel	Micro Saint	WITNESS	Simscript II.5
Tutorial	Not provided	Yes Not thorough enough	No	Yes	Not provided Partially covered in the only manual	No
Getting started	Part of the User Guide	Not provided	Yes	Yes	Not provided	No
User guide	Yes	Yes	Yes	Yes	Yes	Yes
Reference manual	Not provided	Not provided TLI reference manual provided	Yes	Not provided	Not provided	Yes
Index	No Only XCELL+ glossary	Yes Global for all manuals	Yes System concepts	Yes System concepts	Yes System concepts	Yes System concepts
Terminology	Manufacturing	Manufacturing Technical	Manufacturing	General simulation	Manufacturing Technical	General simulation

Table 22.6. On-line user assistance

	XCELL+	Taylor II	ProModel	Micro Saint	WITNESS	Simscript II.5
Model examples provided	Yes	Yes	Yes	Yes	Yes	Yes
Help type	One text screen	Isolated text screens	Hypertext	Limited hypertext	Isolated text screens	Hypertext
Navigation through help facilitated using	Not applicable	Mouse and arrow keys	Mouse point and click on link nodes	Mouse point and click on link nodes	Mouse point and click on cross-reference buttons	Mouse point and click on link nodes
Help text	Short information on system	Complete version of printed material	Differs from printed manuals	Differs from printed manuals	Differs slightly from printed manuals	Differs from printed manuals
Index of topics	Not applicable	Yes	Yes	Yes	Yes	Yes
Search facility within help	Not applicable	Yes. Searches for a first occurrence of a given string	Yes	Yes. Searches for a first occurrence of a given string	Not provided	Yes
Tutorial	Not provided	Not provided	Provided Interactive lessons	Not provided	Not provided	Not provided
Context-sensitive help	Not supported	Only relevant page	Yes	Not provided	Not provided	Not provided
Help on help	Not provided	No	Yes extensive	Yes limited	Not provided	Yes
Printing help text supported	No	No	Yes	Yes	No	Yes
Demonstration disk	Not provided	Yes Elementary	Yes Professional	Yes	Not provided	Not provided

system lack of appropriate feedback makes navigation around the system particularly hard. Only ProModel for Windows offers an adequate level of feedback. XCELL+, WITNESS for Windows and Simscript II.5 for Windows suffer from serious navigation problems. Consistency in use of interaction devices is not applied in XCELL+, Taylor II and WITNESS for Windows. WITNESS for Windows inconsistently uses words like "Cancel" and "Enter". Simscript II.5 for Windows have various inconsistencies across system modules. ProModel for Windows and Micro Saint for Windows have a good screen layout and design. The other four systems have various problems in the way information is presented on the screen. Often extensive use of colour hinders understanding of what is going on (XCELL+ and WITNESS for Windows).

Micro Saint for Windows and Simscript II.5 for Windows use terminology that is too technical. Both systems are developed as general purpose systems that support modelling in various application domains. Therefore, the terminology is not particularly well suited to any domain. Thus, there can be a problem in analogical mapping of the problem to an unsuitable domain. That would cause problems in matching the user tasks. XCELL+, Taylor II, WITNESS for Windows and Simscript II.5 for Windows have problems with modality. The use of modal boxes, which therefore deny the possibility of cancellation, is quite common. In Simscript II.5 for Windows it is not always obvious how to change from one mode to another (e.g. designing a fill-in form and modifying it). XCELL+ can be in several different modes depending on the user selection of the task to be performed. Even though the user is informed which mode is currently on, it is not always obvious how to change to another mode. Only ProModel for Windows gives the user the feeling of being in control.

It seems that the idea of adaptive user interfaces has not yet reached simulation software developers. There is no provision, or if there is it is marginal, for user interface customisation. However, there is the possibility to create new simulation systems for limited domains with a custom-made interface appropriate for the model domain. These capabilities are currently limited to bespoke programming that requires a substantial development effort. Sometimes user interface development can be facilitated using an object-oriented approach that reduces development time. An example is Simscript II.5 that provides ready-made user interface object templates like menus, forms, etc., supplied in the C language library.

After we had examined user interfaces to those simulation software we are in a position to make some general observations. First of all it has to be stressed that all simulation systems are designed for a limited specialist community and for the presumed needs of that user population. This narrow targeting seems to justify an appalling lack of regard for the potential customers. As a rule documentation is highly erratic, written in a technical jargon and rarely organised in any structured manner. If it contains an index (this is not always the case) it usually requires the user to know the exact terminology used to be able to find the topic of interest. Even though four of six examined systems were manufacturing oriented we find that these systems, except in using a more appropriate terminology and thus reducing the memory load of the user, do not provide any more usable modelling environment for manufacturing problems than the general purpose simulation systems.

In the next section we examine what sort of changes in simulation systems will be beneficial in improving their usability. We identified five areas: the simulation environment; data input; simulation experiments; presentation of output results; and user support and assistance. We recognise that some of the suggestions are too expensive to implement or premature for the current state of research. Nevertheless, the list can serve as a source of ideas and a basis for further research in this area.

22.5   Proposed Improvements

An essential aid in model development can be facilitated by selecting model components which are relevant to the model builder's modelling requirements. Pidd (1992b) also advocates that the model builders should be given the freedom to lay out the screen display by use of interaction devices, choosing how to represent the entities as the simulation proceeds from a provided set of icons. Our proposal is that simulation environment, regardless of the system's problem domain, should provide model developers with the following:

1. A facility to design and/or choose a problem domain.
2. A support for data input/model specification.
3. A support for visual simulation.
4. A support for simulation statistics/results.
5. User support and assistance.

22.5.1   A Facility to Design and/or Choose a Problem Domain

During the definition of a new problem domain the user will be given the opportunity to select graphical representations of the domain entities from a library of icons supplied by the vendor. The structural context in the model should be expressed clearly, so that the graphical representation makes visible the relations in the model like the dependency or non-dependency of activities or events. If the user cannot find suitable icons, a facility should be provided to either modify existing icons, to draw new icons or to import icons from some other drawing package or from icon libraries. This provision would enable the user to choose either a more 'realistic' or preferred graphical representation of the model's entities and, therefore, promote a positive attitude on his or her part. If the familiar graphical representations are used to model a problem the user's memory load would be reduced.

All system-supplied problem domains would come with default values relevant to respective problem domains. When the user creates a new problem domain there should be a facility that enables the specifying of default values for the new domain. It should be also made available for the user to make changes of default values in any other problem domain in the list. This provision would reduce the time and effort necessary to specify subsequent models in the same domain. It will also reduce the possibility of making errors by either preventing the user to enter non-valid values or by preventing the user omitting any data necessary to carry out the model execution. Similarly, the user will have a facility available to choose which statistical data will be collected as a default for a problem domain. The domain can be either a new one or an already existing one. Presentation preferences can also be made as default values for a problem domain. This provision would facilitate the flexibility of the modelling environment to better suit the needs of a particular problem being modelled.

There should be a facility that enables changing the system environment to suit the developer's preferences and saving the preferred environment for future use. Changes in environment can include elementary changes such as, for example, background colour, placement of application tool bars and menus, placement and size of application windows, and dialogue boxes, text font types, etc. More advanced changes can include changes in the main application menu like, for example, changing selection names, selection order, adding selections to the menu, etc. In addition, users should be supported to tailor fill-in forms by changing form layout, colour or by including additional labels. The user should be given the opportunity to choose a preferred navigation technique, or to design navigation shortcuts setting his or her own commands for such shortcuts. If the user is given the freedom to tailor the environment to carry out tasks in a desired, or familiar, way the effectiveness with which the tasks are performed will increase. This flexibility of interaction will also promote a positive attitude towards the system.

22.5.2 A Support for Data Input/Model Specification

There is room for a great deal of improvement in the domain of data input and/or model specification that would improve existing simulation systems. We have already mentioned that data validation is supported in only two of the six examined simulation systems. None of the systems offers database capabilities for keeping multiple variations of a model. Data input forms, if available, are generally poorly designed. There is no help provision for individual data fields. Importing data files is supported in four of the examined systems. The format of imported data is usually an ordinary ASCII text file. Therefore, there is much to be improved in the way the simulation data are communicated to the systems. The following list represents features that every simulation would benefit from, some of which are already reported on in Kuljis (1994): data independence; modeless dialogue; facilities for representation of complex data structures; data validation facilities; on-line help facility; and facilities to accept data from some of the major database and spreadsheet software.

It is important that each part of the system preserves the independence of the interface part from the processing part. This requirement is particularly important for the data input or model specification. The metaphor for internal data representation should not determine the metaphor on how the data are presented to the user. Data independence is essential if flexibility of interaction is to be provided.

When providing interaction through which data input is provided to the system it is important to let the user escape an endless loop if he or she wants to abandon the current operation/procedure. Modal dialogue boxes can be quite off-putting and, if used in a system, they have to be supported by adequate guidance as to how to respond to a request.

Simulation models can have complicated logic with complex interactions amongst their entities that is not always supported by the data input facilities of the existing simulation systems, especially for new problem domains. The large volume of data, data complexity and provisions for keeping the definition for more that one model configuration calls for sophisticated data storing facilities, possibly a database management system, which in addition supports data integrity. Mathewson (1989) recognises the value of database facilities to enable the user to carry over some of the experiences and benefits of previous models. The proposed provision would promote the effectiveness of the system enabling the user to relatively easily handle the data required to specify a model.

Data validation has several aspects: validation of a single input against a permitted range of values; validation of the overall consistency of data; and validation of the logic of the system. Validation of a single input is simple and, if not already provided in the system, can easily be added. The valid data range or set that was supplied by the user, or the vendor, can be used. The problem can be how to check the overall data consistency. If the data are kept using a database system some of the inconsistency can be resolved by the inherent database facilities. Of course, the consistency of data that influences the logic of the model cannot be checked. If a system has data validation facilities, errors related to data being out of a valid range can often be prevented. This provision increases user confidence in the system and the effectiveness of the system.

The end user can be aided in using the system if the system provides help facilities. These facilities can be implemented in the different levels of the system. At the lowest level help can be provided for each individual input and for general usage of the system. Examples of valid values can be provided at least for the fields which are not provided with default values (it is not always obvious which default values will be appropriate, and if inappropriate default values are supplied they can confuse the user). At a higher level, help can be provided to explain the consequences of a particular action or set of actions, explanation of error messages and explanation of some more specialised concepts, e.g. the statistical concepts used. On-line help can be invaluable if pre-emptive (modal) dialogue is used in a system. A good on-line help provision is important in promoting effectiveness, learnability and a user's positive attitude towards the system.

Companies that keep most of their data on micro-computers use either a database or a spreadsheet. It would be convenient to use the data in that format for the simulation model specification rather than inputting it again in some other format required for some particular simulation software. File compatibility with the market leader databases and spreadsheets would therefore be a very desirable facility. If the user already has data, required for the modelling, stored in some other application, the proposed provision would enable a fast data transfer and therefore increase effectiveness and promote user willingness to use the system.

22.5.3   A Support for Visual Simulation

Many authors argue that the advantages of visual interactive simulation include better validation, increased credibility (and hence model acceptance), better communication between modeller and client, incorporation of the decision maker into the model via interaction, and learning via playing with the VIS. Swider et al. (1994) feel that animation can provide convincing evidence that model behaviour is representative of the system under study. Cyr (1992) sees the advantage of using animation in its ability to demonstrate problems with the model itself which would otherwise be difficult to detect. Kalski and Davis (1991) point out that summary statistics sometimes do not show the active interactions of processes in a system, and they advocate the use of animation as an aid to the analyst in identifying the system status under which, for example, bottlenecks occur. There are many animation proponents in the simulation community, especially the software vendors, claiming the benefits of animation. However, there is very little published empirical evidence which would suggest how to design effective animation. There are many problems in clearly depicting the model behaviour through an animation display.

The problem is recognised by O'Keefe and Pitt (1991) who found that the acquisition of more formal evidence will provide a better scientific basis for research and development in VIS, and, more importantly, it will aid the provision of guidelines on pragmatic issues such as animation design, display preference and required interaction style. The authors advocate that VIS should be made more flexible and less constraining. Flexibility in interactions and different types of displays should allow the VIS to be usable irrespective of the users cognitive style, as long as each type using the VIS can have access to their preferred display. Carpenter et al. (1993) conducted an experiment with 47 subjects to examine how well the animation communicated the operation of the simulation model. The subjects identified problems more accurately in less time when viewing animation with movements than without movements.

Another experiment examined the role of animation in communicating invalid model behaviour. Swider *et al.* (1994) used 54 subjects to obtain objective and subjective measures in determining which combinations of animation presentation and speed were best for displaying violations of model assumptions. The objective results indicated that the slower presentation speed was superior to the faster speed and that animation with moving icons was superior to animation with bar graphs. Based on the results of this study, Swider *et al.* (1994) recommend: the use of pictorial display with moving icons for simulation models with moving entities; the facility to set the presentation speed to make discrete differences visible; and to avoid overloading the user with too much visual information.

The results of the above studies are not surprising, and they match our intuition and common sense. However, their importance is in substantiating our intuitive judgement with some more concrete evidence. Animation with moving icons is often used in current simulation systems, even though presentation of animation is often not well thought out. Ideally, it may seem desirable to present information on the screen that has characteristics similar to the objects we perceive in the environment. The visual system could then use the same processes that it uses when perceiving objects in the environment. Graphical means of description must be given preference over written ones because they present information in a more compact manner. Factors that contribute towards the meaningfulness of a stimulus are the familiarity of an item and its associated imagery. The graphical representation of constructs for different applications should give definite information about the type of model component it represents, such as waiting queues, customers or servers in queuing systems or stores, or suppliers in store keeping systems (Kämper 1993).

Designing manufacturing applications, as suggested by Preece *et al.* (1994), might benefit from the use of realistic images in helping the users design and create objects. However, they anticipate that there might be a problem in the high cost of real-time image generation, and that for the actual needs of an application such a degree of realism is often unnecessary. Nevertheless, we believe that it can help if some approximations of real-life objects are used. Stasko (1993) recommends that animation should provide a sense of context, locality, and the relationship between and after states. Furthermore, that the objects involved in an animation should depict application entities and that the animation actions should appropriately represent the user's mental model. If these recommendations were followed, the effectiveness, learnability and the enthusiasm of a wider user population to use simulation systems might increase.

Animation speed in simulation systems is commonly made adjustable by their users. There are some problems with the animation speed that are not envisaged by the software developers. Simulation software is built for a particular hardware configuration and therefore for a particular processing speed (in MHz). The speed of animation (moving icons) is dependent on the computer processor speed. Hardware developments are much faster than software developments and by the time simulation software, based on a particular configuration, has reached the market it may well happen that the market has already adopted much faster computers. The user will probably install software on a much faster computer than it was intended for. Even though the user may have a facility to change animation speed, the slowest available speed may still be too fast for an animation observer. Therefore, simulation software developers have to pay attention to that aspect and provide a facility that can cope with speed irrespective of the processing speed. This will enable the user to understand what is happening in the model and hence promote the overall usability of the system.

The eye-catching, appealing nature of animation can tempt designers to apply too many facets to an interface. Animation is, however, another attribute in which the often quoted design principle "less is more" does apply. Nevertheless, if the screen design is kept clean, simple and well organised some redundant information can be quite useful to the user. The moderation principle is something that many simulation system developers should learn about. User interfaces that have screens crowded with too many objects, large numbers of offensive colours and incompatible colour schemes is more of a rule than an exception. To enable 'good' design for animation, the tools that facilitate graphics design should be made sophisticated enough to support such developments. Therefore, tools should: provide a greater number of drawing object templates; provide an extensive colour palette (at least 64 colours) and colour aiding facility; support modification of graphic objects (erasing parts of graphics, filling whole or parts of graphic objects with colours or patterns, resizing, rotating, flipping, etc.); provide on-line help; combining several graphical objects into one; and so on.

22.5.4   A Support for Simulation Statistics/Results

In each model, special components are necessary to carry out statistical computations. The model builder should have the choice to combine such statistical components, dependent upon his or her computational requirements, with those representing the real system. In order to make plain the difference between these 'artificial' objects and those representing the real system. Kämper (1993) advises that the artificial objects should be represented by an icon which clarifies the character of such objects. Graphical coding can provide a powerful way of displaying quantitative data. In particular, graphs are able to abstract important relational information from quantitative data.

Considerable effort has been invested in the presentation of simulation results. Often this effort lacks proper insight into the particular needs of simulation systems. Even though much has already been done in graphical representation of simulation results, there are still issues that need to be tackled to improve the usability of simulation systems, some of which have already been reported by Kuljis (1994): inter-connectivity of the results, explanation facilities, representation of results independent of the processing (i.e. interface independence); a facility to modify graphs; facilities to save results in files compatible with the major database and spreadsheet packages; and a facility to print tables and graphs.

A simulation is a computer-based statistical sampling experiment. Thus, if the results of a simulation study are to have any meaning, appropriate statistical techniques must be used to design and analyse the simulation experiment. Law (1983) points out that the output processes of virtually all simulations are non-stationary (the distributions of the successive observations change over time) and auto-correlated (the observations in the process are correlated with each other). Thus, classical statistical techniques based on independent identically distributed observations are not directly applicable. Summary statistics sometime do not show the active interactions of processes of a system. There is a need for some logical connection of the isolated statistical results. Such a facility should provide insight in the reasons for the particular behaviour of the simulation experiment.

An Activity Cycle Diagram (ACD) might provide the logical inter-connectivity to underpin type structures using similar links to those used in hypertext systems for presenting output analysis, a navigation system and the interrelationships. Some preliminary research has already been carried out to see how machine learning techniques can supply the links amongst dependent variables (Mladenic et al. 1993). The proposed facility would benefit the users with a better understanding of the model behaviour and therefore promote the effectiveness of the system. The effectiveness of any decision support system, like for example a simulation system, is determined mostly by the extent to which it actually aids its users in the decision process.

In the case where a simulation system is developed for an end user, there is a need to provide an explanation of the simulation results. Regardless of how attractively these results are presented, end users often lack the mathematical background necessary for understanding the simulation results. As Bell (1991) points out, "replacing numbers with multi-coloured graphics does not necessarily improve the usefulness of the display for decision making". It is questionable which method would be best suited for this purpose as every interpretation depends on the model specification. For example, O'Keefe (1986) considered expert systems as a possibility for taking the role of explaining model results to the user. Mathewson (1989) recognises the need to aid the user in the interpretation of results which are stochastic, and proposes a knowledge-based system to take this role. Mladenic et al. (1993) see role of machine learning as an aid the interpretation of simulation results. Any such provision would greatly improve learnability and therefore the effectiveness of simulation systems.

Every simulation system, especially one developed for the end user, should enable the display of simulation results independently from the processing. This means that the results can be examined after or during the simulation run. The sequencing of the results display should be left to the user, hence providing the user with greater flexibility in using the system.

While viewing the graphical representation of simulation output, the modeller often finds that the graph representing the data is not appropriate to communicate accurately a particular simulation outcome. Even though the modeller may have had a chance to set the graph type and scaling whilst specifying simulation output prior to the simulation experiment, he or she cannot predict what the output data will be. Therefore, the modeller should have a facility after the simulation experiment, or if dynamic graphs are used during the simulation experiment, to modify the graph type and scaling to an appropriate form for the actual data. This would provide the user with more flexibility in using the system and enable him or her to present information in a form that better suits his or her preferences, or that improves the understanding of the results.

Very often the results of a simulation experiment can give an insight into the company's operating practices and serve as a decision support tool. Statistical results can be incorporated in company documents and reports. This is not always easily or elegantly done with existing simulation software. It would be convenient to have files containing the simulation results exported into a company standard spreadsheet, so that an adequate graphical presentation can be undertaken, and the results can be incorporated into documents using a company standard word processing package. It would probably be useful to have a facility to export the statistical data into the most popular databases. The proposed provision would help the user to use the output data in a way that is convenient and familiar to him or her, and therefore promote a positive attitude towards the system.

Printing graphs is still not a common facility in simulation systems whereas printing tables is usually supported. However, it is often useful to have printouts of simulation output. Many modellers resort to printing the screen which is awkward, or to grabbing screen images. The latter is achieved using either Windows clipboards, or DOS screen capture software, or other similar facilities. This provision would help the user to have the results of a simulation available for later use. It can make it possible to conduct comparative analyses of several model scenarios. Therefore, this facility would promote effectiveness. Like the previous facility, this provision would also promote a user's willingness to use the system.

22.5.5   User Support and Assistance

User manuals for simulation systems are usually poorly written and need a lot of improvements. Of the six simulation systems we have examined only two provide a 'Tutorial' (Taylor II and Micro Saint), three provide 'Getting Started' (XCELL+, ProModel for Windows and Micro Saint) and two provide 'Reference manuals' (Pro Model for Windows and Simscript II.5). An index is provided in all of them except XCELL+, but it usually lists only system concepts using a particular simulation system's terminology. Generally, terminology used in the user manual is too technical. Examples, if provided, are not followed throughout the development process and are therefore of not much use. On-line help very rarely provides help for all facilities and tools in the simulation environment. Context-sensitive help is a rare commodity (it is only provided in Taylor II and ProModel for Windows) and is almost unheard of for system messages (i.e. error messages). An on-line tutorial is provided only in ProModel for Windows. Demonstration disks are provided for three of the examined systems Taylor II, ProModel for Windows and Micro Saint, and of these three only ProModel provides a professional and carefully thought out product. We will only make suggestions on ways of providing more appropriate user support such as extensive use of interactive on-line tutorial help, customisation of user interfaces to suit a particular class of users, adaptive user interfaces and intelligent help.

On-line help is usually in the form of text screens which are descriptive or prescriptive in their nature. They concentrate on what and how. Rarely do they tackle the question as to why some action could be appropriate or beneficial, or what would be the consequences of a particular action. If interactive on-line tutorials are available as an option within help screens, much ambiguity and many answers to "what-if" questions would be resolved. It is easy to integrate animation in these tutorials as well and, thus, provide the full power that tutorials can offer. A good interactive tutorial help can greatly improve system learnability, and therefore also its effectiveness.

End users have unique habits, preferences, idiosyncrasies and working styles. Attempts to force end users to change these styles usually results in end-user frustration and decreased productivity. Larson (1992) advocates that all end users of an application system should not be forced to use the same user interface; user interface designers can customise the user interface to the habits and styles of user classes, rather than force the user to tailor his or her working style to the user interface. Multiple styles of user interfaces can be supported by careful design of an application's functional operations and by customising the user interface to the needs of end users in each class. The ability to customise the user interface by the user promotes usability by providing more flexibility in using the system, and by providing a more effective environment for its user.

22.6   Potential Benefits of the Proposed Improvements

Regardless of whether the simulation systems are data driven simulators or simulation languages, it is becoming common to provide some sort of integrated model building environment. However, the experience we have gained during this research convinced us that the model development process is generally not well supported. Therefore, the improvements in simulation systems that we advocate in this chapter aim to promote better modelling environments. Such provision of completely self-sufficient simulation environments is important for the following reasons:

- it reduces the development time;
- it supports application consistency;
- it can aid the developers throughout the development cycle;
- it can support model completeness;
- it can provide checks of model validation.

That such an effort is desirable, if even not crucial, for wider use of simulation as a modelling technique can be supported with the fact reported by Wu (1992). He provides information that there seems to have been little increase in the use of simulation modelling since 1975, and speculates that if the surveying methods that gave this result are to be trusted one of the reasons for this may be that simulation modelling is too sophisticated and time-consuming to accommodate quick decisions in a dynamic environment. The reasons for the large amount of time required to construct simulation projects Wu (1992) attributes to a lack of expertise in simulation methodology.

The users of simulation software are often experts in special application fields. Kämper (1993) points out that these users, being laymen in information science, should be supported as much as possible by the simulation tool. The areas of concern are: validation, the development of simple models and the development of complex models which contain, for example, non-typical phenomena in a special problem class. She advocates that the simulation tools should support the model builder in the first phases to become familiar with the tool, and in further work to model more complex phenomena without being forced to learn new concepts of model building. She sees the development of task-specific user interfaces which relate to the respective knowledge as an aid to modelling. Bright and Johnston (1991) point out the necessity of 'ease of use' of simulation software. They see 'ease of use' as a combination of structural guidance in the model development process, error prevention, help provision and the rate at which familiarity with the software is gained. However, they are concerned that the provision of these requirements in visual interactive modelling software will hinder generality and reduce its power.

Suggested improvements listed in Section 22.5 would make model specification a much easier and faster process. The expertise required to model a real system will not be as demanding. Fast model development and experimentation with the model in the time-constrained rapidly changing environment will be better facilitated. The users will be given the flexibility to tailor many aspects of the simulation environment to their own preferences. Particularly, the provision of sophisticated on-line help utilities that are more task and problem oriented would foster system learnability and promote more positive users' attitude. Proposal for improvements in visual modelling are particularly important in promoting usability of simulation systems. When the objects involved in an animation depict application entities and when the animation actions appropriately represent the user's mental model the effectiveness, learnability and the enthusiasm of a wider user population to use simulation systems might increase. Hence, all four usability dimensions will be better supported.

22.7   Conclusions and Future Research Directions

Although current simulation systems can be quite sophisticated and often provide leadership in the applications of new technologies (e.g. the use of animation) we recognise that there is a lot of scope for improvements. We examined six representative simulation systems in terms of their usability. We identified both good practice and usability defects in these systems. Based on these observations we proposed improved integrated simulation environments that facilitate: design of problem domains; better support for data input/model specification; better support for visual simulation; better support for simulation statistics/results; and better user support and assistance. Such provision will enhance overall system usability, and promote wider acceptance and application of the simulation modelling approach for a variety of problems. Even though the development of models in the manufacturing domain is slightly better supported than models in other domains, this advantage is not so significant as to require manufacturing systems to be considered separately. The potential benefits of such improvements are reduced model development time, less need for expertise in simulation methodology and the wider applicability of simulation.

There are almost endless possibilities for future research. This is partially due to the complex nature of simulation systems in which many relatively new developments are involved and, hence, are not much researched into. It id due, partially, to the comparably new research area of human–computer interaction. Therefore our proposal for future research is just a small sub-set of the possible research directions in this area.

It would be particularly interesting to conduct an evaluation of the usability of existing simulation systems and a comparable analysis of the results. These comparable results may indicate what the important factors that determine the usability of such systems are. We should not assume that the factors used for the general usability criteria and often cited in the human–computer interaction literature apply equally to the domain of simulation modelling. Another potentially fruitful study could be an examination of how symbolic versus 'realistic' animation influences modelling performance, i.e. how it affects the decision making of the modeller.

Many simulation systems use some sort of diagrammatic technique to represent the logic of the problems being modelled. However, it is unknown whether the technique chosen in a system has any influence on the final model validity. An evaluation of different diagrammatic techniques in usability terms is another area that might provide better insight into the relationship between model representation, its validity and the specification of the model that evolves in the process. We have mentioned that the majority of simulation systems often use graphics to represent the results of a simulation experiment. However, the basis for using a particular graphical technique to depict the numerical results is often questionable. It would be valuable to evaluate how the different graphical techniques influence an analysis of simulation output, and how this is manifested in the conclusions that the modeller or the decision maker infers from the output provided.

The above research proposals deal mostly with the evaluation of simulation systems that are already available. These studies would undoubtedly be valuable for providing some sort of criteria and guidelines for future developments. However, more exciting research lies in the development of new paradigms and new technologies. We propose some enhancements to simulation modelling environments. Many of these proposals would require further research to be practical. This particularly applies to the development of aids for output analysis that would also provide some analysis of the interdependence of simulation output results. Related to this is the development of suitable graphics that can support representations for multidimensional data.

References

Bell, PC (1991) Visual interactive modelling: Past, present and prospects. *European Journal of Operational Research*, **54**(3): 274–286.

Booth, P (1989) *An Introduction to Human–Computer Interaction*. Hove: Lawrence Erlbaum Associates.

Bright, JG and Johnston, KJ (1991) Whither VIM? – A developers' view. *European Journal of Operational Research*, **54**(3): 357–362.

Carpenter, ML, Bauer, KW, Jr, Schuppe, TF and Vidulich, MV (1993) Animation: What's essential for effective communication of military simulation model operation? In *Proceedings of the 1993 Winter Simulation Conference*. London: Institute of Electrical and Electronic Engineers: 1081–1088.

Conway, R, Maxwell, WL, McClain, JO and Worona, SL (1990) *User Guide to XCELL+ Factory Modeling System*. San Francisco, CA: The Scientific Press.

Cyr, RW (1992) Using animation to enhance a marine-terminal Monte Carlo simulator, In *Proceedings of the 1992 Winter Simulation Conference*. Institute of Electrical and Electronic Engineers: 1000–1003.

Jones, S (1988) Graphical interfaces for knowledge engineering: An overview of relevant literature. *The Knowledge Engineering Review*, 3(3): 221–247.

Kalski, DR and Davis, AA (1991) Computer animation with CINEMA. In *Proceedings of the 1991 Winter Simulation Conference*. Institute of Electrical and Electronic Engineers: 122–127.

Kämper, S (1993) A systematization of requirements for the user interface of simulation tools. *Systems Analysis and Modelling Simulation*, 11(2): 107–119.

Kuljis, J (1994) User interfaces and discrete event simulation models. *Journal of Simulation Practice and Theory*, 1(5): 207–221.

Larson, JA (1992) *Interactive Software. Tools for Building Interactive User Interface*. Englewood Cliffs, NJ: Prentice-Hall.

Law, AM (1983) Statistical analysis of simulation output data *Operations Research*, 31(6): 983–1024.

Law, AM and Kelton, DW (1991) *Simulation Modeling and Analysis* (2nd edition). New York: McGraw-Hill.

Mathewson, SC (1989) The implementation of simulation languages. In *Computer Modelling for Discrete Simulation*. Pidd, M (Ed.). Chichester: John Wiley: 23–56.

Micro Saint Builder (1992) CA: Micro Analysis and Design Simulation Software, Inc.

Mladenic, D, Bratko, I, Paul, RJ and Grobelnik, M (1993) Using machine learning techniques to interpret results from discrete event simulation. In *Proceedings of the 15th International Conference on Information Technology Interfaces*. Zagreb, Croatia: University of Zagreb Computing Centre: 401–406.

O'Keefe, RM (1986) Simulation and expert systems – A taxonomy and some examples. *Simulation*, **46**(1): 10–16.

O'Keefe, RM and Pitt, IL (1991) Interaction with a visual interactive simulation, and the effect of cognitive style. *European Journal of Operational Research*, **54**(3): 339–348.

Paul, RJ and Balmer, D (1993) *Simulation Modelling*. Bromley: Chartwell-Bratt Ltd.

Pidd, M (1992a) *Computer Simulation in Management Sciences* (3rd edition). Chichester: John Wiley.

Pidd, M (1992b) Guidelines for the design of data driven generic simulators for specific domains. *Simulation*, 59(4): 237–243.

Preece, J, Rogers, Y, Sharp, H, Benyon, D, Holland, S and Carey, T (1994) *Human–Computer Interaction*. Wokingham: Addison-Wesley.

ProModel for Windows (1993) Orem, UT: Promodel Corporation.

Shackel, B (1991) Usability – context, framework, definition, design and evolution. In *Human Factors for Informatics Usability*. Shackel, B and Richardson, S (Eds). Cambridge: Cambridge University Press.

Shannon, RE (1975) *Systems Simulation – The Art and Science*.Englewood Cliffs, NJ: Prentice-Hall.

Simscript II.5 for Windows User's Manual (1993) La Jolla, CA: CACI Products Company.

Stasko, JT (1993) Animation in user interfaces: Principles and techniques. In *User Interface Software*. Bass, L and Dewan, P (Eds).Chichester: John Wiley: 81–101.

Swider, CL, Bauer, KW, Jr, and Schuppe, TF (1994) The effective use of animation in simulation model validation. In *Proceedings of the 1994 Winter Simulation Conference*. Institute of Electrical and Electronic Engineers: 633–640.

Taylor II Simulation (1993) Tilburg, the Netherlands: F&H Logistics and Automation B.V.

Thomas, LJ, McClain, JO and Edwards, DB (1989) *Cases in Operations Management. Using the XCELL+ Factory Modeling System*. Redwood: The Scientific Press.

Visual C++ (1993) Microsoft.

Windows Simscript II.5 User's Manual (1993) San Diego, CA: CACI Products Company.

WITNESS User Manual Release 307, Version 7.3.0 (1991) Redditch, UK: AT&T Istel Visual Interactive Systems Ltd.

Wu, B (1992) *Manufacturing Systems Design and Analysis*. London: Chapman & Hall.

Subject Index

Author Index